THE URBAN IMPACT ON
AMERICAN PROTESTANTISM
1865–1900

The Urban Impact on American Protestantism 1865–1900

BY

AARON IGNATIUS ABELL

Professor of History in Nazareth College, Rochester, New York

ARCHON

Hamden   •   London

1962

To

MY MOTHER AND FATHER

PREFACE

THIS work, a revised doctoral dissertation at Harvard University, is a generalized study of the religious and social effects of urban development on American Protestantism. The rapid transition from rural to urban conditions of life in the generation following the Civil War brought Protestants face to face with two different yet closely related problems. To a far greater degree than farmers and small townsmen, the wage-earning masses expected religion to establish ultimately a more equitable economic and industrial order. At the same time the cities called upon religion for vast amounts of immediate aid in the way of spiritual and social service. Moreover, each situation bore a complementary relation to the other. Accordingly, the present volume not only treats of the genesis and evolution of the two trends, but also attempts to clarify as precisely as possible the correlations between them.

Materials for this study — chiefly newspapers, periodicals and reports of religious societies and institutions — were furnished by the Widener Library at Harvard, the Library of the Episcopal Theological School of Cambridge, the Boston Public Library, the New York Public Library, the Library of Union Theological Seminary of New York and the Library of Congress. To the officers and assistants of these institutions I am indebted for many helpful suggestions and innumerable courtesies. For their critical reading of the manuscript I wish to thank Professor Paul H. Buck of Harvard; Dr. Blake McKelvey, Assistant City Historian of Rochester, New York; Professor Bert James Loewenberg of Sarah Lawrence College; and Professor James O. Wettereau of Washington Square College at New York University.

I am under deepest obligation to my teacher and stimulating counselor, Arthur M. Schlesinger. He turned my attention to social history as a field of study, suggested the present investigation and guided every stage in its progress. Without his unfailing interest and searching criticism the volume would not have reached completion. I also take this opportunity to acknowledge publicly my profound sense of gratitude to my wife, Elizabeth Schell, who cheerfully assumed the burden of preparing the text for the press.

A. I. A.

CONTENTS

I. THE CITY AS A NEW CHALLENGE TO PROTESTANT
   CHURCHES   3
   The urban religious problem — Protestant difficulties: neglect of
   the social and spiritual needs of the poor; lack of organization for
   social purposes; sectarian divisions — The urban challenge accepted: the program of the American Christian Commission;
   proposals for coöperation, evangelical and liberal; the program
   of the Christian Labor Union.

II. THE GENESIS OF PROTESTANT SOCIAL SERVICE,
    1865–1880   27
    Humanitarian churches: undenominational; the efforts of William
    A. Muhlenberg and William Welsh among Episcopalians; Home
    Evangelization among Congregationalists — Extra-parochial asso-
    ciations: non-sectarian city missions; Unitarian unions for Chris-
    tian work; Episcopal city missions, guilds and workingmen's
    clubs; Lutheran, Methodist, and Episcopal work for immigrants
    — The Young Men's and the Young Women's Christian Associa-
    tions — Temperance reform: "Gospel temperance movement";
    denominational temperance societies — Training of city mission-
    aries: undenominational training schools; the deaconess move-
    ment, Episcopal, Lutheran, and Methodist.

III. SOCIAL CHRISTIANITY AND THE LABOR CHALLENGE,
     1880–1900   57
     Emergence of industrial warfare — Alienation of workers from
     organized religion — Labor and its friends favor social Christian-
     ity — Washington Gladden's advocacy of social Christianity —
     Social Christianity in the church congresses — The Christian So-
     cialists — Social science as a factor in the socializing of Protestant-
     ism — Quickening interest in scientific philanthropy.

IV. SOCIAL CHRISTIANITY: DIFFUSION AND EXPANSION,
    1880–1900   88
    Coöperation for social Christianity: American Congress of
    Churches; Evangelical Alliance; Convention of Christian Work-
    ers; Brotherhood of Christian Unity; League of Catholic Unity
    — Growing cohesion among liberals: American Congress of
    Liberal Religious Societies; increasing activity of Societies for
    Ethical Culture; Union for Practical Progress; The Christian
    Social Union; American Institute of Christian Sociology; The
    Church Association for the Advancement of the Interests of
    Labor; The Brotherhood of the Kingdom; the understanding
    between labor leaders and Christian Socialists.

V. THE SALVATION ARMY IN AMERICA, 1880–1900 . . 118

The Army's religious and social program — Obstacles facing the
Army in the United States — Factors in its eventual success —
Philanthropic endeavor: the Slum Brigade and outgrowths; the
"Social Scheme"; additional social service — Secessionist move-
ments.

VI. THE INSTITUTIONAL CHURCH MOVEMENT . . . 137

Socialized missions: influence of the Convention of Christian
Workers; mission and tract societies; missions to counteract
intemperance and prostitution — Representative institutional
churches: (Episcopal) St. George's and St. Bartholomew's, New
York; (Congregational) Fourth Church, Hartford, Plymouth
Church, Indianapolis, Berkeley Temple, Boston, and the Jersey
City Tabernacle; (Presbyterian) Bethany, Philadelphia, and Mad-
ison Avenue, New York; (Baptist) Baptist Temple, Philadelphia,
and the Judson Memorial, New York; (Methodist) Wesley
Chapel, Cincinnati, and the Metropolitan Temple, New York;
(Unitarian) All Souls', Chicago; (Universalist) Every Day
Church, Boston — The Open or Institutional Church League.

VII. COÖPERATIVE PHASES OF THE INSTITUTIONAL CHURCH
MOVEMENT 166

Methodist Church extension and city mission societies — Dutch
Reformed Church missions and churches in New York — Boston
Fraternity of Churches (Unitarian) — Congregational city missionary societies — Presbyterian city mission work — Baptist city
missions: influence of the American Baptist Home Missionary
Society — Denominational handling of the immigrant — Episcopal missions and church clubs — The federation of churches
movement.

VIII. THE AUXILIARY FORMS OF PROTESTANT SOCIAL SERVICE 194

The deaconess movement — New Trends in Young Men's and
Young Women's Christian Associations — The Sunday school —
The young people's movement — The brotherhood movement —
The sisterhood movement.

IX. CHANGING TRENDS IN THE SEMINARIES 224

Decline of the ministry and the seminaries — Pedagogical reform
— Social science at Harvard, Andover, and Hartford — The
sociological movement: in Congregational seminaries; in Presbyterian seminaries; in Baptist seminaries; in Episcopal schools;
in Lutheran seminaries; in Unitarian and Universalist schools.

X. THE BALANCE SHEET 246

BIBLIOGRAPHICAL ESSAY 256

INDEX 265

THE URBAN IMPACT ON
AMERICAN PROTESTANTISM
1865–1900

CHAPTER I

THE CITY AS A NEW CHALLENGE TO
PROTESTANT CHURCHES

THE rapid growth of industrial cities after 1865 burdened religion to the breaking-point. From the days of William Ellery Channing, early in the nineteenth century, to the present, Protestant social prophets echoed the theme that, while urban life was synonymous with material and intellectual progress, it could show few corresponding triumphs in the moral field. On the contrary, the city was the hot-house of every cancerous growth — of new evils like industrial war and class hatred and of the older evils of pauperism and crime, of intemperance and vice. These maladies in the body politic threatened social pestilence as cities sprawled over the industrial regions, particularly the North Atlantic States and the Middle West. During the forty-year period, 1860–1900, the number of cities of eight thousand or more inhabitants increased from 141 to 547, and the proportion of townsfolk from a sixth to nearly a third.

In these cities foreigners by birth or parentage comprised over two-thirds of the population. Whatever his religious antecedents, the newcomer did not readily conform to customary religious and moral standards. "If a Protestant, he often becomes indifferent," observed Charles Loring Brace of the New York Children's Aid Society. "Moral ties," he continued, "are lessened with the religious. The intervening process which occurs here between his abandoning the old state of things and fitting himself to the new, is not favorable to morals and character." [1] Yet the immigrant was only partly responsible for his moral plight. The enlarging factory system by separating employer and employee weakened human relations in the world of

[1] *The Dangerous Classes of New York* (New York, 1872), pp. 34–35.

work, where mainly the basis for healthy social life must subsist. Machine industry rewarded owners and brain workers at the expense of manual workers who often lacked sufficient income for the necessities of life. Low wages and high rents forced large numbers of the working class, mainly immigrants, into crowded slums which undermined good home life and other supports of virtue. Many slum dwellers, of course, led exemplary lives, but they all faced conditions which encouraged immorality and crime. "The poor," as Theodore Parker had said, "are ignorant and wretched and vicious not from choice but from necessity." [2]

In these circumstances, enlightened moralists concluded that remedial measures must improve not only the people's character but also their wretched environment. Yet Protestant Christianity, bound by doctrine and tradition to spiritual regeneration alone, did not adopt a satisfactory program of social ethics until late in the century. By rigidly separating body and spirit and denying religious value to the former, Protestant thought necessarily ignored the problem of human welfare in the great cities. This attitude led to tacit approval of the rising craze for amoral wealth-getting. For while Protestant theory disparaged material things, most Protestants loved comfort and worldly goods, the possession of which they regarded as the sure sign of Divine favor. Until the mid-eighties the urban poor scarcely figured in Protestant missionary tactics, which continued to angle for the support of the enormous rural and urban middle class. "If there are heathen in the lanes," said the Presbyterian General Assembly in 1869, "there are heathen in the stately avenues also." [3] Even the Baptist and Methodist faiths, once religions of the poor, now displayed almost frantic solicitude for the spiritual welfare of the rich.

Happily, a few Protestants in the early urban period roundly

[2] John Haynes Holmes, *The Social Message of Theodore Parker* (Boston, 1913), p. 9.
[3] *Minutes*, p. 293.

denounced unchristian social behavior. The most scholarly and convincing, though not the first, of these critics was Stephen Colwell of Philadelphia, Presbyterian and welfare economist. In profound studies published in the early fifties, he detailed the historical background for his faith's outright encouragement of greed and selfishness.[4] If the Protestant reformers, through force of circumstances, had, properly, stressed questions of truth, they had unjustifiably "overlooked in their readings of the New Testament its imperative injunctions of brotherly kindness." By its emancipating influence the Reformation gave Protestants leadership in knowledge, art and industry: "All Europe and the world," he said, "soon felt the activity and life infused into business by Protestant energy." But the religion of the Reformation had failed to control its unleashed vitality, especially "in the form of that intense selfishness which is manifested in the pursuit of wealth and power." On the contrary, Protestantism had compromised with worldly men, who without becoming Christians "are officers in the temporal affairs of the congregations, and exercise no small control in all their concerns." In these ways religion had "assumed many of the maxims and practices of business."[5]

Nor did Colwell believe that Protestants were ready to cease idolizing wealth and to begin cultivating a genuine love of neighbor. He thought it significant, for example, that English-speaking Christians had neglected to write even one adequate treatise on Christian charity to refute the rank materialism pervading the political economy of England and America.[6] He noted, too, that Americans clung to a relief system that humiliated and regimented the poor instead of sympathetically aiding them. Protestants persisted in believing that human sufferings were "the penalties of idleness, disease or other similar causes,

---

[4] *New Themes for the Protestant Clergy* (Philadelphia, 1851); *Politics for American Christians* (Philadelphia, 1852); and *The Position of Christianity in the United States* (Philadelphia, 1854).

[5] *New Themes for the Protestant Clergy*, pp. 111, 118, 123–124, 127, 129–130.

[6] *Ibid.*, pp. 141 ff.

in a great measure the fault of the sufferers." [7] But the suffering poor had rejected this view and along with it the Christianity which championed it. Colwell also suspected that Protestants were losing interest in the purely religious welfare of the poor. "The Gospel is sent to the heathen of far distant lands, but the heathen at home are neglected," he complained.[8]

In respect to spiritual neglect of the poor, the shortcomings of Protestantism were more evident than in the broad field of social policy. All could see that as the working class crowded into the industrial quarters the old parochial churches sought congenial sites on the great avenues up town. When the Civil War ended nearly a half-hundred important congregations had already deserted lower New York, and soon after Bostonians were leaving historic meeting houses for sumptuous edifices in the Back Bay. The new locations in New York did not result from mass removal of congregations, charged the anonymous author of *Startling Facts*, but "in every case originated in the change of residence of a few of the wealthier families." [9] The plain churches, another critic pointed out, desired to "follow in the steps of the rich churches as fast as they dare. . . ." There was in the poorer parishes, he said, "the same extra attention paid to the rich . . . and the same thrusting of the poor into nooks and corners." [10]

Contempt for the poor took on a more substantial form in the "fashionable" churches erected after 1865 in the leading cities. The new edifices were small, costly structures, ornate on the outside and richly sombre in their interior arrangements. Moreover, galleries for non-church members, so characteristic of earlier ecclesiastical architecture, were lacking. Professional choirs and quartettes, often procured at great expense, replaced simple music and congregational singing. The ministers seldom

---

[7] *Politics for American Christians*, p. 26.
[8] *New Themes for the Protestant Clergy*, p. 179.
[9] Quoted in "Religion in New York," *Cath. World*, III (June 1866), 382–383.
[10] F. N. Zabriskie, *And the Poor Have the Gospel Preached to Them* (New York, undated), pp. 14–15.

⊔iscussed spiritual issues of interest to the harassed multitudes. "We have heard sermons in these churches," wrote James Parton, the journalist, "which had not a single allusion to modern times, to modern modes of sinning and living." [11] If comparatively few congregations attained the full fashionable status, many exhibited an exclusive spirit, resulting in the progressive alienation of the wage-earning class, especially the caste-conscious immigrants.

Yet the Catholic Church prospered in cities. Its communicants numbered twelve million by 1900, of whom five-sixths were urban immigrants, mainly Irish and Germans.[12] Of the several factors entering into the Church's growth, the chief one was its sympathy with struggling humanity. Though anxious to convert the privileged groups, Catholics always stressed their ministry to the poor. For example, the Paulist Fathers, under the direction of their founder, Isaac T. Hecker, established their central parish in the midst of Irish shanties in New York City. "Thus a movement designed to convert Mr. Emerson and his friends, and the educated people of America," wrote Parton, "was made, first of all, to minister to the spiritual wants of the poorest and most ignorant people living in the Northern States!" [13] Aside from helping progressive Protestants to combat anti-social economic attitudes, the Catholic Church sponsored in its own right an excellent social program, including careful pastoral oversight, fund-raising abroad, the founding of schools and philanthropic institutions and after 1880 a vigorous Americanization movement.

Though many Protestants were ready for a similar program, the religious bodies to which they belonged were largely indifferent to applied Christianity. Societies mainly for inculcating spiritual truth, the Protestant congregations stressed preach-

[11] "Henry Ward Beecher's Church," *Atlantic Mo.,* XIX (January 1867), 39.
[12] Gerald Shaughnessy, *Has the Immigrant Kept the Faith?* (New York, 1925), esp. pp. 171, 251.
[13] "Our Roman Catholic Brethren," *Atlantic Mo.,* XXI (April–May 1868), 432–451, 556–574.

ing and left the applications of religion to Christians in their individual capacities. The "motive energy" of Protestantism, social reformers untiringly pointed out, was "not in the collective body but in the individual soul." [14] Thus the Protestant churches did not supply leadership or guidance to members interested in charity and works of mercy. As a result, indiscriminate alms-giving widely prevailed among Protestants, acting either individually or through secular associations into which they were wont to channel their gifts. If philanthropy of this type supplied some of the material needs of the poor, it denied them the stimulus of human sympathy, education and religious training. What with idleness, poverty and vice increasing in a young, prosperous country the "remedial power of Christ's Gospel and Church has not been wisely and efficiently applied," [15] complained an influential religious magazine. The churches also suffered. The poor could not feel deep attachment for congregations which did their giving and loving by proxy. "It is not for lack of mutual love that modern Christianity is most defective," concluded a New England clergyman. "It is rather for want of an adequate and direct channel for its communication." [16]

Before 1865 only the Young Men's Christian Associations had combined a social with a spiritual ministry to a conspicuous degree. Though the first American Association arose in Boston as late as 1851, two hundred or more were functioning at the outbreak of the war. They secured board and employment for young men as they arrived in the cities and urged them to perform their religious duties faithfully. Moreover, in these early days when the congregations were still indifferent to the poor and other forms of Christian effort were not as yet formulated, the Associations cared for all age and sex groups, estab-

[14] "Modern Romanism and Modern Protestantism," *Christian Examiner*, LXXIV (January 1863), 109.
[15] "Church Work in Large Cities," *Church Rev.*, XVII (April 1865), 40.
[16] J. Colver Wightman, "The Apostolic System of Church Finance," *Baptist Quart.*, V (October 1871), 400–01.

lishing mission Sunday schools, nursing the sick and alleviating the usual run of human distress. Amazingly effective in these fields, they exerted a wider influence, being chiefly responsible for the great religious revival of 1857–1858 and wholly so for the United States Christian Commission through which Northern Christians mitigated the horrors and discomforts of the battle-field. The Associations were a convincing demonstration of what organization with a sustained purpose and flexible methods could do for religion and philanthropy.[17]

Not alone philanthropy but the broad field of social action as a whole suffered from Protestant failure to apply religion. In the years immediately after the war, no evil was more alarmingly apparent than business dishonesty. Worldly men and professed Christians alike threw moral caution to the winds, partly because corporate industry centered their attention on money-making to the exclusion of ethical and humanitarian considerations. The fact that manufacturers and traders as members of a corporation approved fraudulent practices which they personally abhorred was notoriously evident. Moreover, the new business techniques were morally confusing to many conscientious Christians. "The complexity of modern commercial operations," as E. L. Godkin explained, "is so great, the line between what is fair and what is foul so faint . . . that it is often very difficult for a man to say himself whether he is acting honestly or not, and much more so for a bystander." [18] Though this situation was distressing, light did not radiate upon it from the rural-trained ministry to whom social ethics was "mere morality" of no religious significance. Yet intelligent citizens agreed that only as "morality supported by religious sanctions" came to be taught in the pulpits "with far more system, far more detail, far more urgency and far more study

[17] R. R. McBurney, *Historical Sketch of the Y.M.C.A.* (New York, 1886); John W. Dodge, "Young Men's Christian Associations and the Church," *Congregational Rev.*, VIII (September 1868), 440–52.
[18] "The Church as a Reformatory Agent," *Nation*, June 16, 1870, p. 379.

on the part of the preachers" — only then could religion put an
end to dishonesty and fraud.[19]

Protestants also needed applied ethics in their dealings with
the poor as wage-earners. Under the factory system workers
discovered that organization helped to keep wages above subsistence levels and in other ways to advance their interests.
This experience, along with socialist doctrine, the democratic
tradition and the conviction that the "achievements of science"
made poverty no longer necessary, nourished in the post-war
years a firmly rooted labor movement. The growing solidarity
of labor challenged directly the Protestant gospel of individual
regeneration. The average worker devoted so much of his time,
energy and surplus earnings to his trade union that he necessarily lost interest in the church. Moreover, trade-union policies
determined the religious attitudes of the working class. Though
the ministry "deals with individuals, not organizations . . .
the individual thus addressed," said Bishop Matthew Simpson,
"is influenced by these associations which may either help or
retard the power of the pulpit." [20] As the congregations leaned
more and more to the employers' side, the unions urged wage-
earners to abandon Protestant Christianity.

Still another factor retarded Protestant adjustment to cities.
The prevailing "sect system" was inconsistent with the proper
utilization of religious resources. Thus denominational competition for the patronage of the rich in the favored neighborhoods
partly accounted for the exodus of congregations from the
slums and the lower-middle-class districts. What with every
sect loudly proclaiming itself the exclusive Church of Christ,
the obvious remedy — coöperation — seemed a hopeless dream.
Yet champions of unity appeared early on the scene, the ablest
being the Reverend William A. Muhlenberg, an Episcopal
pioneer in hymnology, education and charity. He called himself
an "Evangelical Catholic." The term signified that Christianity

---

[19] "The Education of Ministers," *ibid.*, April 20, 1871, p. 272.
[20] *Lectures on Preaching* (New York, 1879), p. 268.

was neither inward spirit nor abstract truth, but a divine institution in the world with agencies for every legitimate human need. In order that all Christians might the more easily work together for the common welfare, Muhlenberg urged them to view the church "simply as the Congregation of the Brethren of Christ." [21] In this spirit, progressive Protestants associated immediately after the civil conflict, for it was evident by then that cities challenged religion to liberalize its economic attitudes and to organize for social service and ethical teaching.

Thought and action centered around, first, systematic plans for urban missionary endeavor, based upon a thorough study of religious conditions in representative cities; secondly, agitation for the unification of Protestant forces; and thirdly, an adequate solution of the industrial problem. Of the various associations emerging to consider these questions, the most fruitful and significant was the American Christian Commission. Although the United States Christian Commission of Civil War days disbanded early in 1865, the leaders in the autumn of that year decided upon a similar body for peace-time service in cities. James E. Yeatman, a noted public figure of St. Louis, who had presided over the Western Sanitary Commission, suggested the new organization. In his widely read *Circular of Inquiry*, he thoroughly analyzed the urban challenge, pointing out the fascinations of the city for rural folk and stating that the Catholic Church seized upon cities in order, as he believed, "that she may take possession of the nation." He especially stressed the comparative ineffectiveness of Protestant churches in urban communities. The difficulties were, he summarized, "want of knowledge of their moral condition; lack of organization of the wealth, piety and labor which exist there; need of experimental knowledge of the best agencies and how to perfect organizations already formed; and want of trained, tried, permanent laborers in the various spheres of city labor." [22]

[21] *Evangelical Catholic Papers*, I, 459.
[22] American Christian Commission, *Document No. I* (New York, 1867), pp. 9-11.

Impressed by the importance and timeliness of Yeatman's analysis,[23] one hundred and nineteen "widely known, active and influential ministers and laymen of different denominations," [24] called an organizing convention. "We have fallen away," they said, "from the simplicity and entire consecration of the early Christians. At first, every disciple was a missionary and every church a missionary society." The time had come, they believed, for union, not for any ecclesiastical purpose, but for "aggressive Christian efforts." The convention, meeting at Cleveland in September, 1865, and finding Protestantism facing formidable dangers in cities, established a permanent Commission to work out, if possible, satisfactory solutions. Among the Commission's first acts was the appointment of two secretaries, John H. Cole and F. G. Ensign, "to collect information concerning mission work in cities. . . ." Their report the following year, based on personal investigation in thirty-five representative cities, assembled data relative to the growing need for humanitarian church work in cities, the American philanthropic situation viewed as a whole, the activities of the churches as missionary congregations and, finally, the question of using women as missionaries. Though not exhaustive, this report presented the first truly significant picture of Protestant prospects in urban America.[25]

Its crisp conclusions cleared away the mists of ignorance and misunderstanding which had hitherto shrouded the whole subject. No longer, for example, could Protestants justify their indifference to urban problems by alleging that they existed only in a few large cities. "Greatly as these cities differ in most respects," said the secretaries, "certain causes are in operation, to a greater or less extent in each, that necessitate special missionary effort." Common to all cities were the multiplied

---

[23] But see the *Congregationalist*, Sept. 22, 1865, p. 150, and the *Church Rev.*, XIX (January 1865), 637–38 for misunderstandings and misrepresentations of the movement.

[24] *Congregationalist*, Sept. 15, 1865, p. 146.

[25] *Document No. I*, pp. 12, 19–20.

temptations in the way of "debasing" amusements; the facilities for committing and concealing crime; the tenement-house with its blighting effect on home and child life; the heterogeneous populations which increased vice and pauperism; and, lastly, the growing neglect of church attendance. The secretaries assured their Protestant constituency that "no mission field is more necessitous, none more easily accessible, none which appeals to so many interests of the Christian patriot and philanthropist as this in our very midst." [26]

In twelve cities with an aggregate population of over five hundred thousand, the secretaries found that Protestants were only beginning to unite in societies for religious and humanitarian purposes. Mission chapels were not numerous, although "the efficiency and success with which some are conducted," the secretaries reported, "go far toward relieving the worst features of moral destitution in our large towns and reveal the way by which very much more might be accomplished if these efforts were extended." As for the congregations, only a handful were missionary in the apostolic sense of providing for both temporal and spiritual needs. St. Mark's Protestant Episcopal Church in Philadelphia and the First Presbyterian Church in Utica were examples. Though there were others, it "is too evident," the investigators lamented, "that they are the exception rather than the rule, and that in very many churches but little is done for those who neglect the house of God." The unprogressive character of American philanthropy explained partly, they were convinced, the feebleness of Protestant missionary enterprise. If some cities provided for the relief of nearly every form of human suffering, others utterly passed by "entire classes that should be the object of Christian philanthropy" — a situation especially applicable to "vagrant children, inebriates, discharged convicts and fallen women." [27]

The secretaries' investigation confirmed the opinion long held by the best students of urban life that the poor missionary

[26] *Ibid.*, pp. 20–23.   [27] *Ibid.*, pp. 24–25, 35–43.

showing of Protestant churches issued from ignorance and lack of organization as well as from social indifference. It was surprising to see "how little is generally known as to the principles involved and the results of experience already gained in the management of charitable institutions." Though many Christian people were interested in progressive types of social service, they did not possess "positive knowledge as to the best means of reaching the ends desired." Nor could they easily obtain it since a comprehensive library or collection of philanthropic reports did not exist in America.[28] As an example of the mischievous effect of this condition, the secretaries referred to the low esteem in which the churches held women missionaries. Despite the usefulness of female assistants, all the cities visited except New York and Boston could muster only twenty-eight women in actual service — a fact due not merely to prejudice but to the absence of information and training.[29]

Through various means the American Christian Commission, in the sixties and seventies, popularized its program. A department of foreign correspondence, headed by the Reverend George C. Holls of Mt. Vernon, New York, assembled the literature detailing the "experience developed in European societies and institutions," among them the Congress of Inner Missions in Germany and the Reformatory and Refuge Union of Great Britain. The Commission secured access to thousands of Protestant Christians through its monthly newspaper, *The Christian at Work*, founded in 1868 to promote aggressive Christianity.[30] More important were the Christian Conventions, local, state and national, held at frequent intervals and reaching the rank and file of the churches as well as the missionary experts. These assemblies discussed the necessity for thorough district visitations of the poor, the use of churches

---

[28] *Ibid.*, pp. 25–27.

[29] *Ibid.*, pp. 44–46, for the pioneer work of the Boston City Missionary Society (Congregational) in this branch of religious service.

[30] *Ibid.*, pp. 30–31; *Annual Report*, 1869, pp. 18–20; *ibid.*, 1870, p. 22.

for humanitarian purposes, the formation of Christian associations, lay preaching, open-air preaching, the rescue of social outcasts, and the promotion of Christian union.[31]

In urging these reforms the many conventions were primarily responsible, the Commission claimed, for the remarkable awakening to urban religious needs. The national Convention at New York in 1868 sounded the keynote of the Christian social theme. The Reverend J. T. Duryea, of the New York City Mission and Tract Society, was sure that "Christian people were beginning to realize the startling fact that the Gospel was not presented to every creature," in either city or country. Dwight L. Moody, the lay evangelist, denounced fashionable Christianity, contending that "opera-singing in the churches" would never interest the masses. Nearly all speakers strongly favored free churches and women church workers. In the course of an eloquent plea for sisterhoods and deaconess institutions on the German Protestant model, the Reverend George W. Washburn stated that the "theory that woman has no place in the Church deprives America of two-thirds of its Christian force." The discussions in other conventions were similar in tone, a speaker in an Illinois convention, for example, saying that the "church is doing nothing, it is a beautiful machine, but it stands cold, dead, useless."[32] Though severe, the criticism was constructive in intent, aiming to persuade church members to obliterate class lines from religious life. To this end, the first New York State Convention demanded lay effort and suggested to pastors, "especially those in our more densely populated communities that they seek out and employ all such talent in their congregations as they shall believe to possess qualifications for this important and pressing work."[33]

[31] *Independent*, Jan. 21, 1869, p. 2; *ibid.*, May 1, 1873, p. 562; *Church Union*, June 19, 1869, p. 1; *ibid.*, July 24, 1869, p. 1; *ibid.*, Oct. 23, 1869, p. 5; *Congregationalist*, Dec. 14, 1866, p. 198; *ibid.*, Feb. 6, 1868, p. 44; *ibid.*, Nov. 28, 1867, p. 237; *ibid.*, Nov. 26, 1868, p. 377.
[32] *Cumberland Presbyterian*, Nov. 26, 1869, p. 9.
[33] Y.M.C.A. of New York, *Report*, 1868, pp. 63–64.

Though it afforded a fine object lesson in Christian coöperation, the American Christian Commission left to other groups
the task of explaining the advantages of associated effort. Thus
the lay evangelists, under Moody's leadership, stressed Christian union as an integral part of their program of restoring
apostolic Christianity. "It is the claim of unsectarian character
which this movement makes," as one preacher observed, "that
gives it vitality and strength before the people and brings to it
a large measure of the success with which it has been
crowned." [34]   More explicitly, the American branch of the
Evangelical Alliance, formed in 1867, made planning for Christian union the sum and substance of its existence. When six
years later the World Alliance Conference convened in New
York, the venerable Muhlenberg was on hand to insist that the
church must exhibit "the Divine Brotherhood . . . if she is to
make headway in the world." [35]   Charles Hodge of Princeton
explained that the church's unity must come from faith in Christ
rather than from beliefs about Him. Hodge was surprisingly
radical in stating that membership in one congregation involved
the right of membership in every other congregation. "The
terms of church membership," he insisted, "are prescribed by
Christ, and cannot be altered — we are bound to receive those
whom He receives." [36]

Though keeping intact their organization and religious life,
the various denominations seemed willing to subordinate their
creedal differences to the larger interests of social Christianity.
Thus, in successive councils after the war, the Congregationalists refused to enforce Calvinism and "made Evangelical Christianity the basis of church union. . . ." [37]   In the Protestant

[34] W. T. Moore, "Modern Revivalism," *Christian Quart.*, VIII (January
1876), 54.
[35] "The Lord's Supper in Relation to Christian Union," *Evangelical Alliance
Conference* (New York, 1874), p. 183.
[36] "The Unity of the Church Based on Personal Union with Christ," *ibid.*,
pp. 139–141.
[37] *Christian Union*, Jan. 24, 1872, p. 108.

Episcopal Church the rising tide of sympathy and tolerance broke down the walls of bitter theological controversy. During the seventies both the High Church and the Low Church groups extended the olive branch, recognizing each other as legitimate types of religious thought, with something to contribute to the common welfare not only of the Episcopal Church but of Christendom at large.[38] By suggesting that the "Church is more catholic than any of its members can possibly be,"[39] the friends of peace finally silenced contentious churchmen. So complete was the reconciliation that the keynote of the General Convention of 1880 was "not the restatement of dogma, but the urgency of Christian work."[40]

Several congresses, leagues, alliances and conferences arose to direct these brotherly impulses. The first in point of time was the Church Congress of the Protestant Episcopal Church, the outgrowth in 1874 of recently formed church clubs in New York, Boston and New Haven. In New York City, for example, the Latimer Club, later the Church Conference, in its meeting at Calvary Church, found in missionary topics a bond of common interest before which theological differences receded into the background.[41] At a joint meeting in New Haven, in May, 1874, the clubs decided to hold a Congress at the autumn General Convention. Though bishops and theological professors frowned upon the movement, moderates of all parties favored it as a necessary supplement to the General Convention, which as a conservative body left "almost untouched the wide field of the church's practical life."[42] A well-known religious journal noticed that in its first session the Congress tried to advance truth through moral influence rather than through

[38] Ibid., Sept. 16, 1874, pp. 203–204; ibid., Nov. 11, 1874, p. 367.

[39] Ibid., March 2, 1882, p. 201.

[40] Edmund Guilbert, "The General Convention," Christian at Work, Nov. 11, 1880, pp. 908–909.

[41] Church and State, Feb. 28, 1874, p. 3.

[42] Julius H. Ward, "The Utility of the Church Congress," Church Rev., XVIII (January 1875), 57–58.

ecclesiastical authority — a new trend certain of rapid growth.[43] The Reverend Samuel Osgood observed that the second Congress "was strongly in favor of generous, practical work and humane, comprehensive culture. There was little of dogmatic temper and perhaps too little of distinct theological and religious teaching." [44]

Likewise, progressive folk in other denominations formed deliberative bodies: the Alliance of the Reformed Churches Throughout the World Holding the Presbyterian System, in 1875; the Free Lutheran Diet in America, in 1877; the Methodist Ecumenical Conference, in 1879; and the Baptist Congress for the Discussion of Current Questions, in 1882. While aimed immediately at understanding and ultimately at consolidation among closely related denominations, they also exalted the ideal of union among all Christians. Even so stalwart a Methodist as the Reverend J. M. Buckley, editor of the *Christian Advocate*, was ready by 1891 to say that the church of the future would be all-inclusive, confining its creed to a few essentials of salvation and leaving the rest to individual judgment and private conscience.[45] The essays and discussions in the periodic meetings of these various groups embodied, perhaps, the most constructive religio-social thinking in the United States before 1900.

The Christian unity movement could not, of course, expect direct support from the numerous people who had lost faith in historic Christianity.[46] Liberals in the strict sense of the term, these religious heirs of the Transcendentalist movement divested Christianity of all orthodox meaning and viewed it simply as one of the great, though imperfect, religions of the world. As humanitarian nationalists, they did not believe that the Christian church was "large enough for this independent,

[43] "Episcopal Prospects," *Christian Union*, June 17, 1874, p. 479.

[44] "The Church Congress in New York," *ibid.*, Nov. 7, 1877, p. 393.

[45] "The Methodist Council," *Church Work*, vol. III (November 1891), No. 1.

[46] See Charles Eliot Norton, "The Church and Religion," *No. Amer. Rev.*, CVI (April 1868), 376–396.

sturdy, vigorous America. A native religion, not fetched from beyond the seas, a religion universalized by the genius of American liberty, must yet," they thought, "supplant the narrow and cramping Christianity of the churches."[47] They favored free, socially responsible religion. One of their brilliant leaders, Francis E. Abbot, urged all Protestants to "cease these everlasting exhortations about salvation from imaginary devils and drive out the devils of ignorance and vice and pauperism. Secure by reforms the *Right Social Conditions* for virtue and intelligence," he pleaded, "and then stimulate each poor devil to try once more with the aid of your sympathy and strong helping hand."[48]

Ethical culture was the earliest phase of liberalism's constructive character. Its leader, Felix Adler, was the son of Rabbi Samuel Adler of Temple Emanu-El in New York. Though trained in Germany for a rabbinical career, young Adler decided that Judaism as well as the other organized faiths had outlived their usefulness. Believing that the moral motive alone could be made permanent and fruitful in religion, he organized in New York in 1876 a Society for Ethical Culture. Within the following decade similar groups were formed in Philadelphia, Chicago and St. Louis.[49] Although the movement originated with a great Jewish leader, it was otherwise of a non-Jewish character, its members and leaders coming mainly from the ranks of the Free Religious Association and of the liberal Christian churches. Thus, the heads of the Societies outside New York were of Gentile heritage, who as religious thinkers repudiated Christianity on both intellectual and social grounds. Through a radical reconstruction of religion they hoped to check the evil tendencies in American life.[50]

The liberal philosophy furnished support and authority for

[47] Quoted in William Reed Huntington, *The Church Idea; An Essay Toward Unity* (New York, 1870), pp. 116–17.
[48] *Index*, March 4, 1870, p. 5.
[49] W. L. Sheldon, *An Ethical Movement*, pp. xi–xiii.
[50] F. Adler, *Creed and Deed* (New York, 1877), pp. 167–169.

the movement. Ethical culture stressed freedom in order that religion might appeal to the moral ideal, which after all was the only subject worthy of reverence. In no sense a materialist, Adler did not deny immortality, but, believing that it could not be proved, he refused to build ethical law upon it. Otherwise, any undermining of belief would destroy the sanction for good conduct. He felt, also, that the social objectives of liberalism required organization and that, in this respect, the Ethical Societies stood for a new departure. The liberalism of the past, he declared in 1879, "was merely negative," centering in the influence of strong personalities. But the new liberalism "must pass the stage of individualism, must become the soul of great combinations." [51] He wished the Societies for Ethical Culture to combine the freedom of the liberals with organization akin to that of the Roman Catholic Church.[52]

Most liberals approved the venture. Thus Octavius Brooks Frothingham of New York, president of the Free Religious Association, disbanded his congregation in 1879. In a farewell sermon, he declared that "the era of individualism is drawing to a close. . . . It seems to me that the world is on the verge of an era when organization will be invoked to work out our problems." [53] He commended the Society for Ethical Culture as a logical successor to his own society. Francis E. Abbot agreed with Frothingham, seeing in the ethical movement the realization of the "ten years' ideal" of Free Religion.[54] When the *Unitarian Review* pronounced Adler's work a "retreat," William J. Potter of New Bedford replied that by organizing "on the foundation of ethical culture and moral idealism," "modern radicalism proves its advance on preceding forms of the same spirit, which were mainly destructive." [55] Social re-

[51] Free Religious Assoc., *Report*, 1879, pp. 42–43.
[52] *Creed and Deed*, esp. pp. 170–171.
[53] *Index*, May 8, 1879, pp. 222–223; J. Coleman Adams, "Certain Intellectual Tendencies in America," *Universalist Quart.*, XVI (October 1879), 377–378.
[54] *Index*, Feb. 20, 1879, p. 90.
[55] "Is it Retreat or Advance?" *ibid.*, Sept. 11, 1879, p. 439.

form, especially industrial education and the social settlements, received intelligent, persistent support from Ethical Culturists. The program of the American Christian Commission, along with agitation for coöperation, disclosed the missionary and humanitarian aspects of the urban challenge. There remained for study and interpretation the industrial problem which underlay all social ills. Though a growing number of Christians recognized the problem, only a few thoroughly analyzed it. Among these were the men who organized in 1872 the Christian Labor Union of Boston on a platform reading as follows:

The Christian Labor Union of Boston is composed of persons who seek to obey Jesus Christ's command, "Follow Me," and to secure obedience to it in the conduct of every form of human labor. It adopts the Bible principles of the Hebrew church in its relations to Land, Labor and Capital. It assumes that Jesus Christ founded no new church, but that He came to expand the one then existing into perfect form, by laying aside its cumbrous ceremonial, and unfolding to their fulness those spiritual principles in it which pertained to the temporal life of man as well as bringing man into a right relation to God. Believing that the poverty of the poor is very largely the cause of their absence from the churches, and of the low moral condition of some of them, the Christian Labor Union aims at least to point out that cause distinctly.[56]

The leaders in this first definite attempt to join Christianity and the labor movement were E. H. Rogers of Chelsea, Massachusetts, T. Wharton Collens of New Orleans and Jesse H. Jones, Congregational pastor at North Abington, Massachusetts. Rogers, a Methodist, was labor's foremost champion in the General Court, making, for example, the brilliant minority report in favor of an eight-hour working day and steering to passage the bill for creating the Massachusetts Bureau of Statistics for Labor.[57] Collens, jurist, Utopian socialist and devout Roman Catholic, largely financed the Union, besides

---

[56] *Equity*, April, 1874, p. 8.
[57] Carroll D. Wright, "The Growth and Progress of Bureaus of Statistics of Labor," *Jour. of Soc. Science*, No. XXV (December 1888), pp. 1-5.

writing extensively in its interest.[58] Jones, a graduate of Harvard and of Andover Seminary, was one of the first ministers to become aggressively identified with the cause of labor. He served a term in the General Court, worked for the State Labor Bureau and helped organize the Knights of Labor. Lofty purpose and sustained intellectual power characterized his many books and published sermons.[59] As chief writer for the Christian Labor Union, he edited its two small newspapers, *Equity* and the *Labor Balance.*

Though Rogers, Collens and Jones led the movement, the labor reformers as a whole supported it, including such prominent figures as Ira Stewart, George E. McNeill and Wendell Phillips. The Eight Hour League Convention of 1874 declared that the Christian Labor Union "deserves and should receive the warmest commendation of all labor reformers." [60] This endorsement is not surprising, for the Union championed the enlarging viewpoint of humanitarians, that industrialism, by subjecting workers to the power of capital, had degraded them into wage serfdom. Much was made of the incompatibility of industrial despotism on the one hand with political democracy on the other. "The Labor problem," said Jones, "is, How shall America grow out of an industrial system, all hostile to her political system, into an industrial system in harmony therewith?" [61] In an address before striking workingmen in 1873, he advised them to "carry the New England town meeting into the management of all affairs of work and wealth, where men work in joint interests together." [62]

---

[58] *The Eden of Labor; or the Christian Utopia* (Philadelphia, 1876); "View of the Labor Movement," *Cath. World*, X (March 1870), 784–798.

[59] See especially his autobiography, *Joshua Davidson, Christian* (New York, 1907); *The Kingdom of Heaven* (Boston, 1871), and *The Bible Plan for the Abolition of Poverty and the New Political Economy Involved Therein* (Boston, 1873).

[60] "Eight Hour League Convention," *Equity*, June 1874, p. 20.

[61] "The Labor Problem — A Statement of the Question from the Labor Reform Side," *Internat. Rev.*, IX (July 1880), 61.

[62] *Joshua Davidson, Christian*, p. 129.

As a further elaboration of its program, the Union, somewhat on the analogy of the Marxian socialists who wished to destroy a so-called surplus value, proclaimed "labor cost" as the "just limit of price." The value of an article, Collens contended, was determined by the amount of labor time expended upon it.[63] Though the leaders believed that labor legislation would promote a more equitable distribution of wealth, they stressed labor organization as the chief means of compelling capital to agree to industrial democracy and coöperation. There could be no peace and justice, said Jones "until organized labor fronts organized capital and brings it to terms." When that occurred, the two parties could "ascertain what is for their mutual benefit," and, each yielding here and holding there, "work out together their common welfare."[64] These proposed reforms were necessary to uproot the pagan property system — the "embodied anti-Christ of our times," as the Union called it.

The Union bitterly complained that, while Christianity as the ideal of human brotherhood offered a true solution of the industrial problem, the churches were not only indifferent but antagonistic. "The great body of rich churches, if forced to the issue," said Jones, "would . . . deliberately set up some form of paganism, rather than submit to the thorough preaching of the truth . . . concerning property." At most, the church taught men how to dispose of wealth; but it refused to teach them how morally to acquire wealth. "So the church says that, to build a theological seminary is serving God; and she accepts half a million of money from a man [Daniel Drew] who got it by the most iniquitous service of Mammon, and *names the seminary after the man*."[65] Perverted attitudes on the part of Protestants towards the problems of property and wealth stemmed, the Union said, from the Reformation doctrine that religion lacked authority in temporal affairs.[66] The Protestant

---

[63] "The Measure of Hardship," *Labor Balance*, October 1877, pp. 6–8.
[64] *Joshua Davidson, Christian*, p. 128.   [65] *Ibid.*, p. 206.
[66] E. H. Rogers, *Like Unto Me* (Boston, 1876), p. 15.

Church, as Jones contended, fostered a separation between politics and religion: "Protestantism, not only does not teach, but it strenuously denies that Jesus was a secular leader." [67] To correct this misinterpretation of Christianity, the second public meeting of the Christian Labor Union, in May, 1875, resolved that the God of the Bible "sets forth in that book a two-fold work. . . . One branch is to cure men in their innate tendency to evil, and is called Regeneration . . . the other branch is to establish in the earth that divine order and conduct of human society which Jesus Christ called the Kingdom of God." [68]

The Union agreed that Protestants rightly emphasized the first doctrine, the doctrine of Eternal Life. Yet they did not fully understand it, for they generally interpreted it as referring to a future world when its real meaning was the life of Jesus Christ in the soul. The essential characteristic of the Christly life was love, good will to others, a disposition "which ultimates in service through sacrifice." Jones pointed out that individual regeneration in this sense had social significance. "As the spirit and life in the heart is for others," he said, "so the structure of the community is such as to enable all persons in it to move about more freely to help and serve one another." For Jesus, even though He sanctioned spiritual methods only, meant his kingdom to "be a literal world-empire here on the earth." That kingdom was in deadly conflict with the industrial system of modern Christendom. The changes wrought by God in human hearts would inevitably effect a social revolution, peaceful if those in power would allow, but violent, as in the slavery contest, if they resisted. [69]

By whatever means effected, the coming economic order would be "a form of society" making "provision for the common wants of all." [70] In the light of this probability the churches

---

[67] *Equity*, August 1874, p. 36.   [68] *Ibid.*, June 1875, pp. 17-18.

[69] *Joshua Davidson, Christian*, pp. 31-33, 40-45, 119, 244.

[70] *Labor Balance*, October 1877, pp. 4-5.

must reëxamine their policies. Although the Union approved the program of the American Christian Commission, it urged the congregations to stress justice instead of charity. Let ministers expend time on shortening the hours of labor, on establishing coöperative institutions and on securing to every family an inalienable home; and they "will find to their astonished delight that our north streets will begin to change, and will in due time pass away, and that all missions to them will cease, for they will be no longer needed." [71] When the Y.M.C.A. of New York aided unemployed workers to replace other workers on strike to resist a wage cut, the Union formally protested, accusing the Association of "helping the poor to eat up the poor. . . ." Charity of this kind, the Union claimed, was "doing more to alienate the poor from the Gospel of Jesus than all the infidel publications of the world could do without it." [72]

The Christian Labor Union did not expect to see economic individualism immediately displaced. Industrial czars had been ordained in the nature and unfoldment of human society. "I know," said Jones, "that without them the capacities of man for coöperation on any scale commensurate with his destiny could never have been developed." [73] In this view, the problem of winning industrial democracy was the task of educating society in the principles of equity. In the existing state of religious opinion, the Union did not believe that Protestantism could be of great assistance. But the leaders hoped that eventually the church would champion labor reform. Change would come, said Rogers, "*indirectly* through the associated action of the members of the church of Christ, in mutual care of each other's pecuniary welfare, thus gradually leavening society with the principles of the Decalogue and the motives of the Gospel." [74] To this end, the Union advised the congregations

[71] *Equity*, April 1874, pp. 2–3.
[72] *Ibid.*, March 1875, p. 7.
[73] "The Labor Problem — A Statement of the Question from the Labor Reform Side," *loc. cit.*, p. 58.
[74] *The Hope of the Republic* (Boston, 1886), p. 3.

to form mutual benefit societies. Their success would be "the first step in retrieving the pernicious error that the church was designed to be a purely spiritual organization." [75] In thus correlating charity or social service with its sweeping program of industrial reconstruction, the Union set out the full meaning of social Christianity.

Though the new trends in Protestant thinking seemed revolutionary, they were no more than wise reactions to a changing social scene. For if America was to be "preëminently a nation of cities," religion could expect its rural ideals and techniques to be modified. Although the rural and urban middle classes continued to support a purely spiritual religion, the poorer folk of the great cities called upon Christianity to champion their industrial demands and to provide agencies for their social and moral welfare. Sensing the situation, the more progressive Protestants organized for the purpose of bringing about a thoroughgoing religious readjustment. While the Christian Labor Union made clear the long-range implications of social Christianity, the American Christian Commission was of far greater significance, displaying the seriousness of the urban crisis in terms of immediate religious problems and suggesting social-service methods. Its plan and philosophy of action were so comprehensive that all kindred subsequent movements could be but elaborations or specializations. Of special importance for its guidance of "Christian work" in the early days, it created a tradition of religious and social sympathy which influenced all later social movements in Protestant America.

[75] *Equity*, February 1875, p. 4.

CHAPTER II

THE GENESIS OF PROTESTANT SOCIAL SERVICE
1865–1880

PROTESTANTS attempted to solve urban problems mainly through social service. Though they realized as time passed that fundamental changes in the economic and political constitution of society were necessary, they were always more immediately interested in the humanitarian and spiritual phases of human welfare. From the outset, the city mission providing both physical and moral aids to the poor held the foremost place in social Christianity. By 1880 urban missionary effort embraced five closely related types of philanthropy: (1) the humanitarian endeavor of various congregations; (2) the support of city missions through extra-parochial associations, denominational and undenominational; (3) the organizations for handling special groups in the population, especially youth; (4) the efforts to combat peculiar forms of evil, notably intemperance; and (5) the successful plans for the training of city missionaries. Together, these services constituted what for want of a better term may be called the Protestant religio-social system.

Since the congregations were the unit-cells of Christianity, their willingness in large numbers to care for the poor would be the measure of Protestant ability to serve the city. Men identified with the American Christian Commission — Dwight L. Moody and clergymen like Thomas K. Beecher, Theodore L. Cuyler, Howard Crosby, Samuel J. Nicholls and Stephen H. Tyng, Jr. — were among the first to enlarge the scope of church work.[1] The most resourceful and dramatic of these leaders

---

[1] *Document No. 8*, pp. 27–31, 47–49; W. H. Daniels, *D. L. Moody and His Work*, pp. 103–108, 119–120.

was the Reverend Thomas K. Beecher, pastor of an independent Congregational church in Elmira, New York, from 1850 to 1900. He induced his wage-earning parishioners in the early seventies to erect a costly structure splendidly equipped for social service as well as for worship. The varied facilities of this church, among them free baths for the "unclean of the congregation," led Mark Twain, Beecher's brother-in-law, to write that we "are going to have at least one sensible, but very, very curious church in America." Another admirer writing after Beecher's death, pronounced his church "one of the first, if not the very first, People's Palaces ever erected." [2]

More influential, perhaps, was Stephen H. Tyng, Jr., who earnestly pleaded for the return of the churches to the ideals of primitive Christianity and proved himself an excellent organizer at Holy Trinity Church, New York, in the fifteen years after the war. Planning to adjust the family church "to the demands of a new life and a changed condition of society," [3] and commencing in 1864 with a Pastoral Aid Society and two additional organizations, one each for men and women, Tyng perfected one of the great mission churches of America. Church members at Holy Trinity were valued chiefly for their ability to influence the indifferent, the destitute and the outcast. Tyng always entrusted his helpers with full responsibility, removing those who proved inefficient. But since he assigned men in accordance with their secular callings — for example, physicians to care for the sick and lawyers to protect the rights of the poor — he seldom experienced difficulty. [4] Thus managed, Holy Trinity appealed to all lovers of humanity, and when in 1878 it encountered financial trouble, New York philanthropists endowed it with an annual income for the "support of

---

[2] Samuel L. Clemens (Mark Twain), "A New Beecher Church," in *Curious Dreams and Other Sketches*, pp. 34–38; W. S. B. Mathews, "A Remarkable Personality — Thomas K. Beecher," *Outlook*, March 10, 1906, pp. 555–761.
[3] "Ecclesiastical French Flats," *Independent*, Feb. 22, 1877, p. 1.
[4] Stephen H. Tyng, Jr., "Our Church Work," *ibid.*, Nov. 8, 1876, p. 372; *ibid.*, Nov. 15, 1876, pp. 392–393; *ibid.*, Nov. 27, 1876, p. 412.

undenominational, evangelistic and humanitarian work among the poor of New York City." [5] Fate was less kind to Dr. Tyng himself. Ruining his health by overwork, he was forced in 1881 to retire permanently from the ministry.

These successful churches were undenominational, professing only faith and discipleship in Jesus Christ. But the angry condemnation which greeted similar churches showed that public opinion was not yet ready for a creedless Christianity. Thus, during the seventies ministers like W. H. H. Murray of Boston, David Swing of Chicago and Edward Eggleston of Brooklyn were obliged to abandon their humanitarian congregations. In the eyes of Eggleston, his venture was "the Church of the Christian Endeavor," but to most people it was "the Church of the Holy Ambiguity" that "believes nothing, teaches nothing, has no opinions and admits all possible opinions as to the truth and falsehood of Christ's Gospel and way of salvation." [6] The various attempts to organize congregations on a simple Christian basis no doubt encouraged the denominations to bestir themselves. The Protestant Episcopal Church, for example, increasingly subordinated theological interests to the more constructive tasks of urban religious extension. "There is no better way of helping the city poor in their temporal distresses . . . ," wrote the *Church Review*, in 1855, "than by establishing Free Churches in every destitute part of our cities." [7] Within a few years the official agencies, such as the General Convention, the Diocesan Conventions and the Board of Domestic and Foreign Missions, were earnestly studying social problems and formulating plans to solve them. Toward the end of the period, in 1874, the more active leaders formed a national Free Church Association to promote the movement within and without the Episcopal communion.

The Reverend William A. Muhlenberg contributed most to

[5] *New York Tribune*, Dec. 17, 1877, p. 8; *ibid.*, Feb. 25, 1878, p. 2.
[6] Quoted in *Christian Union*, May 19, 1875, p. 422.
[7] "City Missions," VIII (October, 1855), 393–394.

the early Episcopal social movement. His Evangelical Catholic principles, as has been pointed out, nourished the coöperative spirit among Protestants. As early as 1845 he had founded in New York the Church of the Holy Communion whose free pews and novel benevolent adjuncts strongly appealed to the plain people. Moreover, the outgrowths of this church were quite important. In order to insure proper oversight of the poor, Muhlenberg in defiance of Protestant opinion established an order of deaconesses, the first in the English-speaking Protestant world. In 1857 these women took charge of Muhlenberg's recently established St. Luke's Hospital. Since false, non-interventionist theories kept government indifferent to the plight of tenement dwellers, Muhlenberg designed a "Christian industrial community" or "rural settlement" to relieve a few victims and to serve as an object lesson in applied social science. In 1870, St. Johnland, as the community was called, opened on a pleasant site a few miles up the Hudson, and, in addition to the cottages, included a church, a home for crippled children and a home for the aged.[8] In these ways Muhlenberg showed, as one of his followers said, "that one work of the church of God for man is to teach and feed and heal." [9]

Another pioneer was William Welsh, a Philadelphia merchant, who had long devoted his main energies to religion and philanthropy. Such varied activities as church extension, Sunday school teaching, religious journalism and the founding of young men's institutes had enlisted his interest before humanitarian impulses began stirring in the Protestant Episcopal Church. Appointed the first manager of the Episcopal Hospital in 1850 Welsh had made it a social and religious center, from which men and women went out to care for the needs of the people in their homes. When experience at the hospital showed

[8] Annie Ayers, *William Augustus Muhlenberg*, 4th ed. (New York, 1889), p. 208, *passim; Christian Union*, Jan. 29, 1885, p. 25; *Outlook*, Dec. 19, 1896, p. 1144.
[9] William Adams, "A Policy for the Church in the Nation," *Church Rev.*, XXX (October 1877), 532.

the surprising effectiveness of Christian sympathy between classes as a method of religious extension, Welsh decided to apply it to his own parish, that of St. Mark's in the Frankford suburb. Though the parish was located in an industrial section occupied chiefly by English immigrants, it did not have in its membership a single male wage-earner. But systematic lay effort, first with the wives of immigrants and then with their husbands, broke down the cold formality of the regular parishioners and won the confidence of non-churchgoers. Four committees, dealing with the young and old of both sexes, persuaded two hundred workingmen to join the Bible classes and nearly seven hundred families, mainly of the laboring group, to worship in the church. Nor did these amazing increases in membership involve any resort to degrading almsgiving of the usual sort.[10] Toward the end of the century, an Episcopal minister truly said that "few parishes have become so well known throughout the country as St. Mark's." It was a "model parish in the number, variety and the success of its parochial activities."[11]

The Congregationalists, whose churches in New England had long suffered from the migration of members to the frontier and to the cities, also took steps to enlarge the scope of church work. They repeatedly spoke in the post-war years of Home Evangelization, which meant, they said, that the congregations must organize with a view to bringing all persons, whatever their social status, within reach of religious influences. The church was to be not an end in itself but a means to the Christianization of society.[12] In the words of the Reverend A. S. Chesebrough of Connecticut, the church in its work must be "intensive as well as extensive, it must leaven and transform human character and human society."[13] Though the National Council,

[10] M. A. DeW. Howe, *Memoir of William Welsh* (Philadelphia, 1878), pp. 4-17.

[11] G. W. Shinn, *King's Handbook of Notable Episcopal Churches*, p. 67.

[12] Leonard Bacon, "Home Evangelization," *Congregational Quarterly*, IV (April 1862), 199-212.

[13] *Home Work, or Parochial Christianization* (Boston, 1867), p. 84.

meeting in Boston in 1865, recommended a program of home evangelization for every church, it had neither authority to enforce its proposals nor means to encourage their adoption. But the scheme was taken up in some of the State Associations, particularly in Massachusetts. In 1865 the General Conference, with the assistance of the State Home Missionary Society, launched a plan for developing the full power of the church. Daniel P. Noyes resigned as Secretary of the American Home Missionary Society to become State Secretary of the Committee on Home Evangelization, feeling that the ministers and churches "are not insensible to the approval of new and serious responsibilities" — problems in the solution of which the popular virtue would be tested even more severely than it had been during the war.[14]

The Committee in Massachusetts as well as those in other States collected statistical data which revealed a high average percentage of church neglect, and probed into its causes. These included the inevitable dislocations incident to radical changes in population, the widespread antipathy between foreigner and native-born and the costliness of public worship.[15] Yet caste rather than cost was the main factor. Thus, in 1868, a committee of Boston ministers reported that the "difficulties in the solution of the city problem are not financial, but purely moral. When not resolvable into unbelief, they are to be summed up in this, that the rich and poor have no just feelings toward one another, and do not like to worship God together." No solution was possible until it was recognized that the "church is an institution for humanity, not for a caste."[16]

The Committee on Home Evangelization in Massachusetts drew up plans of work for the congregations, pointing out some

[14] *Congregationalist*, Jan. 13, 1865, p. 5.

[15] General Conference, *Minutes*, 1863, pp. 22–24; *ibid.*, 1866, pp. 62–63, 70; General Association, *Minutes*, 1869, pp. 46–47; Maine General Conference, *Minutes*, 1860, pp. 6–7, 63; *ibid.*, 1862, p. 63; Leonard Bacon, "Our Home Heathen and How to Reach Them," *New Englander*, XVIII (November 1860), pp. 998–1019.   [16] General Association, *Minutes*, 1868, p. 49.

of the things which church responsibility for communities involved.[17] It stressed the necessity for supervising the sick and the poor. Large numbers of poverty-stricken people, said the *Report* for 1871, had been alienated "because in their affliction they were not visited," and "neglected children are daily becoming a peril to the State as well as a grief to all the good, by reason of a similar lack of timely care." As a means of overcoming this difficulty the committee suggested that churches organize women into companies of visitors "for the relief of the poor, the sick, unprotected children and all others who may be accessible to neighborly benevolence — such companions designed for both a temporal and spiritual ministry." [18]

Though the majority of churches and ministers in Massachusetts either opposed or failed to grasp the significance of the State Association's plan, an increasing number caught its essential spirit. The Reverend James M. Whiton of the First Congregational Church in Lynn pointed out in 1873 that the movement was a "protest against the extreme individualism of ultra Protestantism in favor of the New Testament conception of the Church as both 'a household and a working band' " and that the idea "is slowly but surely taking possession of pastors." [19] Whiton himself first championed social Christianity under the auspices of the Association. Prompted by Noyes, he and his young assistant, the Reverend Joseph Cook, arranged a series of meetings at the congregation in 1870–1871 for the purpose of promoting "a true labor reform." Addresses were given by prominent civic leaders and labor representatives of Massachusetts, among them George E. McNeill of Boston who was pleased to see "an orthodox Congregational Church open its doors for the free discussion of this industrial question." Though the remedies proposed by the various speakers were moderate and reasonable, the manufacturers of Lynn refused to

[17] *Ibid.*, 1872, pp. 51–53.   [18] *Ibid.*, 1871, pp. 45–47.
[19] "Church Activities in Massachusetts," *Congregationalist*, March 13, 1873, p. 82.

participate in the meetings or to adopt the suggested reforms — a rebuff which many socially minded churches were to suffer in the following years.[20]

Another leader notably efficient in church management was George R. Leavitt, pastor of Pilgrim Congregational Church in Cambridgeport, Massachusetts. Developing his church from a mission chapel, Leavitt avoided dependence on men of wealth and, opening the pews to all, relied upon the voluntary gifts of clerks and wage earners. Convinced that "organization is just as important to a church as to a business enterprise or to an army" and that its "fruits are just as certain," he created a General Committee of Work to direct five separate departments of religious activity.[21] Observers ascribed the congregation's almost continuous revivals of religion and the amazing growth in membership to his wise repudiation of dualism in the religious field. Under Leavitt's leadership, "men were made to feel the breadth of their social life and its corresponding obligations in the home, the city, the nation and the world," said the Reverend Samuel W. Dike. "The moral sense had been developed on every side in a practical way," he pointed out, "so that there was something to respond to the faithful preaching of the central doctrines of the Gospel."[22]

Outside the Episcopal and Congregational groups, few parishes engaged in humanitarian endeavor before 1880. Extra-parochial activity gauged better, perhaps, the rising social interest, since Protestants realized in much the same way as the Catholics did that isolated congregations were too weak to sustain the whole religious burden. Associations of broader scope were therefore deemed essential. One expression of the wider need was the thirty or more undenominational mission

[20] James M. Whiton, "The Churches on Labor Reform," *ibid.*, Dec. 22, 1870, p. 401; *ibid.*, Feb. 9, 1871, p. 61.
[21] George R. Leavitt, *A Brief History of Pilgrim Congregational Church, Cambridgeport, Massachusetts* (Boston, 1885), p. 2, *passim*.
[22] "The Religious Problem of the Country Town," *Andover Review*, II (August 1884), 129.

societies which by 1880 were active in both the larger and the smaller cities. The earliest of these bodies were tract societies which social changes had forced to broaden their work. "The migration of churches . . . ," said the New York City Mission and Tract Society in 1866, "from the lower and other parts of the city and the changes that have taken place in the population remaining, have gradually led to the establishment of what are usually denominated mission stations." These centers, located in all the lower wards of the city after 1852, looked after the most elementary temporal needs of the people. At the end of the war the New York Society drew up a well-rounded mission scheme, defending it as within the nature and design of Christianity.[23] The Brooklyn Tract Society, also convinced that the churches were not "equal to the emergency," assumed the mission status in 1858 as the Brooklyn City Mission and Tract Society.[24] When experience showed that converts made through preaching services and relief work did not value membership in the wealthy congregations, the several societies organized churches for them.[25]

But the handful of independent undenominational missions were more successful in attracting popular attention and were, therefore, of more significance for future social development. Among these were the Five Points Mission and House of Industry in New York, dating from 1850; the Howard Mission for little Wanderers in New York, founded in 1861; the North End Mission in Boston, formed in 1867; and the Water Street Mission in New York, opened in 1872.[26] They were alike in that

[23] New York City Mission, *City Evangelization* (New York, 1866), pp. 49–55, 66–69.

[24] *Annual Report*, 1856, pp. 9–13; *Brooklyn City Mission and Tract Journal*, 1867, p. 5; *ibid.*, November 1874, pp. 2–3.

[25] *Ibid.*, 1867, p. 5; *Christian Union*, Feb. 11, 1880, p. 131; *ibid.*, April 14, 1880, p. 347.

[26] "The Five Points House of Industry," *Amer. Church Monthly*, III (March 1858), 216–222; *ibid.* (April 1858), 289–297; *ibid.* (May 1858), 350–360; Henry Cammann and H. N. Camp, *The Charities of New York, Brooklyn and Staten Island*, pp. 435–440, 490–496.

they provided first for the material needs of humanity. "This we believe to be the Biblical way of reaching the heart," said the Managers of the North End Mission. "Till the cravings of hunger are satisfied, we cannot develop the moral nature." [27] The needs of women and children were given special attention through several agencies both remedial and preventive in character. The Five Points Mission, besides a working women's home, had seven buildings for welfare work; the Howard Mission erected model tenements and a hospital for sick poor children; and the North End Mission purchased a home for the training of children. These enterprises played up their nonsectarian character, the North End Mission declaring itself "thoroughly catholic" and "too great to be sectarian." [28]

The Water Street Mission, the outcome of a spectacular anti-prostitution campaign,[29] owed most to the arresting personality of its founder, Jerry MacAuley. Born in Ireland in 1837, he had come to America at the age of thirteen and grown up under his grandmother's care in the Fourth Ward in New York City. Exposed to temptations on every side, he became a tippler and petty thief in early boyhood, obtained, in rapid succession, the higher degrees of gambler, drunkard, burglar and what not, and at the age of nineteen faced a fifteen years' sentence. In prison the forces of goodness had their first chance at Jerry; he was converted by the "awful Gardiner," an ex-prize fighter. In 1864 he was pardoned, but on returning to the Fourth Ward he resumed his criminal career, only to be finally redeemed by the agents of the Howard Mission.

The public interest in Water Street suggested to MacAuley the founding of a permanent mission. Applying for advice and help to prominent clergymen and wealthy church members, he met with mortifying coldness or refusal. He received aid, however, from A. S. Hatch, the Dodge family and the Methodist

[27] *North End Mission Magazine*, I (January 1872), 17–18.
[28] *Ibid.*, I (April 1872), 3.
[29] Oliver Dyer, "The Wickedest Man in New York," *Packard's Monthly*, I (July 1868), 37–49; "The Water Street Mission," *ibid.*, II (February 1869), 56–7.

camp-meetings. Soon after incorporating the mission, Jerry secured a substantial well-equipped three-story brick mission house, and had also the assistance of his wife as a Bible reader. Though the institution specialized in the reform of social outcasts, it did not forget the dire poverty of tenement families of the neighborhood. In the wider fields of service, MacAuley succeeded in closing the most notorious dens of the vicinity. The property being owned by the rich, he could get no aid from the police, but finally he worked out his own system by which his converts secured evidence against offenders and appeared as witnesses in the courts. In this way the dens were broken up one by one "until they became as scarce as they had once been plentiful." [30]

A rescue agency, the mission emphasized lively evangelistic services in which MacAuley was expert. His preaching, as all lay preaching, tended to be direct and conversational. His speaking was described as "a strange melange of earnestness, experience, humility and wit, with not the least attempt at eloquence and apparently no study of effects." [31] Unlike many men of his type, however, he avoided pious pretension and mission cant. He simply told how God had been successful with him. That his methods won approval was attested at his death in 1884, when he was given the largest private funeral in the history of New York City. In reclaiming social outcasts he had been remarkably successful, and often his converts followed his example in various other cities. His influence upon the cultured classes was no less pronounced. They, too, were "converted" in the sense that many of them resolved to devote their lives to the welfare of others.[32]

In the denominations, extra-parochial activity was quite apparent. Unitarians, for example, formed Unions for Christian

---

[30] R. M. Offord, *Jerry MacAuley, An Apostle to the Lost*, pp. 44–45, 70–71.

[31] Coleman E. Bishop, "Jerry MacAuley and His Work," *Chautauquan*, V (April 1885), 391.

[32] S. H. Hadley, *Down in Water Street, passim.*

Work as a natural outgrowth of sermons and moral instructions by prominent ministers in theaters and music halls. Begun in 1865 by the Reverend George H. Hepworth of Boston, these meetings were held in several sections of the country, everywhere appealing to non-churchgoers. Unitarian leaders explained in the National Conference that the movement arose to compensate partly for the failure of the churches to provide properly for the spiritual needs of urban communities. The Conference members clearly realized that the social inequalities of the new industrialism expressed themselves religiously in an aristocratic church system. "We cannot divorce our ecclesiasticism from property," insisted William B. Weeden, "the church must devise a method to give it healthy action." This was all the more necessary because the wage-earning class, which had little interest in churches, would wield a very strong influence in another generation.[33]

The first Union for Christian Work, formed in Providence in the spring of 1868, was followed by similar ones in Boston, New Bedford, Salem, Brooklyn, Lowell, Cambridge, New York, Chicago and San Francisco. Since they were substantially alike, a few words about the Providence Union, in which Weeden was the guiding figure, will delineate the movement. The Union "required no declaration of belief, but laid its foundation in the simplest form of creed: 'The object of the members shall be to do good and to grow better.' " The equipment of the Union included rooms for reading and instruction, and a commodious hall for lectures and entertainments. A reporter for the *New York Tribune* wrote in 1870 that the Union "is really a church, a school, a free library, a lyceum, a charity, a social club, all in one. . . ." This social service was esteemed, not only as excellent in itself, but because it gave religion an unusual appeal. "If the clergyman who in his study bewails the decline of the church," concluded Weeden, "would break into life outside his limits, he would see where

[33] *Annual Meeting*, 1868, pp. 58–65, 90–92.

the real power of the church lies, and comprehend its invincible strength." [34]

Though leaders in the Protestant Episcopal social movement relied largely upon the parish church, they also recognized the "necessity of organized mission work extra parochial in all large cities." [35] Accordingly, city mission societies were formed, beginning in the early fifties, in New York, Baltimore, New Haven, Charleston, New Orleans and elsewhere.[36] By 1856 the General Convention could call attention "to the rapidly extending work of city missions, and to the large provision making for the relief of the poor and the afflicted in our principal cities." [37] Thus in Baltimore, the House of Industry, founded in February, 1856, furnished lodgings and meals, and sought work for the unemployed. Generally, however, conventional charities were the outcome. The Society in Brooklyn, for example, became the Church Charity Foundation in charge of an orphan's home, a home for the aged and a hospital. The remarkable array of Episcopal philanthropic institutions coming into existence during the fifties and sixties was as a rule the result of city missions.

The New York Protestant Episcopal City Mission was the agency for much of the denomination's early social service. The Mission was the outcome, in 1864, of an earlier organization, in which the Reverend William and Mrs. Richmond and others had proffered religious solace to the recipients of the city charities. Finding strictly religious work and the existing charities of the city woefully inadequate to the needs of women and children in every state of degradation, Mrs. Richmond supplied the necessary agencies: the House of Mercy, the Home of the Homeless, the Sheltering Arms, the Infant Asylum and St.

[34] Weeden, "Report on Christian Union," *ibid.*, 1870, pp. 106, 111–113.
[35] W. H. Jefferys, *The City Mission Idea* (Philadelphia, 1922), pp. 15–16.
[36] *Journal*, p. 214.
[37] *Ibid.*, 1853, pp. 253, 263; *ibid.*, 1859, pp. 256, 266–267, 312; *ibid.*, 1862, pp. 181, 192–193; *ibid.*, 1868, p. 336; *ibid.*, 1871, p. 440; *Amer. Church Monthly*, II (April 1857), 317; *ibid.*, II (June 1857), 474–475.

Barnabas House.[38] In order to provide separate treatment for outcast women the Episcopal parishes of New York launched an agitation in 1866 for a "midnight mission." Circulars were sent out, public meetings held and sermons delivered in many of the churches, those of Muhlenberg being the most effective. By 1868 the Protestant Episcopal City Mission had in all seven institutions whose work, while largely concerned with the temporal welfare of the neglected classes, was "animated throughout by a spiritual motive." [39]

Closely associated with the city mission movement among Episcopalians were the brotherhoods or guilds which sprang up in various cities during the fifties and federated into the Brotherhood of the Protestant Episcopal Church. Unlike the English guilds which stressed art and sacramental devotion, the ones in America were relief societies.[40] An interesting outgrowth of the guilds was the workingmen's clubs, of which twenty-two were formed before 1885 when the first Congress of Workingmen's Clubs and Institutes was held. Typical of these clubs was the pioneer one, formed in Philadelphia by William Welsh in 1870. Like the guilds, it provided poor relief, but in addition it arranged systematically for instruction and recreation. Although the club was managed by an executive committee from St. Mark's Church, there was no religious qualification for membership, any eighteen-year old of good moral character being privileged to join. The workingmen's clubs helped to counteract the virus of aristocracy in church life by epitomizing the principles of true Christian charity and by pointing the way to the solution of social problems through association.[41]

[38] "Church Missions in New York," *Church Rev.*, XIV (January 1861), 359–370.

[39] *Spirit of Missions*, XXXVII (January 1872), 351; *ibid.* (July, 1872), 421–422; *ibid.* (August 1872), 479–480; *ibid.*, XXXVIII (February 1873), 91–92.

[40] *Church Rev.*, XI (May 1858), 334–37; *ibid.*, XVII (October 1864), 394–409; *Journal of a Convention of the Brotherhood of the Protestant Episcopal Church* (New York, 1853), pp. 7–15.

[41] Congress of Workingmen's Clubs, *Workingmen's Clubs and Institutes in the United States* (New York, 1885); J. G. Holland, "A New System in City Churches," *Scribner's Monthly*, VIII (June 1874), 241–242.

Though in this period few of the largest denominations undertook systems of city missions, they realized that in establishing elementary charities they were furthering this aspect of religious extension. Thus, in 1870, a Presbyterian Alliance was formed in Philadelphia "to combine the interests and energies of the Presbyteries in thorough and systematic work for the evangelization of the masses." When offered property for a hospital, the Alliance accepted it in the conviction that the "Christian idea of ministrations to the destitute, sick and suffering of our race is that which combines bodily relief with spiritual benefit." [42] Some of the denominations, notably the Lutheran, devoted special attention to immigrants. To this end, the Synods of the General Council in 1873 established a home for them in New York City which, in the next twelve years, cared for over eighty-five thousand people. Aside from spiritual instruction, the home temporarily lodged immigrants, handled their money, forwarded them to their friends and relatives and helped them to secure employment. The Synods in the Synodical Conference had, in addition to several immigrant missions in New York and Baltimore, the excellent Lutheran Pilgrim House in the first-named city. Some other Synods later followed these examples. The Swedish Lutheran Churches in 1881 furnished a home for Scandinavian immigrants in Brooklyn; the Augustana Synod in 1893, a Swedish Emigrant House in New York City; and the Southern Synods in 1900, a German Immigrant Home and Seaman's Mission in Baltimore.[43]

Likewise, to some extent, Methodists combined a social with a spiritual ministry in their missionary activity among Germans and Scandinavians. Thus, during the centennial of American Methodism in 1866, John H. Ockerhausen gave twenty-five thousand dollars for an Immigrant House in New York City. With the aid of the German New York Port Mis-

[42] Presbyterian Hospital in Philadelphia, *Annual Report*, 1873, p. 10.
[43] Helen M. Sweeney, "Handling the Immigrant," *Catholic World*, LXXVII (July 1896), 504 ff.; *Stall's Lutheran Year Book*, 1885, pp. 92, 97, 110; Bureau of the Census, *Benevolent Institutions*, 1910, pp. 198, 224.

sion Home Association, it helped both immigrants and seamen by giving board, handling money and securing employment. Though successful, the House was discontinued in 1877. Scandinavians received similar service from a bethel ship, the *John Wesley*, in charge of the beloved Pastor A. G. Hedstrom from 1845 to 1877. This agency was "an asylum for destitute immigrants, supplying for them at once bed, board, table, wardrobe and sanctuary. It was a labor agency for hundreds, thus blessing not only the stranger but those who employed him." [44]

Though the Protestant Episcopal Church, like most denominations, failed to establish port missions and immigrant homes, it realized that the newcomers needed special attention. For the English immigrant, slow to adjust himself to the voluntary system of church support, the Anglo-American Church Emigrant's Aid Society was formed in 1855 to supply letters of introduction and to subsidize pastors and teachers.[45] In helping the Protestant Episcopal Church, the Church of England was but following the example of Roman Catholics in Europe who raised large missionary sums for their bishops in America. By presenting their "Memorial" for a more flexible church service to the General Convention of 1853, Muhlenberg and his friends showed their great interest in the movement to make Episcopalianism attractive to immigrants, especially those of Lutheran heritage. Before 1880 some of their hopes had been realized.[46] The Church German Society, formed in New York City in 1874, furnished the means for training German-speaking ministers to serve as assistants in the regular congregations. This plan proved successful in several places, notably at Grace Church, New York, which became known as a center for far-

[44] J. M. Reed, *Missions and the Missionary Society of the Methodist Episcopal Church*, II, 434; Missionary Society of the Methodist Episcopal Church, *Report*, 1866, pp. 147–148; *ibid.*, 1881, p. 246; *ibid.*, 1873, pp. 162–163.

[45] William Adams, "The Church and Our Foreign Population," *Church Rev.*, XI (July 1858), 242–243.

[46] *Journal*, 1853, p. 182; *ibid.*, 1865, pp. 361–363; *ibid.*, 1868, p. 458; *ibid.*, 1871, pp. 289–290; *ibid.*, 1880, pp. 157–160; Muhlenberg, "An Exposition of the Memorial," *Evangelical Catholic Papers*, I, 109, *passim*.

reaching missionary operations among Germans in all parts of the city.[47]

In much the same way as immigrants, the thousands of homeless young men and women who responded to the lure of the city needed that careful attention which only extra-parochial organization could supply. Even more than the independent city missions, the Young Men's and Young Women's Christian Associations owed their remarkable growth to the failure of the city church to provide for social needs. At first these organizations, especially the Y.M.C.A., cared for the poor generally, but as a result of discussion and experiment in the years immediately following the war, they decided to restrict their activities mainly to middle-class youth of the respective sexes. The Y.M.C.A., with its task thus lessened and specialized, had by 1880 over sixty well-equipped buildings to supply the religious and social demands of young men. Recognizing that the Y.M.C.A. was performing a function beyond their power, ministers and denominations after some hesitation acquiesced in its existence. The General Assembly of the Presbyterian Church, for example, endorsed it in 1877 as "a perfect adaptation of the church to a peculiar situation." [48]

The building program of the Y.M.C.A. showed vitality largely because substitutes were needed for the splendor of the gin palaces, casinos and theaters. American Christians had begun to see, as the Reverend William G. Blaikie of Scotland said in 1870, "that if the devil is to be fought with any purpose, the war must be carried on regardless of expense." [49] Other influences, however, encouraged the movement, among them the brilliant example of the New York Association, the improved organization worked out by the Albany Convention of 1866, and splendid leadership. The New York Association,

[47] *Report*, 1881, pp. 3–5; *Spirit of Missions*, XXXVIII (October 1873), 605–607; *ibid.* (December 1873), 742; *ibid.*, XL (June 1875), 351.

[48] *Minutes*, 1877, p. 58.

[49] "America and the Americans," *Sunday Magazine*, II (December 1870), 159–162.

reorganized in 1864 by William E. Dodge and others, persuaded New Yorkers to provide it with a massive structure in which after 1869 it carried out, in the face of inertia and prejudice, a four-fold program — "the improvement of the spiritual, mental, social and physical conditions of young men." [50] The Executive Committee of the national Association popularized this policy through its field work and its *Association Monthly*, a magazine published for three years, beginning in 1870. "Till the building crisis is passed," it warned, the branch Association "is simply an experiment." [51] To this same end, the several State Associations brought pressure upon the local Associations. [52] All this would have availed little without the leadership of strong personalities, many of whom were members of the American Christian Commission. Of these, Moody contributed most, especially in finance, raising for the Associations in the course of his life over a million dollars. [53]

The Associations did not adhere strictly to their specialized field. The New York Association, for example, organized in 1872 a Bowery Branch to coöperate with the City Mission and Tract Society in providing poor relief. Led by John Dooly, it established a soup kitchen, a lodging house and an efficient employment bureau. [54] The Chicago Association was for years a real city mission society, using its building to promote "the spiritual, intellectual and social improvement of all within its reach, irrespective of age, sex or condition." [55] Though many branches inclined toward a similar policy, experience showed the specialized policy to be more conducive to growth and in-

[50] *Annual Report*, 1872, pp. 28–29; *ibid.*, 1881, pp. 19, 26; *Nation*, March 15, 1866, p. 327.
   [51] I (June 1870), 132; K. A. Burnell, "How to Secure Association Buildings," *ibid.* (July 1870), 172.
   [52] *Ibid.*, II (November 1871), 214; *ibid.*, I (January 1871), 16; *ibid.*, I (July 1870), 176.
   [53] William R. Moody, *The Life of Dwight L. Moody*, pp. 118–119, 466–481; W. H. Daniels, *op. cit.*, p. 124.
   [54] *Annual Report*, 1874, pp. 20–21; *ibid.*, 1877, pp. 70–72.
   [55] Richard C. Morse, *My Life With Young Men*, pp. 66–67; Daniels, *op. cit.*, pp. 87, 122–125.

fluence because, for one thing, it avoided conflict with the churches.[56] When Moody in the late seventies agreed to the circumscribed work, victory for the special policy was assured. In 1882, the Chicago Association, the last of the mission strongholds, capitulated.

The Young Women's Christian Association, though smaller than the Young Men's Christian Association, was truly a sister organization in that it directed its main energies to supplying the needs of middle-class women. Like its masculine counterpart, the Y.W.C.A. grew rapidly in the first decade after the war.[57] The federation of the various Associations in 1871, no doubt, stimulated growth and expansion as did likewise the conventions sponsored by the American Christian Commission. Thus, in the large convention at Pittsburgh in 1867, Moody explained the dire need for concerted action and organized the women of the city into an Association which soon assumed large proportions. But H. Thane Miller, a blind lay preacher and educator of Cincinnati, was to be the apostle of the Y.W.C.A. Several of its branches, the ones in Cincinnati, St. Louis and Philadelphia, for example, resulted directly from his heartfelt eloquence.[58] Whatever the diverse origins of the Associations, they all bestirred themselves to provide home facilities and educational opportunities, to which physical training was added after 1880.[59]

Predominantly a preventive movement, the Y.W.C.A. had little time for general mission work. But a few, notably those in Pittsburgh and Utica, specialized in this field. The Pittsburgh Association initiated a visitation system preparatory to

[56] Amos Hill Coolidge, *The Relation of the Y.M.C.A. to the Church*, pp. 3-4, 11-12; R. R. McBurney, *Historical Sketch of the Y.M.C.A.*, pp. 53-54.

[57] Elizabeth Wilson, *Fifty Years of Association Work Among Young Women, 1866-1916* (New York, 1916), pp. 22-35.

[58] *Association Monthly*, II (November 1871), 223; W. R. Moody, *op. cit.*, pp. 50-51, 54-55, 159-60.

[59] *Ibid.*, pp. 37-38, *passim*; Boston Y.W.C.A., *Annual Report*, 1871, p. 16; *ibid.*, 1889, pp. 15-16; Y.W.C.A. of New Haven, *Annual Report*, 1884, pp. 23-24; *ibid.*, 1887, pp. 10-11; *Christian Union*, Feb. 6, 1892, p. 270.

the fulfilling of its purpose "to improve the moral, intellectual and social condition of women and children." In the winter of 1868 the visitors reported a startling condition: young women of unblemished character, without friends, home or lodgings, forced to seek permission of the mayor to sleep in public institutions. Thereupon the Association hastily devised a refuge — The Pittsburgh Home for Destitute Women. Within a short time other institutions were established — the Home for Working Women, the Home for Aged Protestant Women, and the Sheltering Arms, a reformatory where the erring could be given the proper care. By 1874 the Association had seven distinct branches of philanthropic and religious endeavor, and property for its performance worth seventy-five thousand dollars, twice as valuable as that possessed by any other branch.[60]

The Association in Utica, while primarily for "young women dependent upon their own exertions for support," saw fit to broaden its efforts. It established sewing schools for women and children, a hospital and bureaus of employment. In addition, it became virtually a charity organization society for the city.[61] Other Associations followed in the footsteps of Pittsburgh and Utica, for example, Cleveland, which founded in 1868 a home for fallen women and, somewhat later, a day nursery and kindergarten. The beginnings of charity organization in Cincinnati — its Board of Associated Charities — grew out of the Association's mission work. The Minneapolis Association handled the relief work of the evangelical churches for twenty years.[62] In this early period, says an official historian of the Y.W.C.A., "many relief organizations had their origin in women's Christian associations." [63]

[60] Women's Christian Association of Pittsburgh and Allegheny, *Annual Report*, 1870, pp. 14, 16; *ibid.*, 1871, pp. 31–32, 43–45; *First Annual Report of the Pittsburgh Home for Destitute Women*, April 1869 (Pittsburgh, 1874), pp. 3–5; Boston Y.W.C.A., *Annual Report*, 1874, p. 16.

[61] *Illustrated Christian Weekly*, Oct. 16, 1875, p. 502.

[62] Bureau of the Census, *Benevolent Institutions 1910*, p. 234; Wilson, *op. cit.*, pp. 58–59.

[63] *Ibid.*, p. 56.

Protestants devised special organization to deal not only with particular groups but also with peculiar evils, especially intemperance. The conviction that work for temperance should be included among the functions of the church figured prominently in the revival of interest in the liquor question after the war. The National Temperance Society and Publication House, formed in August, 1865, advanced the cause, though less notably than the "gospel temperance movement" and the "Women's Crusade," both of which began in the early seventies.[64] Francis Murphy, an Irish-American, whose career and personality strikingly resembled Jerry MacAuley's, led the gospel temperance agitation. Disgusted with the "will power" panacea of the professional reformers, he advanced association, based on human and divine love, as the only satisfactory substitute for the saloon. "Drunkards were social people," who, as he artlessly put it, needed "some pleasant way of spending an evening." In the wider sense it was necessary, he said, "to cultivate the public sentiment and inoculate the community with the Gospel of Jesus Christ." [65]

Several denominations also organized to aid the temperance cause. The conviction in the various sects that religion and temperance were inextricably connected found clear expression, for example, in the meeting of the Congregational Council of 1865. A committee reported its satisfaction with the "revival of temperance efforts in a Christian spirit, and on the scriptural principles of self-denial for personal safety and the good efforts of others." It saw in them "just one method of that home evangelization in which this council is so deeply and properly engaged, and that, too, a method indispensable to the complete success of that divine work of evangelization." [66] The Presbyterians were first to adopt definite measures, adding in 1880 a Permanent Committee on Temperance to the committees of the

[64] W. H. Daniels, *The Temperance Reform and Its Great Reformers*, pp. 435–454. [65] *Christian Union*, March 27, 1878, p. 266.
[66] *Debates and Proceedings*, p. 480.

General Assembly. The special report justifying this action declared that "it is not only an eminently Christian work, but one which may well call for special exertions, and specific forms of work on the part of the church itself." [67] The Reverend John Hall, on informing the various synods of the new departure, defended it on the theory that intemperance, being associated with drinking customs and the legislation of the federal government, was a social rather than an individual evil. Hence an exception ought to be made to the widespread conviction "that the preaching of the Gospel and the missionary work of the church are adequate to meet the demands of all moral work." [68] While not properly supported by the General Assembly, the Permanent Committee succeeded, nevertheless, in equipping the synod and presbyteries and, to a lesser extent, the local churches for effective effort.[69]

The social reformers in the Protestant Episcopal Church formed the Church Temperance Society. Though they did not sympathize with the total-abstinence program, they were interested in plans of a more moderate nature. The discussion of the subject, "The Prevention and Cure of Drunkenness," before the Church Congress in 1876, showed influential Episcopalians as favoring concerted effort for the reform of the low and the fallen. The Reverend R. Heber Newton proposed that a society, similar to the one in the Anglican Church, be formed to "make room in its broad platform for those who seek the common end, while allowing in different sections the employment of different methods." [70] Within the next few years regional meetings and parochial societies prepared the ground for the fruition of Newton's suggestion. Finally, in 1881, Robert Graham, a prominent worker in the Anglican society, lectured throughout the country, awakening such interest that several ministers

---

[67] *Minutes*, 1881, p. 356.
[68] *Ibid.*, 1882, pp. 226–227.
[69] *Ibid.*, 1885, pp. 816–817; *ibid.*, 1886, p. 228.
[70] Episcopal Church Cong., *Papers, Addresses and Discussions*, 1876, p. 237.

under the Reverend B. F. DeCosta's leadership hastened to institute the Society.[71]

Though the Methodist Episcopal Church did not form a committee of national scope until 1912, the General Conference as early as 1864 advised preachers to speak specifically on temperance subjects, and in 1868 authorized the annual conferences, when they deemed it wise, to employ a minister to devote his whole time to agitation.[72] The National Council of Congregational Churches in 1883 appointed a Standing Committee on Intemperance, the stimulus coming from the General Association of Massachusetts whose State Committee on Home Evangelization had since 1875 urged temperance reform as a special branch of mission work.[73] The Unitarians were now ready for a similar course. While the National Conference had in the years after the war frequently discussed the subject, no action was taken until Christopher R. Eliot, pastor of the Meeting House Hill Society in Boston, instituted two societies in his church — one for adults and another for children. In his remarkable address entitled "Why, What and How," he showed that temperance bodies in the individual churches were the only effective protest against unfavorable conditions and the best means for encouraging and helping those in need of aid. The success of Eliot's work attracted the attention of the National Conference which in 1886 set up the Unitarian Church Temperance Society.[74]

The denominational temperance societies pleaded continuously for the enforcement of existing liquor laws and for the enactment of new ones looking to the restriction or elimination of the liquor traffic. But Protestants were more willing than

---

[71] B. F. DeCosta, "The Protestant Episcopal Church," *One Hundred Years of Temperance*, pp. 380–381.

[72] Henry Wheeler, "Relations of the Methodist Episcopal Church to the Cause of Temperance," *Meth. Quart. Rev.*, LVIII (October 1876), 639–643.

[73] *Minutes*, 1875, pp. 56–57; *ibid.*, 1884, p. 35.

[74] *Lend a Hand*, I (October 1886), 632–633; *ibid.* (December 1886), 759; *Christian Register*, June 2, 1887, pp. 338–339.

formerly to give physical welfare an important place among the methods of reform, recognizing that intemperance was a result as well as a cause of social disorder. The prevention of drunkenness, as R. Heber Newton said, was "to be reached by a general advance along the whole line of progress, physical, social, mental and moral, in accordance with the laws of nature." [75] During the frenzied temperance campaign in Pittsburgh in the winter of 1876–1877, the reformers cared for the temporal needs of people. As a contemporary said of the crusade, "There has been a settled principle attending it, that men must have full stomachs to keep sober, and that clothing for the ragged and work for the idle was a prominent accessory to reformation." [76] In Philadelphia a lodging house and, in other cities, inebriate homes and coffee houses were established. Murphy supported these plans and enlisted Joshua L. Bailey, the Quaker coffee-house promoter, as a co-laborer. The Woman's Christian Temperance Union, formed in 1874 to conserve the fruits of the crusade, also aided. Its plan of procedure, presented at the first meeting by Frances E. Willard, included, besides Gospel temperance meetings, juvenile temperance societies, antitreat leagues, coffee rooms and houses for inebriate women. In the following years the Union's program expanded to the full extent of social mission work.

The last factor in the Protestant religio-social system, the training of lay helpers, also began in this early period. The American Christian Commission had emphasized its importance, saying that Americans ought to have at least one institution "to educate those who would follow Christ in a life of labor among the poor, the criminal and the outcast." [77] In the late sixties the Y.M.C.A. began preparing men for efficient Christian service through laymen's institutes and Bible classes. [78]

[75] Episcopal Church Cong., *Papers, Addresses and Discussions*, 1876, p. 236.
[76] Young Men's Temperance Union of Pittsburgh, *Brief History of the Great Temperance Movement* (Pittsburgh, 1887), p. 21.
[77] *Document No. 8*, pp. 5–6.
[78] K. A. Burnell, "Laymen's Institutes," *Association Monthly*, I (May 1870),

From 1870 date the undenominational training schools. The Reverend Stephen H. Tyng pioneered in this as in other branches of religious endeavor. He raised several thousand dollars in 1870 to equip the Home of the Evangelists, which he termed "a short cut to the ministry." He reported in 1876 that the institution had graduated fifty men, all pledged, ministers and laymen alike, to toil for the welfare of the neglected classes.[79]

A similar institution, the Tabernacle Lay College in 1872, grew out of the Reverend T. DeWitt Talmage's Brooklyn Free Tabernacle. Securing a commodious building and a resident faculty of professors and lecturers, the college offered excellent courses on the Sunday school, city missions, management of orphanages and prisons, and the training of nurses and deaconesses.[80] Institutions for women also sprang into existence, the most important being the Training Home for Christian Workers, established in New York in 1870, and renamed Bethany Institute in 1872. In charge of the progressive Reverend A. G. Ruliffson, the school provided both instruction and practice. The former consisted largely of thorough Bible drill and lectures on missionary techniques of the social type. Training in the use of these was afforded by service in the city missions under charge of experienced missionaries. Drawing students from all denominations in every section of the country, Bethany by 1892 had graduated nearly four hundred women.[81] In Chicago, Moody likewise undertook to prepare women for Christian service, setting up in the early seventies a Bible School for the Training of Evangelists. His world-wide career not permitting him to remain in active charge, he placed it under

---

141; "The Laymen's Institutes," *ibid.* (July 1870), 173; *ibid.* (August 1870), 204.

[79] *Association Monthly*, I (April 1870), 89; *Congregationalist*, Feb. 1, 1872, p. 42.

[80] T. DeWitt Talmage, *Sermons*, Second Series (New York, 1873), pp. 10-11.

[81] *Annual Report*, 1872, pp. 4-15; *ibid.*, 1873, pp. 5-6; *ibid.*, 1877, p. 8; *ibid.*, 1892, p. 6.

the management of Emeline Dryer, formerly dean of women at the Illinois State Normal. This enterprise was also quite successful.[82]

The movement fared less well in the denominations. In the Protestant Episcopal Church, for example, the more conservative members met the cry for trained women missionaries with clever epithets — "Protestant Sisterhoods," "Puseyite Nuns," and others equally damaging to argument and reason. But Muhlenberg's example was followed by Episcopalians in several cities and dioceses, and the question of extending recognition was thoroughly discussed in the General Conventions from 1868 to 1880. Meanwhile, in 1867, William Welsh had opened in Philadelphia the Alonzo Potter Memorial House to train women for nursing, mission work and teaching in parish schools. Though not requiring a vow of celibacy or a distinctive dress, the institution resembled in other respects the deaconess houses of Europe.[83] But additional institutions of this kind, as well as official sanction for organized women's work, had to await a more favorable occasion.

Lutherans in this period planned to associate trained women with the development of charitable enterprises. The leader was the Reverend William A. Passavant, who learned of the Kaiserswerth deaconesses in 1864 while attending in London the first meeting of the Evangelical Alliance. With a youthful enthusiasm which he retained to the end of a long, busy life, he set about laying the foundations for a similar system in America. In his newspaper, *The Missionary*, establshed in 1851, he cogently directed the attention of Lutherans to the problems of cities. Soon he had founded the pioneer Lutheran charities — a hospital in Pittsburgh and an orphan asylum at Zelienople, Pennsylvania. Expecting these charities to be managed by women, Passavant persuaded Theodore Fliedner, the founder

---

[82] W. H. Daniels, *D. L. Moody and His Work*, pp. 186–188.

[83] *Spirit of Missions*, XXXII (February 1867), 141; *ibid.*, XXXIII (July 1868), 510, 514–515.

of the Kaiserswerth institutions, to bring deaconesses to America. Though a beginning was made and one American woman, Katherine Louise Martens, was consecrated a deaconess, the work did not thrive, the German women returning home and Miss Martens gaining no associates. The widespread prejudice against public religious activity by women proved too powerful to be easily overcome.[84]

Prejudice apart, this early experiment failed because Lutherans lacked well-equipped foundations to employ a large number of women. Accordingly, Passavant redoubled his efforts, becoming responsible, either directly or indirectly, for all the early Lutheran charitable institutions. In addition to Passavant Hospital in Pittsburgh, he founded the Lutheran Hospital of St. Louis in 1853, the Passavant Memorial Hospital in Chicago in 1865 and the Passavant Hospital at Jacksonville, Illinois, in the same period. He also encouraged an increase in the number of orphan asylums. Thus the Wartburg Orphan Farm School at Mt. Vernon, New York, the second of its kind in the Lutheran Church, opened in 1864 as the direct outcome of his efforts. Lutheran philanthropy, under his direction, rapidly responded to meet the new social demands. The nine institutions in 1865 mounted to forty-three by 1885 and to seventy-five by 1894.[85] The efficiency of these institutions owed most, perhaps, to the Reverend George C. Holls, who in 1851 came fresh from an assistantship at Dr. J. H. Wichern's celebrated orphan homes at Hamburg, Germany. He soon won the attention of Dr. Passavant who chose him to manage the first of the American Lutheran orphanages. Ten years later, in 1864, he headed the establishment at Mt. Vernon, New York. By applying the scientific principles of Wichern, Holls measurably advanced

[84] G. H. Gerberding, *Life and Letters of W. A. Passavant*, pp. 24-248; C. Golder, *History of the Deaconess Movement in the Christian Church*, pp. 251-256.
[85] J. E. Bushnell, "Child-saving Institutions," *Luth. Quart. Rev.*, XX (July 1890), 289-298; *Lutheran Almanac*, 1865-1868; *Annual Cyclopedia*, 1893, p. 465.

the movement for a more adequate policy of child training in the United States.[86]

Several prominent Methodists likewise proposed to introduce the German deaconess system. Bishop Matthew Simpson, who had learned first-hand of this service during his repeated trips to Germany, was the foremost advocate. The task of agitation, however, fell to a group of women, of whom Mrs. Annie Wittenmeyer of Philadelphia was most influential. On her return in 1870 from a visit to Kaiserswerth, she established a newspaper, *The Christian Woman*, and lectured widely, appealing to women to consider their duty to the sick, the poor and the forlorn. She was ably assisted by Mrs. S. M. D. Fry of Ohio, who in a series of articles in the *Ladies' Repository* showed that the Greek and Roman Catholic Churches owed much of their social influence to the benevolent activity of women. We need, she said, "not only amateur charity ladies, but an organized force trained in those ministering functions which have their root in woman's nature." [87]

Early in 1868 a special agency, the Ladies and Pastors' Christian Union, was formed under Mrs. Wittenmeyer's leadership to prepare the ground for deaconess establishments. Having as its object "the employment of Christian women in coöperation with the regular ministry in the extension of the Redeemer's Kingdom by works of religion and charity," the Union actively engaged for a time in family visitation, tract distribution and in the relief of the poor. By 1876 there were forty conference auxiliaries and nearly four hundred local societies with a membership of over nine thousand, many of the societies having operated since the beginning of the movement. In the late seventies, however, the Union rapidly lost ground for the reasons that the General Conference refused financial aid and the congregations lacked missionary zeal.[88] Nevertheless, by arous-

[86] Henry Barnard, *George Charles Holls, A Memoir*, p. 4, *passim*.
[87] "Ancient and Modern Sisterhoods," XXXII (October 1872), 245.
[88] Gen. Conf., *Journal*, 1872, pp. 445–446, 737; *ibid.*, 1876, pp. 639–640;

ing the interest of large numbers, the Union fertilized the soil for the great deaconess harvest after 1885. The dozen or more charitable institutions organized between 1864 and 1881 worked also to the same end.[89]

Altogether, the years 1865–1880 carried Protestant social service through the embryonic processes of growth. The religious spirit had ceased to be predominantly meditative and was becoming each year increasingly charitable and reformatory. The changing attitude chiefly expressed itself, as Henry Codman Potter said in his review of the period, in "that missionary work which consists in building mission chapels and in humane and philanthropic agencies which go along with them."[90] City missionary societies and similar extra-parochial associations were mainly responsible for this activity. The Protestant congregations possessed enormous resources for promoting human welfare, but they had remained, with few notable exceptions, indifferent to social distress. Though interested in the young, unmarried middle class which flocked to the cities, they were not equipped to meet its manifold needs. Whereupon the two undenominational Associations had nobly come to the rescue. Some lay people, particularly women, had trained for missionary service, but the plans for deaconesses after the European model failed in the face of inertia and prejudice. After the war the churches renewed their interest in the temperance crusade in accordance with principles which seemed more reasonable and sane than those followed in the pre-war years.

By 1880 many Protestants had grasped the religious significance of urban development. The mid-century controversy centering around Stephen Colwell, the ideas advanced by the Christian Labor Union for solving the industrial problem and the comprehensive plans of the American Christian Commission

---

J. H. Potts, "Ladies and Pastors' Christian Union," *Ladies' Repository*, XXXVI (May 1876), 394–395.

[89] Bureau of the Census, *Benevolent Institutions: 1910*, p. 86, *passim*.

[90] "Church Life and Work," *Christian Union*, April 6, 1881, p. 324.

for urban missionary endeavor — all these showed that Protestants understood the implications of Christian social reform. If, as it seemed, they had scarcely begun to reduce theory to practice, the explanation could be found in the capital fact that they still lacked genuine social sympathy and earnestness. In the absence of a serious class struggle, Protestants, in a spirit of good-natured apathy, had allowed the urban religious problem to go unsolved. But all apathy was soon to end before the thunder of ruthless social war which resounded over the horizon of the eighties and nineties.

CHAPTER III

SOCIAL CHRISTIANITY AND THE LABOR
CHALLENGE, 1880–1900

AFTER 1880 Protestants infused new energy into their humanitarian program. At last thoroughly alive to the religious importance of the social problems, they reproached themselves for having neglected them in previous years and struggled somewhat frantically to make amends for the lost time. The enormous acceleration of urban growth lay at the bottom of the growing Protestant emphasis on social Christianity. The total urban population increased fifty per cent during the eighties — a rate of advance six times faster than that of the seventies. Since pauperism, crime and grinding poverty kept well ahead of urban increase, the only rational recourse of the churches was to a comprehensive system of social service. Immigration continued to mirror urban development: in the single decade of the eighties over five million newcomers arrived, most of whom crowded into the industrial centers. These folk required special consideration from Protestants, for being predominantly "newer" immigrants from Central and Southeastern Europe, they lagged far behind the "older" immigrants in education, familiarity with democratic ideals and loyalty to Protestant Christianity.

The aspect of urban expansion which seemed most alarming to Protestants was industrial conflict. Though natural under the wage system and constantly in evidence, economic warfare did not assume menacing proportions until the machine and the factory became dominant in the productive process. Before the end of the eighties this long anticipated situation widely obtained. As its chief social result, the number of wage-earners rose during the decade from two and three quarter millions to four and a quarter millions — a numerical increase exceeding that of the two previous decades combined. But the economic position of the working people did not correspondingly improve. As compared with the employers who controlled the new industry, the workers actually retrogressed. Machinery and corporate organization utilizing immigrant labor made American capitalists, in the words of a New York merchant, as independent of American workingmen "as the imported slaves made Roman patricians independent of Roman laborers." [1] By combining in pools and trusts, the masters of capital succeeded not only in suppressing cut-throat competition but also in imposing exhorbitantly high prices upon the consuming public and slashing wage-cuts upon their employees.

But, in the manner of an inexorable law of physics, the oppression and tyranny of the business groups provoked countermeasures on the part of labor and its many allies who hated monopoly and special privilege. Workingmen perfected fighting organizations; and, beginning in 1877 with the striking railway employees, staged repeated insurrections against capital. The series of nation-wide strikes during the Great Upheaval of 1884–1886 and the Homestead and the Pullman troubles of the early nineties were embittered struggles symbolic of the growing and, as it seemed to many earnest persons, the permanent estrangement of the two classes. Adding fuel to the flames were such additional ingredients of industrial warfare as lockouts, black lists and boycotts of every description, all widely used after 1885. Out of the heat and fury of the conflict emerged a remarkable degree of working-class solidarity. To bringing about this result, the fraternalism of the labor unions directly contributed, notably the Knights of Labor which essayed with much temporary success the difficult task of forging both skilled and unskilled workers into one all-inclusive body. If, in the end, the workers organized along craft lines, that fact only

---

[1] Francis B. Thurber, "Lay Criticism on the Ministry and Methods of Church Work," *Homiletic Rev.*, VIII (April 1884), 412.

meant that they were adjusting their methods to the needs of the moment. What really mattered was that the wage-earners by various means had attained a consciousness of their special interests and a resolute determination to do battle for them.

The workers for the most part steered clear of the radical social philosophies, asking only "a fair day's wages for a fair day's work." If at one with the Socialist Labor party in opposing the country's "despotic system of economics," [2] they instinctively shunned the party's doctrinaire Marxian program and alien leadership. Though more favorably impressed with Henry George's scheme for socializing land rents and Edward Bellamy's proposal for nationalizing all industry, the workers did not affiliate in large numbers even with these natively inspired movements. Nevertheless, the socialist agitation served to embitter labor against capital and to awaken many outside the wage-earning ranks to the social dangers of industrial warfare, for socialism threatened to rationalize the strong drift toward anarchy and violence in the economic field. In the early eighties anarchists, affiliated with the International Working People's Association, gained considerable influence in the Socialist movement, all parroting with John Most, their leader, the fiery refrain, "Lead and powder alone can make us free." In their Pittsburgh Manifesto of 1883 they resolved to exterminate the capitalists by force, if necessary, and to destroy those allegedly capitalistic institutions — the state, the family and the church. "I have labored for three years to prevent the shedding of blood," reported John Swinton, the New York socialist, in 1885, "but it cannot be helped. It is sure to come." [3] Sharing Swinton's apprehensions were some of the best minds of the land, including Professor Richard T. Ely and the Reverend R. Heber Newton. When in May, 1886, during a labor

[2] M. Kaufman, "The Progress of Socialism in the United States," *Economic Review*, I (January 1891), 49.

[3] A. H. Bradford, "Socialism from the Socialistic Standpoint," *Independent*, Aug. 27, 1885, pp. 1096–97.

riot at Haymarket Square, Chicago, a bomb hurled by unknown hands killed one policeman and injured many others, the whole nation realized the portentiousness of the situation.

Yet, anarchy, actual and potential, was less to be feared than its inevitable outcome. Unless promptly checked, chronic disorder would undermine the people's heritage of liberty. Sooner or later, as many thinking persons realized, an orderly society of some kind would arise to pacify the warring elements. Though many patriots expected a socialist despotism, wiser heads discerned that tyranny, if it should displace democracy and freedom, would take a capitalist form. Newton warned in 1886 that it "would not require many panics for Property to cry aloud for some strong man to come forth as the savior of society." [4] As industrial war gripped the land, distinguished conservatives wavered in their support of democracy. "I confess I expect no Caesar," said the Reverend Roswell D. Hitchcock after the strikes of 1877. "But then I expect to see this communistic madness rebuked and ended. If not rebuked and ended, I shall have to say, as many a sad-eyed Roman must have said nineteen hundred years ago, *I prefer civilization to the Republic.*" [5] If drastic social reform within the democratic-Christian framework was the effective antidote to dictatorship, neither capital nor labor, as Newton remarked, seemed ready to subordinate its narrow, selfish interests to the common welfare. Capital refused to concede that change must come — "that we are in the midst of a period of economic and social transition" from a predominantly competitive to a largely coöperative society. Labor also was at fault for "its failure to recognize that this evolution of the higher economic and social order is to be brought about not through cataclysm, but through a gradual, orderly, peaceful, natural development out of the present system." [6]

The cleavage between the two forces would not have widened

[4] *Present Aspects of the Labor Question* (New York, 1886), p. 42.
[5] *Ibid.*   [6] *Ibid.*, pp. 42–43.

so far had the non-economic bonds of social cohesion come into full play. In some of the older countries, a common cultural life dulled the sword's edge of industrial strife, but in America, where the employer was generally a native and the employee nearly always an immigrant, folk sentiment intensified the hates of the factory and the market place. The cause of industrial peace gained nothing from the growing number of folk who, while standing between capitalists and laborers and putting humanity before wealth and greed, were not alive to their social responsibilities. In England and Germany, Professor Ely pointed out, brave men of exalted natures had helped to maintain the unity of civilization by throwing themselves into the breach. But with us, he said, "comparatively few have realized their duty in this matter, and it is doubtful if history records any more rapid social movement than this ominous separation of the American people into two nations." [7] The democratic, casteless tradition accounted largely for the hesitancy of the intermediate groups in taking on the tasks of social mediation: they feared that any assumption on their part of responsibility for the weak and the poor would be mistaken for patronage and condescension.

The Protestant churches did not share these scruples, rightly so. They were not, however, well prepared to mediate between the classes because by preferring capital to labor they were alienating the workers from organized Christianity. During the eighties several clergymen carefully investigated the religious habits of the various occupational groups, invariably finding that wage-earners attended Protestant services in much smaller proportions than other classes. From a study of the census returns for 1880, Washington Gladden concluded that from a fifth to a fourth of the nation's families depended upon wages for a livelihood. Knowing however, that in his own congregation, the First Congregational of Columbus, Ohio, only a tenth of the attending families belonged to labor constituencies, he

[7] *The Labor Movement in America* (New York, 1886), pp. 112–14.

sent questionnaires to representative workingmen, business men and professional people of the city to obtain, if possible, an accurate picture of the situation. The replies "make it all too evident," he said, "that the proportion of working people who attend church is much smaller than the proportion of church goers in the entire population." [8] In Pittsburgh and Allegheny, Alexander Jackson supervised a religious census in 1888 which strikingly confirmed what Gladden and others had discovered. It revealed that business, professional and salaried men who comprised less than ten per cent of the population made up over sixty per cent of the male membership of the Protestant churches.[9]

Although, as a result of these and similar studies, Protestants now conceded that the workers were hostile to the churches, they continued to harbor the idea that class conflict was not a factor in the situation. To some, the close association between Protestantism and wealth was altogether natural since true religion insisted upon the virtues of honesty, industry and thrift which led as a rule to material prosperity. Thus the Reverend Mr. Jackson dismissed the whole subject with the crisp remark that "Evangelical Christianity pays." Many explained that the workers were outside the churches because of the natural depravity of man (without attempting to explain why employers were less depraved) or because of the perversity of loud-mouthed labor agitators. In all these conjectures Protestants shunned the true explanation, namely, the bearing of social antagonisms upon religion. As late as 1892 the overwhelming majority of Congregational pastors in the Bay State believed that industrial discontent had "little or no effect upon the attitude of the workingmen towards the churches." [10]

[8] "The Working People and the Churches," *Independent*, July 23, 1885, pp. 944–945.
[9] Alexander Jackson, "The Relation of the Classes to the Church," *ibid.*, March 1, 1888, pp. 258–59.
[10] John P. Coyle, "Report of the Committee on the Work of the Churches," Gen. Assoc. of the Cong. Churches in Mass., *Minutes*, 1892, p. 30.

Workingmen thought differently. They had lost confidence, they reiterated, in a church that was in active or passive alliance with their oppressors. Gladden cited the instance of a "tired looking shop girl" in Boston who, in response to a query as to the reason for her failing to attend church, replied: "My employer goes. He is one of the pillars of the church. That's reason enough why I shouldn't go. I know how he treats his help." [11] Swinton, one of the earliest intermediaries between labor and organized religion, charged the clergy with "utter obliviousness" to social questions. In the various struggles of workers for better conditions during the panic years of the seventies, "no clergyman was ever to be found," he said. On the contrary, the ministry preferred "to snuff the odors of fortune and cross their clerical limbs under the banquets of Nabobism rather than do as He whom they pretend to serve did." [12]

The attitude of trade union leaders was quite as emphatic. "My associates," reported Samuel Gompers of the American Federation of Labor, "have come to look upon the church and the ministry as the apologists and defenders of the wrongs committed against the interests of the people simply because the perpetrators are possessors of wealth." People in the churches, whose "real God is the almighty dollar," controlled the ministry, he charged, and used their "exalted positions to discourage and discountenance all practical efforts of the toilers to lift themselves out of the slough of despondency and despair." Methods found by labor to be effective, continued Gompers, "have been generally frowned down upon with contempt, treated indifferently or openly antagonized by the ministers and the apparently staunch supporters of the church." [13]

Incidents of almost daily occurrence convinced wage-earners

[11] "The Working People and the Churches," *Independent*, July 30, 1885, pp. 966–969.
[12] "Views of John Swinton, Lay Criticism on the Ministry and Methods of Church Work," *Homiletic Rev.*, VIII (August 1884), 648–649.
[13] "The Church and Labor," *Amer. Federationist*, II (August 1896), 119–120.

that Protestant opinion was weighted against them. Believing, as it seemed, that God had ordained the existing social system, most ministers preached that poverty resulted exclusively from personal sin and warded off the thrust of workers for justice by confronting them with statistics of their wanton extravagance and saloon-spent wages. If laboring men would only return to the churches "instead of giving so much of their time and earnings to saloons, or to labor associations," suggested the *Congregationalist*, "we are persuaded they would find themselves less frequently pinched by poverty and less in want of real friends than they now are." [14] By slurs of this kind the churches displayed a lack of sympathy and understanding which puzzled and exasperated working people. They likewise resented the prevalent clerical policy of seizing every opportunity to flay employees for their violence and unreasonable demands while either ignoring employers' faults or condemning them in terms so general "that the point and special application are unfelt." [15] The rage of workers mounted to fury when they saw churches directly profiting from capital's ill-gotten gains. For example, Chicago workers sent a committee "to tell their employer that their wives and children were suffering while he was giving one hundred thousand dollars, and from their reduced wages, to a theological seminary." [16]

While rejecting "churchianity" — which they held to be another word for pious fraud and pretense — most workers professed belief in Christianity. Characteristic of this attitude was the New York rally of workmen in the early eighties which in the same of breath hissed the churches and cheered the mention of Christ's name. A committee of the Congregational Churches in Massachusetts found that, in most cases, the wage-earner voiced allegiance to the Great Galilean along with hatred

[14] "Labor and the Church," *Congregationalist*, Feb. 8, 1894, pp. 185–186.

[15] George Dering Wolff, "The Wage Question," *Amer. Cath. Quart. Rev.*, XIII (April 1886), 337.

[16] A. H. Bradford, "Why the Artisan Classes Neglect Church," *Christian Union*, July 9, 1885, pp. 7–8.

of the church which in his opinion had betrayed Him. If the churches "would be faithful to Jesus," he said, "no alienation would exist." [17] To the charge that workers were atheists John Willett, a Michigan trade-unionist, quickly retorted, "We believe much in Jesus and his teachings, but not much in the teachings of his pretended followers." [18] Workingmen opposed the laws of the church, explained James R. Buchanan, a leader in the Knights of Labor, only when they "are in contradiction to the laws of God and humanity." There should be no conflict between religion and the fullest claims of labor; in his view pure, "undefiled Christianity" was in "perfect accord with socialism." [19]

Workingmen also upbraided the clergy for their ignorance of industrial situations. Ely wrote in the middle eighties that the Protestant minister as compared to the Catholic priest had difficulty in being fair to labor. "It was not a difference of good will so much as a difference of knowledge," he said. "The Catholic revealed an acquaintance with the movements of the masses — the Protestant ignorance." [20] After studying typical sermons on the labor question, Swinton concluded that ministers lacked accurate "knowledge of its elements." [21] In the words of another socialist-journalist, the clergy's range of ideas did not extend "beyond profit-sharing or woman's rights, or some reform, which, taken by itself, is no reform at all." [22] Most men in the pulpit were unreasoning optimists, "believing that all things work together for good — or ought to." [23]

Sentimentality was slight comfort to the workers, who ex-

[17] John P. Coyle, "The Churches and Labor Unions," *Forum*, XLII (August 1892), 767.
[18] "Letter from a Workingman," *Christian Union*, Oct. 29, 1885, pp. 7–8.
[19] *Truth*, Nov. 10, 1883, p. 3.
[20] "Socialism," Inter-Denominational Congress, Cincinnati, 1885, *Proceedings*, pp. 89–90.
[21] "Fiddle-de-Dee," *John Swinton's Paper*, April 5, 1885, p. 1.
[22] "Labor and Religion," *Workmen's Advocate*, May 30, 1886, p. 2.
[23] Frank I. Herriott, "The Pulpit and Social Problems," *Homiletic Rev.*, XXIV (September 1892), 266.

pected the clergy to probe industrial life for its ethical meanings. "All we ask of the churches," said Swinton, "is that they
should study the facts." [24] He advised churchmen frantically
seeking to reach the "masses" to "ascertain by some orderly
definite method the conditions of life, the conditions of labor
and the conditions of death of these masses. That will inevitably in course of time give them some notion of their method
of action in the taking of their next step." [25] The Reverend
John P. Coyle, brilliant Congregationalist, stressed the duty of
the clergy to revise "the ethics of property holding for the use
of the men who are preparing to revise its laws." Workers de-
sisted "from immediate action," he said, "by inability as yet to
agree upon practical measures, which inability grows out of the
consciousness . . . that they are facing a problem of immense
difficulty which they are poorly equipped to meet." They were
asking of the ministry, he explained, neither partisanship nor
political leadership, but simply "moral light . . . mere questions of public policy they expect to be able to answer." [26]
Quite naturally, wage-earners were incensed at the clergy, who,
with so splendid an opportunity for service, expended their
energies on theology and in dry, doctrinal sermons wore thread-
bare the old theme of supermundane salvation.

Though highly critical of the churches, the workers' real aim
was not to destroy but to socialize Protestant Christianity.
Even the socialists hoped for a working alliance with Christianity. The orthodox Marxists of the Socialist Labor party held
that the Christian "may embrace the whole of socialism and
still find support in precepts from Holy Writ. . . ." This the
"thoughtful Christian" will do, they ventured, because "he
has before him the fact that his religion has failed to raise the
world out of misery." [27] Socialists of the Nationalist school

[24] A. H. Bradford, "Socialism from the Socialistic Standpoint," *loc. cit.*
[25] "Views of John Swinton. . . . ," *loc. cit.*
[26] "What the Workingman May Ask of the Minister," *Homiletic Rev.,* XXV
(January 1893), 83–84.
[27] Zeno, "Who Are Enemies?" *Workmen's Advocate,* Jan. 10, 1886, p. 1.

spoke to the same effect, their leader, Bellamy, asserting that Christians had "no other choice save either to abjure the present social and industrial system or to abjure Christ." [28] Socialist spokesmen were tolerant of members who affiliated with Christianity. When, for example, Harry Vrooman, the Kansas socialist, abandoned the law for the Congregational ministry, the *Workman's Advocate* (Marxist) was not surprised. "There is not anything in the socialistic philosophy," it insisted, "that will repel a belief in Christianity." [29] Though most socialists considered theology a mosaic of falsehoods, they regarded the dogmas as "of such a nature that they may not interfere with the work of social reform." [30]

Non-socialists were at even greater pains to explain the bearing of religion on social questions. Thus, Henry George in his widely read book, *Progress and Poverty*, synthesized economics, ethics and religion. He joined with other economists in demolishing the wages-fund theory which justified employers in paying labor only a subsistence wage. He acknowledged the existence of economic laws; but he contended that these when truly formulated conformed with a ruling moral principle of fairness and justice. Though faith in God and belief in immortality were requirements of nature and reason, these would continue to elicit scorn from the toiling masses, he said, until the intellectual world ceased teaching that non-human forces were responsible for vice and misery. George had in mind particularly the doctrine of Malthus that God had allowed millions to be born without providing means for their support, and social Darwinism which favored sacrificing weak to strong individuals in the alleged interests of a mythical race perfection. *Progress and Poverty* was in many respects an autobiography of a profoundly sensitive soul. George's story of how his discovery of a true social philosophy had restored his faith in God helped

[28] *New Nation*, Jan. 23, 1892, pp. 50–51.
[29] "Socialist and Preacher," *Workmen's Advocate*, July 6, 1889, p. 1.
[30] *Workmen's Advocate*, Jan. 10, 1886, p. 1.

many orthodox believers to grasp the religious implications of the social movement. In striking contrast to the revolutionary socialists, George and his followers, as the *Nation* said, "present the surprising spectacle of an appeal from Christians to Christianity — of an agitation which professes to be not alone in the interests of justice, but also in the interests and in the spirit of Christianity." [31]

The new scholarship, especially as it touched upon economics, helped to draw religion into the arena of social reform. Taking their cue from the economists of the German and English historical schools, many American students of the subject — for example, Francis A. Walker, Carroll D. Wright, Richard T. Ely and John Bates Clark — rejected the classical political economy, whose "axiomatic principle," they contended, "is selfishness." Not only did the individualism of the old economic science clash with the Christian "law of self-sacrifice," but it also ignored the social and coöperative trends in the world of industry and trade. Thus Professor Clark asserted "that the competitive principle, instead of being supreme and resistless, exists at best by sufferance, is subject to constantly narrowing restrictions, and is liable, in particular forms, to be totally suppressed by the action of that moral force which is, in reality, supreme." Employers and employees had each united in great combinations in order to eliminate, he believed, the brutalities and wastes of lawless struggle. Solidarity within the ranks of capital and labor foreshadowed the socialization of industry, for the same moral force which was bringing to an end the era of anarchy within each group would in due time suppress it between them and usher in a coöperative society.[32]

Professor Ely of Johns Hopkins was the most influential student of the new political economy in its religious aspects. As one of the founders of the American Economic Association in 1885, he drew up the statement of principles which insisted

---

[31] "Workingmen and the Churches," *Nation*, April 2, 1885, p. 275.
[32] *The Philosophy of Wealth* (New York, 1886), pp. 45–46.

"that the conflict of labor and capital has brought into prominence a vast number of social problems, whose solution requires the united efforts, each in its own sphere, of the church, of the state, and of science." In order to win church support for the Association's program, he wrote many excellent articles for the newspapers and magazines as well as several books: *Recent American Socialism* (Baltimore, 1885), *The Labor Movement in America* (New York, 1886), *Social Aspects of Christianity* (New York, 1889), and *The Social Law of Service* (New York, 1896).

He pointedly reminded his fellow-Christians that their actions did not accord with the social ideals of the early church. If Christianity originally had instituted a truly human brotherhood and was still the only effective means of harmonizing divergent interests, the churches had come to terms with the "world," preferring luxury and ease to self-sacrificing care of the poor and acquiescing in the pagan doctrine that classes owed nothing to each other. By confusing socialism with anarchy, Christians had failed to see the positive truths in the socialist movement. Although the socialists wrongly planned to collectivize all productive property, they were right, Ely repeatedly said, in stressing the social principle and in calling for state intervention. In its work of relieving misery and equalizing opportunities, private philanthropy must now have the aid of the state. Ely bespoke religious support for these ideas since "Christianity naturally appeals to the poor man, and throws no obstacles in the way of his efforts to ameliorate his condition. Even from socialism, if thoroughly infused with Christian principles, there is nothing to fear. The Bible has nothing to say against socialistic schemes in themselves." [33]

These sentiments appealed to a growing number of churches and clergy. The *Nation* noted in 1886 that the "labor question is discussed no more frequently and anxiously in the secular

[33] "Christianity the Remedy for Socialism — Letter to the Rev. A. F. Schauffler, May 26, 1884," *Christian Union*, June 26, 1884, p. 605.

press and political gatherings than in the columns of church papers and the debates of religious conventions." [34] The majority of ministers, perhaps, still truckled to the foes of labor, but "many, very many," R. Heber Newton said, were honestly studying the issue and, "in the face of uninterested and naturally prejudiced congregations, trying hard to show wealth the other side of the case." [35]

The progressive clergy, for the most part, acknowledged Washington Gladden as their teacher and leader. Born in 1838 of New England ancestry at Pottsgrove, Pennsylvania, Gladden had spent his early life in privation and poverty. A youth of broad human sympathies, he was aroused by the pre-war humanitarian emphasis in some of the churches, and decided upon college and the ministry. After graduating at Williams he trained privately for his chosen calling and, save for a brief excursion into religious journalism, passed his many years as an active Congregational pastor in industrial communities — Brooklyn, New York, North Adams and Springfield, Massachusetts, and, finally, Columbus, Ohio.[36] Though well-read in social economics, Gladden was mainly impelled by the bitter conflict between employers and employees in his own congregations to examine the industrial situation and "to try and get at the rights of it." [37] Out of this harrowing experience, aided by serious reflection, grew his long list of books on the social question. If the first, *Working People and Their Employers* (Boston, 1876), was "somewhat lacking in comprehension," the others were of high intellectual merit and of great practical interest. The most important were perhaps *Applied Christianity* (Boston, 1886) and *Tools and the Man* (Boston, 1893).[38]

[34] "Home Missions and Anarchism," *Nation*, Sept. 6, 1886, pp. 228–29.
[35] "A Warning to the Rev. Jesse Jones," *John Swinton's Paper*, Nov. 22, 1885, p. 2.
[36] *Recollections*, pp. 1–98.
[37] *Ibid.*, pp. 294–95.
[38] Other important books by Gladden include, *Ruling Ideas of the Present Age* (Boston, 1895); *Social Facts and Forces* (New York, 1897); *Social Salvation* (Boston, 1902); and *Christianity and Socialism* (New York, 1905).

There were, Gladden pointed out, three possible relations between labor and capital: the subjugation of labor by capital through slavery; the warfare between the two under the wage system; and "the identification of labor and capital by some application of the principle of cooperation." [39] Society was in the second of these stages, that of industrial war, because the wage system resulted in unbearable inequalities in the distribution of income. If wealth was rapidly accumulating, "poverty, even pauperism, is increasing still more rapidly," he insisted. It might be questioned "whether the average annual wages of the average workingman will purchase for him any more of the necessaries of life today than it would in the years before the war." With the socialists Gladden agreed that the wage-earners were not sharing fairly in the national prosperity.[40]

Nor would they, so long as the wage system ruled industrial relations, for under that system competition alone determined the laborer's reward through the law of supply and demand. Experience, he contended, had shown that in an age of increasing mechanical appliance there "can never be any equitable or continuous adjustment of the wage question upon the basis of free competition in labor." [41] Labor organization and social ethics alike were relatively powerless to secure justice and peace under the prevailing system. Gladden admitted, of course, that "Christian principle can do much to mitigate the strife, so far as it gains control over the lives of men, but it would be a good while," he predicted, "before the masses of men, whether capitalists or laborers are so fully governed by the Christian law that they will cease to struggle for the advantage and mastery." [42] Some form of partnership by which labor shared in the profits as well as the losses of industry was the only fair and workable remedy. But until such time as this principle was fully accepted, Gladden sanctioned labor's organization for

[39] *Working People and Their Employers*, pp. 44–45.
[40] *Applied Christianity*, pp. 10–15, 63.
[41] *Ibid.*, p. 36.   [42] *Working People and Their Employers*, p. 44.

effective combat. "If war is the order of the day," he said, "we must grant to labor belligerent rights." [43]

Gladden was anxious to steer a course midway between individualism and socialism. Either the one or the other in exaggerated form was to be avoided; in the ideal society both would appear in exact balance. The problem was simple to "socialize the individual." [44] However greatly the *laissez-faire* policy, by removing moral and political controls from economic life, had helped to oppress labor, it did not follow that in the new order all earnings ought to be given to labor. The socialist plan was economically false (in its theory of value), politically impracticable (in requiring a great bureaucracy for its realization) and ethically dangerous (in threatening to thwart unduly the development of character). Gladden pleaded with collectivists to "venture on this path of nationalization cautiously. . . ." [45] "The remedy needed," he insisted, "is not the destruction but the Christianization of the present order." [46]

Gladden increasingly recognized the imperative need for state intervention. He had once used the argument that protection rather than the promotion of human welfare was the legitimate function of government, but "today," he said in 1889, "it seems much less conclusive than formerly." [47] He ventured to predict that when "the King of us all does come into his own, you will discover that he is something more than a policeman." [48] As religious people succeeded in making government more Christian, they should "favor the attempt on the part of the state to improve the condition of its poorest and least fortunate classes." If this was the motive of socialism, it was also the "very spirit and purpose of Christianity." Gladden

---

[43] *Applied Christianity*, p. 125.

[44] "Socialism versus Un-socialism," *Forum*, III (April, 1887), 123.

[45] "The Social and Industrial Situation," *Bibliotheca Sacra*, XLIX (July 1892), 399.

[46] *Applied Christianity*, p. 98.

[47] Nat. Council of Congreg. Churches, *Minutes*, 1889, p. 344.

[48] Quoted in D. M. Means, "Christian Socialism," *Nation*, May 23, 1893, p. 381.

would have government stop Sunday work, limit land ownership, own and operate telegraphs and railways and forbid the accumulation of great fortunes. He believed that this vast enlargement of the functions of government would awaken political interest and thus help to check political corruption.[49]

In the face of suspicious and warring industrial factions and of a half-apathetic public, Gladden scored, nevertheless, some substantial victories. His celebrated address, "Is It Peace or War?" delivered in many cities, impressed both capital and labor. Its eloquent plea for the right of labor organization as a basis for friendly relations between the two parties helped to foster a more reasonable attitude. He was chiefly responsible for ending the difficulties between operators and miners in the Hocking Valley coal region.[50] The attempt of Ohio Congregationalists to conciliate capital and labor was also the work of Gladden. The State Association in 1891, believing that "social problems will never be settled right until settled according to the law of love as manifested in the life and teachings of Jesus," appointed a committee with Gladden as chairman to investigate the industrial situation.[51] The committee held conferences in several cities, at which the representatives of both camps presented their grievances and discussed grounds of agreement. The meetings revealed "an absence of clear thinking on both sides," but did something to remove "prejudices and misconceptions" from the minds of the influential people who attended them.[52] These gatherings stimulated similar religious ventures in other parts of the country during the following years. Gladden's influence derived in large part from certain remarkable personal qualities: an aptitude for economic study, unswerving faith in his cause, a saving sense of humor and a virile literary style.

[49] *Tools and the Man*, pp. 281–302.
[50] J. B. Clark, "Christianity and Modern Economics," *New Englander*, XLVII (July 1887), 59.
[51] "The Social and Industrial Situation," *loc. cit.*, pp. 383–411.
[52] *Christian Union*, Jan. 30, 1892, p. 214.

He also epitomized the prevailing philosophy of socially minded ministers and laymen. With scarcely an exception the country's ecclesiastical bodies issued statements confirming his essential ideas. Thus the church congresses, notably the Episcopal and Baptist ones, discussed social questions from a moderate viewpoint. Episcopalians now abandoned the fiction that employers and employees always possessed identical interests. If there was perhaps no real distinction between the abstractions, capital and labor, there was "in their present condition," one speaker said, "a profound diversity of aim and wish between different men; and it is with these living, breathing factors that a true philosophy has to do." [53] All who appeared before the Congress advised Christians, in the interests of peace and justice, to substitute economic coöperation for economic individualism. They denounced as "a sinful state of society" the prevalent condition in which the only relation between capital and labor was "the payment of wages and the receipt of charity." [54] But many agreed with Abram S. Hewitt that the problem was being solved along lines unknown to, or not approved by, the orthodox political economists. Through organization the armies of labor were becoming powerful enough to force employers to negotiate, and out of this situation should ultimately come a joint ownership of productive property. During this evolution the church, he said, should insist on brotherhood and justice.[55]

In the same spirit the Baptist Congress viewed the labor question in terms of its permanent significance. In 1886 the eloquent layman, James Buchanan of Trenton, New Jersey, pointed out that the combination of capital had provoked a great counter-combination of workingmen, and that this situation, if not subjected to the Christian law, would destroy society. The large vote for Henry George in the New York

---

[53] John N. Galliher, "The Mutual Relations Between Capital and Labor," *Papers, Addresses and Discussions*, 1878, pp. 109–110.
[54] John W. Kramer, *ibid.*, pp. 108–109.   [55] *Ibid.*, p. 99.

mayoralty campaign of 1886 seemed to Buchanan greatly significant, not as an endorsement of his land views but as "a protest strong and emphatic against the greed of Mammon and the selfishness of the strong. . . ."[56] In the changed conditions most speakers realized, with the Reverend Walter Rauschenbusch, that the problem of reform was social, requiring the aid of government and the pressure of public opinion to direct individual energies into right channels.[57] But the stress of the Congress was on Christ like individuals. The "real and ineradicable evil," said David Jayne Hill, "is not social but personal." The main fault did not lie in the constitution of society, but in the perversity of the individual. "It is just here," he believed, "that Christianity becomes a social force of more real meaning than any socialistic theory for the reorganization of society." For Christianity, entering into the motives and impulses of men, "awakens sympathy for the unfortunate and helpless . . . thoughtfulness and sharing of burdens."[58] The Reverend Leighton Williams of Amity Baptist Church in New York also contended that self-sacrifice as practiced by Jesus Christ "is at the basis of all social regeneration."[59]

By stressing the doctrine of self-sacrificing service, Christians meant no more than that a social faith must precede or accompany a social program. So long as a collaborative spirit prevailed in the social world, they were in the main indifferent to the final form of society, some preferring one scheme and some another. Gladden's followers expected the state to regulate large competitive industries and to socialize the natural monopolies. A strong minority among the clergy and laity, led by W. D. P. Bliss, wished to socialize all productive property by ethical, non-Marxian methods. Though trained for the Congregational ministry, Bliss entered the Episcopal Church in

[56] "The Labor Question," *Annual Session*, 1886, p. 50.
[57] "Artificial and Natural Monopolies," *ibid.*, 1889, pp. 55–56.
[58] "Socialism — True and False," *ibid.*, 1885, p. 28.
[59] "Artificial and Natural Monopolies," *loc. cit.*, p. 67.

1886, assuming charge of a parish in South Boston. Impressed by the doctrines of Henry George, the *Christian Union* and English Christian Socialism, he had for some time been fighting the battles of labor.

With the assistance of the Reverend Francis Bellamy, he formed in Boston in February, 1889, a Society of Christian Socialists, somewhat on the plan of the Nationalist Clubs. After imputing to the existing industrial system "the moral evils of mammonism, recklessness, overcrowding, intemperance, prostitution and crime," the Society declared that the "aim of socialism is embraced in the aim of Christianity," and that "the teachings of Jesus lead directly to some form of socialism." [60] For several years the Society published *The Dawn, A Magazine of Christian Socialism and Record of Social Progress.*[61]

Other places followed Boston's leadership, societies being organized in Hartford, New York City and Denver and in the states of Ohio, Illinois and Kansas.[62] A few Christian Socialist centers and churches also sprang up. In Boston in 1890 Bliss formed the Brotherhood and Mission of the Carpenter, which with the aid of the Wendell Phillips Association embarked upon an educational program similar to that of Cooper Union in New York. When overwork forced him to give up the Church of the Carpenter in 1896, a Guild of the Carpenter continued the social and economic aspects of the enterprise.[63] The Reverend E. P. Foster, secretary of the Ohio Society, finding that his congregation did "not want the gospel applied to social and labor questions," established the Church of the Golden Rule and a weekly newspaper, *The Golden Rule*, which the Central Labor

[60] Lawrence Gronlund, "Christian Socialism in America," *Christian Register*, June 3, 1889, p. 380.
[61] See Nicholas Paine Gilman, "Christian Socialism in America," *Unitarian Rev.*, XXXII (October 1889), 345–57, for a detailed account.
[62] For details see "Record of Progress," *The Dawn*, II (May 1, 1890), 39–40; (June 1890), 92–94; (July–August 1890), 164–165; (Jan. 15, 1891), 12.
[63] Katherine Pearson Woods, "The Church of the Carpenter," *Christian Union*, Aug. 27, 1892, pp. 383–84; *The Dawn*, II (November 1890), 316; *ibid.*, VII (Jan. 1, 1896), 5.

Conference of Cincinnati adopted as its official organ.[64] The Reverend W. E. Sillence of Chicago also opened a Christian Socialist Church.

In a manner quite satisfactory to left-wing labor reformers of the period, Bliss steered his movement into socialistic channels. He believed that Christian Socialism was simply "the union of Christianity and essential scientific socialism" [65] — an idea repeatedly stressed by labor spokesmen in their complaints against the church. Though admitting that schemes of social organization were not substitutes for self-sacrifice, experience in a competitive order had shown, he insisted, an incompatibility between the laws of business and the Christian spirit. "While competition, each for himself lasts," he said, "no manufacturer, no employer, can pay the wages he would like." [66] Francis Bellamy believed that, with business maxims contradicting the law of love, "To talk about the principle of brotherhood" was "to treat the laws of Christ with flippancy." But socialism, he thought, would produce an environment "where not only the Golden Rule but the Law of Love will have a living chance." [67] The Christian Socialists were realistic enough to see that the unaided Christian spirit could not overcome every outward circumstance. Bliss and his followers were convinced, as Professor Paul Monroe said, that the teachings of Christ "are impossible of literal application in the present form of society, with the corollary that the present order of society should be changed until such application is practicable." [68]

Though favoring socialism as the final end of society, the followers of Bliss insisted that it be established gradually rather than suddenly. Socialism, as Bliss himself declared, was not a

[64] *Ibid.*, II (July–August 1890), 165; *ibid.* (October 1890), 251; *ibid.* (Dec. 18, 1890), 9.

[65] *What Is Christian Socialism?* (Boston, 1890), pp. 18–19.

[66] *What Christian Socialism Is*, pp. 12–14.

[67] "The Tyranny of All the People," *Arena*, IV (July 1891), 101.

[68] "English and American Christian Socialism: An Estimate," *Amer. Jour. of Sociology*, I (July 1895), 68.

scheme, but an evolving organism, a philosophy of life, to be progressively applied. "Any system that will carry out its principle," he said, "is socialism." [69] With government in America under plutocratic influence, it would be undemocratic and dangerous to introduce a full-fledged collectivism. It could function without peril to popular liberty only as political reform and the social spirit were developed.[70] As means of education, though not as ends in themselves, he favored profit-sharing, coöperation, trade unionism, arbitration and the various forms of municipal ownership. Socialists wanted the new regime to come speedily, but, as the Reverend Philo W. Sprague hastened to explain, the "essential thing" with them was that socialism "is the necessary outcome of a process that is going on in the ethical development of society." [71] From this it is clear that in working for socialism by evolutionary means the Christian Socialists of the Bliss school repudiated "coöperation as an end but not as a method." [72]

The more uncompromising Christian Socialists followed George D. Herron, a spiritual revolutionist. Born in 1863, at Montezuma, Indiana, Herron had spent the first years of his ministry on the home missionary field. His phenomenal popularity began with his address in 1891 entitled "The Message of Jesus to Men of Wealth." Becoming pastor of the Congregational Church in Burlington, Iowa, he preached eloquently on the social question, and organized classes to study primitive Christianity in its relation to human institutions and that "wide divergence from the simple social system of Christ found al-

[69] *What Christian Socialism Is,* pp. 17–18.
[70] *What Is Christian Socialism?* pp. 21–22, 27–28; "Position on Social Order," *The Dawn,* II (Dec. 4, 1890), 15.
[71] *Christian Socialism. What and Why?* pp. 48–49; also his article, "More or Less Inhumanity," *Nationalist,* I (September 1889), 153.
[72] Paul Monroe, *op. cit.,* p. 60. But Monroe in his brilliant and otherwise accurate study erred in thinking that Bliss and his followers actually repudiated coöperation as a method of attaining their goal. He was led astray largely by Austin Bierbower's *Socialism of Christ* (Chicago, 1890), which by portraying Christ's purpose as materialistic and violent was wholly exceptional and in no sense typical of Christian Socialists in America.

most everywhere in modern society." [73] A wealthy parishioner, Mrs. E. D. Rand, swayed by his teaching, established for Herron in 1893 a chair of Applied Christianity at Iowa (later Grinnell) College, which he used for social agitation until 1901. Out of his lectures before audiences, classes and summer gatherings from Maine to California came several widely read books: *The Larger Christ* (Chicago, 1891), *The Call of the Cross* (New York, 1892), *A Plea for the Gospel* (New York, 1892), *The New Redemption* (New York, 1893), *The Christian State* (New York, 1895), *Social Meanings of Religious Experiences* (New York, 1896) and *Between Caesar and Jesus* (New York, 1899). These works were "characterized by vigor of thought, intense enthusiasm, incisive, flashing utterance and an unfailing faith that the central doctrines of Christianity offer the true solution for all the problems, personal, social and political that vex our times." [74]

Economic evils, he said, stemmed from "the crude assertion of an enlightened self-interest as a law of human activity." But this gospel "would have caused the proclaimer to be mobbed in the streets of Athens in the days of Pericles," would have "astonished Moses," and seemed "ancient and barbarous" to Abraham.[75] He believed therefore that the "public ownership of the sources and means of production is the sole answer to the social question and the sole basis of spiritual liberty." [76] But Herron was interested primarily in preparing the way for a radical overturn. "I object to being called a socialist," he explained, "not because socialism is too radical, but because it is too wholly conservative." When the time should come for initiating the new system, More, Rousseau, Marx and Bellamy

[73] Irving Meredith, "American Institute of Christian Sociology," *Congregationalist*, July 27, 1893, pp. 134–135.

[74] "The New Books," *Review of Reviews* (New York), VII (July 1893), 110–111.

[75] "The Message of Jesus to Men of Wealth," *Christian Union*, Dec. 11, 1890, p. 804.

[76] "Between Caesar and Jesus," *The Commons*, IV (May 1899), 12.

would seem "but rude and conservative pioneers on the social frontier." [77] He was mainly an interpreter of Jesus — a religious crusader rather than a political or social reformer. His social views grew out of his profound religious experience. "Spiritual things are to him," as an observer said, "the most real of all things." [78] "Dr. Herron's work," wrote an intimate acquaintance, "has been and is distinctly to take the religious consciousness as it existed, for example, in the minds of such men as Edwards and Finney, and translate it into the social movement of our time." [79]

Though a socialist, Professor Herron stressed the doctrine of sacrifice more than perhaps any other American religious leader. It was the law of the life of God, "the divine order of culture." Just as Christ suffered on the cross for the redemption of mankind, so Christians must sacrifice their own interests for the welfare of others. Thus, the man of wealth "who fails to be a little Christ in the world has made a disastrous and irreparable business failure." [80] The great requisite of the world was failure in the conventional sense. "The redemptive need of civilization, the divinest want of the church," he said, "is not what we call successful men, who are the church's curse, and the nation's corruptors, but strong men willing to fail, that they may prove the justice of love and the social wisdom of sacrifice." [81] Jesus meant society to be an "organized sacrifice." "The state," he urged, "must be the social organ, and society the living organism, to discover how to apply the redemptive forgiveness of Jesus to persons and administer it through institutions." [82] Christianity was "a social ideal based upon the

[77] *Between Caesar and Jesus*, pp. 242–243.

[78] J. K. McLean, "A Kodak View of Professor Herron's Personal Characteristics," *Arena*, XIV (September 1895), 111–114.

[79] Charles Beardsley, "Professor Herron," *ibid.*, XV (April 1896), 784–796.

[80] "The Message of Jesus to Men of Wealth," *loc. cit.*, p. 805.

[81] "The Opportunity of the Church," *Arena*, XV (December 1895), 45.

[82] "A Christian Theory of the Distribution of Wealth," *Congregationalist*, Feb. 22, 1894, pp. 265–266.

sacrifices of service as the natural law of human life,"[83] an ideal rarely understood in Protestant churches.

Although the founders of social Christianity seriously studied the industrial situation, they did not regard it as the only or even the main aspect of the poverty problem. "Back of all economic factors," contended R. Heber Newton, "are other and yet larger factors." He attributed most poverty to hereditary vice and crime and to the inadequate discharge by the state of its social functions — this last "the most important factor in the problem. . . ."[84] But boss rule with its attendant corruption and inefficiency blocked the way to a municipal social service program. With a view to cleaning out the Augean stables of his own city, Newton in 1890 organized the People's Municipal League of New York, in the program of which professional people, the clergy and organized labor displayed interest. The churches were given a large part in the movement because they "hold," wrote Newton, "the moral forces upon which we hope to draw for this task of practical religion."[85] At this juncture the newly elected president of the New York Society for the Prevention of Crime, the Reverend Charles H. Parkhurst, assumed leadership, proved collusion between criminals and the city's police department and led an aroused electorate to victory against the Tammany organization in 1894. If the reform government which followed carried out only a few planks in its platform and was soon driven from power, it excited nevertheless nation-wide interest in municipal affairs and foreshadowed the greater successes of the early twentieth century.

In the meantime, progressive Protestants urged the churches to support non-political social service programs. Aside from the motives of charity, the findings of science prompted the

[83] "The Sociality of Jesus' Religion," *Arena*, XIV (November 1895), 385–386.
[84] *The Present Aspects of the Labor Problem*, p. 51.
[85] "The People's Movement for Municipal Reform," *Independent*, Aug. 7, 1890, p. 1084.

churches to enter the various movements for social betterment. It was now clear that environment, past and present, conditioned all phases of human development. This meant in religious terms that the body, the mind and the soul were interdependent: no one faculty could prosper apart from the welfare of the others. Science insisted that good moral character must rest upon a solid material foundation. "We now know," wrote Josiah Strong in 1893, "that, other things being equal, the more nearly normal the physical life is, the more nearly normal will be the intellectual and spiritual life." [86] If the positive discoveries of science prompted Christians to attend to the non-spiritual background of spiritual growth, they also showed that personality in the final analysis was more powerful than outward circumstance. Thus, only a few social scientists denied that the individual with a strong sense of his freedom and responsibility need succumb to the pauperism, intemperance or crime of his bad heredity or environment.

But the "philosophers" of social science for the most part championed unmitigated naturalism. Herbert Spencer and his host of American followers asserted that men were powerless of their own will either to prevent or to hasten human improvement. By way of reaction religious leaders called for a Christian sociology in which such postulates of social science as law and organism harmonized with Christian personality. The Reverend J. H. W. Stuckenberg, widely known American sociologist, explored the subject with some thoroughness in his treatise, *Christian Sociology*, published in 1880. Other ministers, notably Gladden, Amory H. Bradford, Samuel W. Dike, William J. Tucker of Andover and Francis G. Peabody of Harvard, also pioneered in the field. These thinkers freely conceded that science had helped religion by calling attention to the neglected social aspects of Christianity, and, moreover, that it must determine the method of progress. Science was right, as Tucker said, in claiming that "the advance of society,

[86] *The New Era*, p. 228.

like that of nature, is not sporadic, but gradual and consistent." [87] But the motivation of reform, they contended, is Christian. "What is this dynamic of social reform?" asked Professor Peabody. The "power of the Christian life," he answered, "finding its partial expression in these diverse social movements and correlating them all through its single impulse." [88]

After the middle eighties some of the more progressive magazines made room for systematic sociological discussion. Thus the *Andover Review* in 1885 commenced its "Sociological Notes" under Dike's direction. Three years later the *Homiletic Review*, taking to heart Edward Everett Hale's criticism that religious journalism failed to grapple with present-day problems, introduced social themes into its sermonic outlines and soon after created a Sociological Department with the veteran Stuckenberg as editor. In a similar spirit, the *Bibliotheca Sacra* in 1894 decided to place sociology on a plane with theology, securing as social editors Z. Swift Holbrook and Edward W. Bemis, the former a widely known Mid-Western business man and the latter a brilliant, new-school political economist. Besides supporting industrial reform in the manner of Gladden, the magazine now entered into almost every phase of Christian sociology. Its symposium on the subject in 1895 showed that eminent men in all walks of life welcomed the new discipline. The Reverend George H. Ide of Milwaukee stated the prevailing attitude. Ordinarily he would not associate the word "Christian" with scientific investigation. "Still as Christianity is interwoven with all this phenomena and perhaps is the cause of much of it," he explained, "it does not seem far out of the way to speak of Christian sociology." [89] Although controversy long raged over the precise nature and delimitations of the subject, few well-informed persons denied its existence or value.

[87] "Christianity and Its Modern Competitors," *Andover Rev.*, VI (December 1886), 645–646.
[88] "Philosophy of the Social Questions," *ibid.*, VIII (December 1887), 570–572.
[89] "What Is Sociology?" *Bibliotheca Sacra*, LII (July 1895), 458–485.

Protestant interest in the great problems of industrial reform and social science suggested the likelihood of radical changes in the established social order at some distant day. The immediate result was a more vital philanthropy. That gifts for the relief of the poor prodigiously increased excited little surprise; in the changed conditions that was to be expected of a people whose liberality was proverbial. The really noteworthy development was the new purpose and methods of charity: it now attempted to do its work in a spirit of democracy and fellowship and to view its agencies less as ends in themselves than as means of realizing the ideals of social justice. The old charity had sought, in Professor Tucker's words, "to put right what social conditions had put wrong," but the new seeks "to put right the social conditions themselves." [90] Aside from the early humanitarian churches and missions, the Charity-Organization movement first notably exemplified the improved techniques of giving. Beginning at Buffalo in 1877, societies arose in nearly a hundred and fifty cities by 1900, all aiming to coördinate relief agencies, to check indiscriminate charity and to help the victims of poverty and pauperism to help themselves.

The social settlements — meeting places of the estranged classes in the slums of the greater cities — epitomized the practices and purposes of the new philanthropy. Begun in the late eighties by young college graduates, the settlements rapidly multiplied during the nineties, with social reformers of all types sharing in the movement. In the eyes of many persons, the settlements were object lessons in democracy and social justice. "Such simplicity, joined with comfort, is sought in them," wrote Vida D. Scudder of the College Settlements Association, "as would be possible to all men under a normal distribution of wealth." [91] As the main reason for his founding Andover House in Boston (later South End House) in the early nineties, Pro-

---

[90] "From Charity to Justice," in his *New Reservation of Time and Other Articles* (Boston, 1916), pp. 82–83.

[91] "College Settlements and Religion," *Congregationalist*, May 2, 1895, p. 682.

fessor Tucker cited the need for more sympathy and understanding among the various classes. He did not believe that religion "in and of itself" could give "the social unity, in any community, which is now the most essential element in the change of social conditions." [92]

Many Protestant Christians evidently shared Tucker's view, for several seminaries and congregations opened and managed settlements in which no religious belief was required of the resident workers or the beneficiaries. Though at first most Christians feared that the settlement might prove a deplorable substitute for the church, others contended that, even if the new "instrument of social reform" was not missionary, it was essentially religious in character. In the opinion of one of the more influential church journals, the service of the settlement worker, like that of the friars of old, proceeded from a "belief in the brotherhood of humanity and a sense of the oneness of redeemed mankind in Christ." [93] The friends of the settlement were at great pains to make clear that the religious divergence in all cities precluded technically spiritual work and that the settlement did not claim competence in the church's peculiar field. To complain of the settlement "that it has no sermons, and no prayer-meetings, and makes no public profession of religion," said the Reverend George Hodges, founder of Kingsley House in Pittsburgh, "is like complaining of the physician that he does not wear a surplice and that he carries a medicine-case instead of a Bible." [94]

Though impressed by these arguments, progressive Protestants for the most part preferred to carry on humanitarian work alongside churches and missions. According to the Christian

[92] "The Work of Andover House in Boston," in R. H. Woods, W. T. Elsing and others, editors, *The Poor in Great Cities; Their Problems and What Is Done to Solve Them* (New York, 1895), p. 185.

[93] "The Religious Aspects of Social Settlements," *Churchman*, Feb. 27, 1897, p. 308.

[94] "Religion in the Settlement," Nat. Conf. of Charities and Corrections, *Proceedings*, 1896, pp. 150–151.

view, the first and most important step in social reconstruction was the bringing of the rich and poor together in public worship. As compared with this duty of the church — the disregarding of class distinctions and the making its services available to workingmen — the question of participation in industrial and social reform was of secondary importance. Or more accurately, the church would make its unique and most appropriate contribution to the solution of social problems by insisting that all classes acknowledge spiritual allegiance to Jesus Christ. "The solution of this ecclesiastical problem," wrote a seminary student, "must precede the solution of the industrial problem and prepare for it." [95] Mainly as a means of identifying the poor with the congregations and of symbolizing Christian brotherhood, many Protestants proposed to superimpose philanthropic, educational and recreational features upon the fundamentally spiritual functions of churches and missions. In these religious and humanitarian fields social Christianity was to discover its chief interests.

Yet social Christianity, it should be recalled, was a pervasive, many-sided movement. The truth is that after 1880 Protestants formed contacts, from every fruitful approach, with the new currents in American social life. With the nation in the throes of industrial conflict which seemed likely to terminate in economic despotism, the churches resolved to bring their influence to bear in favor of peace and justice. They were also motivated by an anxious desire to arrest the widespread alienation of labor from Protestant Christianity. Edward Bellamy was justified in stating early in the nineties that "the churches of America are not going to make again, and on a far vaster scale, the mistake they made a generation ago in opposing or ignoring the anti-slavery agitation." [96] Not only the friends, but also the enemies, of the labor movement bore witness to the growing sympathy of

---

[95] John Howard Melish, "The Duty of the Christian Minister in Relation to Social Problems," Christian Social Union, *Publications*, No. 51, July 1898, p. 21.
[96] "The Churches and Nationalism," *New Nation*, Dec. 5, 1891, p. 710.

the clergy with the cause of workingmen. In the eyes of the learned conservative, the Reverend G. Frederick Wright of Oberlin, the unbridled demands of labor resulted from the "misguided sentimentalism and culpable cowardice of the ministry" which no longer preached submission and subordination.[97] Though Protestant social theory still insisted that the spirit of love and self-sacrifice on the part of individuals must animate all reform, it now welcomed the aid of the state, to the extent, if need be, of outright socialism. Yet Protestants steadily refused to limit social Christianity to economic reconstruction. Fundamental as this was, the more immediate aspects of urban poverty offered a more fruitful field for the promotion of social justice. With the new scientific philanthropy at their disposal, the churches could look forward to mighty triumphs. But first they faced the task of diffusing widely their social teachings.

[97] "Ministers and Mobs," *Bibliotheca Sacra*, XLIX (October 1892), 679.

CHAPTER IV

SOCIAL CHRISTIANITY: DIFFUSION AND EXPANSION
1880–1900

HAVING adapted the principles and policies of social Christianity to the needs of the rapidly maturing cities, leading Protestants were anxious to diffuse the new findings. A task so Herculean required the coöperation of all the more experienced religio-social workers. Only by concerted effort could average people be made to realize the urgent need for the church's social program. Moreover, the expansion of the program awaited a further consolidation of spiritual forces. If in spite of sectarian divergence Protestants should unite to study the urban religious situation, they would prepare the way, they believed, for common action over the whole field of social service. Though some favored a single Protestant Church, proposals to this end speedily foundered on the rocks of unreality and prejudice. Many who subscribed to the ideal of organic church unity admitted that the "time is not ripe for an act of union until there is first the spirit of union." [1]

But simple coöperation was as widely favored as organic unity was frowned upon. Thus, the Presbyterians, when rejecting the Episcopal plan of 1886 for church unity, called for "some practical mode of coöperation" to deal with the great social problems — "the care of the poor, the delicate and often disturbed relations of capital and labor, the infusion of Gospel principles into all the affairs of ordinary life, into business, and legislation and the general intercourse of men." [2] The opponents of sectarianism in the various leagues and church congresses led in the movement to popularize coöperative action

[1] T. S. Hamlin, *Denominationalism or Christian Union* (Chicago, 1891), p. 78.
[2] "Appendix XI," *Journal of the Bishops, Clergy and Laity of the Protestant Episcopal Church in General Convention*, 1895, pp. 603–604.

as the remedy for the inability of the denominational system "to grasp vigorously the issues of life in the community and to lead them in large directions. . . ." [3] The Protestant Episcopal Church Congress, discussing in 1890 the subject, "Practical Christian Cooperation with Other Christian Bodies in Rescue Work," agreed that in the whole range of philanthropy religious groups could associate without sacrifice of principle.[4] "If we cannot have an *Incorporation*," said Dr. James McCosh of Princeton, a founder of the Pan-Presbyterian Alliance, "let us have a *Federation*." [5] His carefully elaborated plan, explained the *Christian Union*, was "practically a revival of the parochial system of the old world, modified and adapted to a country without an established church, or recognized ecclesiastico-political parishes." [6]

To this end, evangelical Protestants in the eighties and nineties evolved five organizations to focus religion on social life. These were the American Congress of Churches, the Evangelical Alliance, the Convention of Christian Workers, the Brotherhood of Christian Unity and the League for Catholic Unity. Essentially alike in aim, they differed greatly in size and degree of influence, the second and third being by far the most important.

The Reverend W. W. Newton, an Episcopalian of Pittsfield, Massachusetts, founded the American Congress of Churches in 1884 to do for Christianity as a whole what the church congresses and leagues were doing for denominations. More specifically, the Congress aimed "to promote Christian Union, and to advance the Kingdom of God, by a free discussion of the great religious, moral and social questions of the time." [7] Winning the support of several prominent men, the Congress held two meetings, the first at Hartford in 1885 and the second at

[3] Julius H. Ward, *The Church in Modern Society* (Boston, 1889), pp. 82–83.
[4] *Papers, Addresses and Discussions*, pp. 38–67.
[5] "Federation of Churches," *Christian Union*, Feb. 6, 1890, pp. 189–190.
[6] "Dr. McCosh's Plan," *ibid.*, p. 186.
[7] *Proceedings of the Hartford Meeting*, 1885, pp. 3, 23–25.

Cleveland the following year. The papers read at the first gathering, though contributed by such well-known friends of social Christianity as James Freeman Clarke, Professor George P. Fisher, Bishop A. Cleveland Coxe and Washington Gladden, were of a theoretical character. At the Cleveland meeting the discussions were different, being, as one observer wrote, "more concerned about the living needs of the time than about doctrines, about practice than hair-splitting." [8] In the topics, "The Workingman's Distrust of the Church, its Causes and Remedies," and "Readjustments in the Church to Meet Modern Needs," the Congress considered the Christian theory of reform and its applications. Everett P. Wheeler and Henry George discussed the methods the churches should use to acquire influence with the wage-earning class, and the Reverend Leonard Bacon called for "unity of the churches in their organization to improve the well-being of men in the present life." [9]

Though the American Congress of Churches was short-lived, the Evangelical Alliance was influential until the closing years of the century. Organized in 1867, it had enjoyed only a nominal existence for twenty years. Besides being handicapped by a Calvinistic creed, the Alliance had side tracked social reform to fight free thought and Roman Catholicism, the traditional bogies of the evangelical mind.[10] The new exigencies of Christianity led, however, to a "new departure," foreshadowed by the Inter-Denominational Congress held in Cincinnati in the fall of 1885. This meeting was inspired largely by Josiah Strong whose book, *Our Country*, had already begun to electrify the religious forces of the nation. Attended by prominent leaders like Lyman Abbott, George R. Leavitt, Thomas K. Beecher, Amory H. Bradford, Washington Gladden and Richard T. Ely, the Congress followed an orderly program, discussing first the evils and then the remedies. "While there was

---

[8] *Chautauquan*, VI (July 1886), 603.

[9] *Christian Union*, June 3, 1886, pp. 6–7.

[10] A. Cleveland Coxe, "A Christian Alliance the Demand of Our Times," *Independent*, Feb. 14, 1884, pp. 194–195.

some disagreement in details," wrote an observer, "there was a general agreement that the present industrial system needs radical changes and that these changes are to be wrought by applying to it the principles of Christianity which have already revolutionized the State and the Church." [11] The Congress also took account of the applications of Christian social theory. Thus, the Reverend Frank Russell detailed the astonishing social improvement which had followed systematic care of the poor by the churches in the small city of Mansfield, Ohio.[12]

In the same spirit the Evangelical Alliance resolved to become an instrument for rousing the churches to their social mission. At a gathering in New York of some hundred and fifty religious leaders, summoned in 1886 by William E. Dodge, the new president of the Alliance, the common opinion was expressed that coöperation rather than organic union was the crying need of the hour.[13] The meeting arranged for a national conference and appointed Strong and Russell to the newly established offices of General Secretary and Field Secretary. The eighty-six distinguished men, who called the first conference, alluded to the fact that America was "now beginning to approximate European conditions of society. The existence of great cities, severe competition, an unemployed class, increasing pauperism and crime," it said, "are the occasion and evidence of a wide-spread discontent for which the ballot affords no remedy." The situation required the aid of the Christian Church, which had "not yet recognized its relations to the entire life of the community and the nation." [14]

The three conferences of the Alliance met fully the expectations of all people who wanted the relation of religion to the social question adequately discussed. The conferences in Wash-

---

[11] "Christianity and the Workingman," *Christian Union*, Dec. 17, 1885, p. 6.
[12] "A Religious Census," *Discussions of the Inter-Denominational Congress in the Interests of City Evangelization Held in Cincinnati, Dec. 7–11, 1885*, p. 228.
[13] *Christian Union*, April 15, 1886, p. 20.
[14] *Congregationalist*, Oct. 13, 1887, p. 353.

ington and Boston so thoroughly canvassed the dangers and shortcomings of American civilization that the Chicago conference of 1893 could specialize in presenting "practical methods of Christian work by which the Church might accomplish her social mission and thus meet the great perils and needs of the time." [15] The Alliance insisted that the churches deal less with human creeds and more with human needs.[16] As Dodge put it at the Washington meeting in 1887, if "God and our hopes for the future were blotted out, . . . the model of Christ's perfect life, if it could be imitated by man, and His teachings followed, would make this earth a heaven, and put an end to sin and evil everywhere." [17] President E. B. P. Andrews of Brown believed that religion had so narrowly construed its function that ruin threatened. "Should the church remain as now," he warned, "cold to the masses and their interest, a great Christian labor leader may arise — a Luther and Powderly in one — and Christianity would stride to victory, but its agent would be a new church, with relations to the churches represented in this conference, somewhat like the relations of original Protestantism to the Catholic Church of its time." [18]

As the Alliance diagnosed religious and social conditions, the necessity for an associative program became increasingly apparent. As Christianity assumed social responsibilities, "many things will be found," said Dodge, "which only can be successfully met by a cordial coöperation of all the churches." [19] To some it might seem useless, the Reverend R. S. Storrs of Brooklyn confessed, to "attempt to make good conquer evil and take the place of it in our rapid and turbulent American society," yet there was no "occasion for despair" provided the

---

[15] "Introduction," *Christianity Practically Applied*, vol. I.

[16] *Congregationalist*, Dec. 12, 1889, p. 426; *Christian Union*, Dec. 12, 1889, p. 761.

[17] *National Perils and Opportunities*, 1887, p. 6.

[18] "A Plea for an Enlarged View of the Church's Mission," *Christianity Practically Applied*, I, 341–349.

[19] *National Perils and Opportunities*, 1887, pp. 5–6.

Christian resources of the country were "called into full activity." [20] The realization of the Alliance plan depended upon the ability of local congregations to organize their religious resources — a program which Josiah Strong called federation at the bottom. Federation at the top, he said, "would necessarily be conservative; it could not lead. It could never go faster than the slowest denomination entering in the federation." [21] These local alliances should pursue a three-fold work: (1) coöperation in the study of sociological and industrial problems and in applying Christian principles to their solution; (2) coöperation in teaching the entire population the Gospel; and (3) coöperation for accomplishing needed reforms and for defending cherished American institutions. In order to attain these objectives, which it increasingly stressed, the Alliance drew up a fourteen-point program. A series of pamphlets, prepared by Carl Schurz, Richard Watson Gilder, Woodrow Wilson, John R. Commons and others, proved useful. [22] At first, however, the Alliance centered attention on strictly religious work, such as house-to-house canvassing to end church neglect.

The Alliance entrusted the supervision of its more elaborate plan to Russell, the Field Secretary, who travelled throughout America several times, addressing church groups, summer religious assemblies and theological seminaries. Besides getting State Committees established in New York and Michigan, he succeeded by 1889 in forming alliances in over forty cities, including New York, Philadelphia, Baltimore, Boston and St. Paul. [23] In New York City, the beginnings dated from a great meeting in Chickering Hall in December, 1888. Papers and discussions by prominent leaders confirmed the slight hold of religious agencies on the wage-earning class, and revealed a no

[20] *Ibid.*, pp. 299–300.
[21] Josiah Strong, "Practical Coöperation in Church Work," *Review of Reviews*, VI (October 1892), 301.
[22] *Encyclopedia of Social Reform*, p. 565.
[23] Josiah Strong, "Progress of Christian Coöperation Since the Washington Conference," *National Needs and Remedies*, p. 13.

less determined will to end the clubhouse type of church.[24]   The Reverend Charles H. Parkhurst's resolution providing for systematic visitation was passed and arrangements were made to carry it into effect.   But the New York clergy, still unmindful of social danger, were reluctant "to join forces in any redemptive work." [25]   In other large cities, however, notably Baltimore and Philadelphia, excellent results were obtained.   The Ministerial Union of the latter city in 1888 relinquished its work in favor of a reorganized Evangelical Alliance, which aimed "to reach the entire community with Christian influence, and to apply the Gospel principles of love to the social and religious problems of the day." [26]   A systematic house-to-house canvass reached a million people.   By bringing the denominations and the Citizens' Permanent Relief Committee together in 1895, the Philadelphia Alliance helped to alleviate physical distress.

Beset with great difficulties, the Alliance plan developed slowly.   The active opposition, combined with the inertia and indifference of others, led Strong to say that years would be required "to produce marked results." [27]   While R. Fulton Cutting, chairman of the State Committee of New York, saw in the scheme a means for reconciling capital and labor, the effort to sustain it required a high degree of Christian heroism.[28] Yet the influence of the Alliance method can scarcely be over-estimated.   It revealed religious and social evils, suggested remedies, and stimulated churches to work together in effecting solutions.   In some cases churches which failed to get help from others carried out the project unaided.[29]

[24] *Nation*, Dec. 6, 1888, pp. 447–448.
[25] A. Mackay-Smith, "Practical Coöperation, with Other Christian Bodies in Rescue Work," Prot. Episcopal Church Cong., *Papers, Addresses and Discussions*, 1890, pp. 47–51.
[26] William Charles Webb, "Federation in Pennsylvania," *Hartford Seminary Record*, X (May 1900), 204–205.
[27] "Progress of Christian Coöperation Since the Washington Conference," *loc. cit.*, p. 17.
[28] "Coöperative Religious Work in New York State," *National Needs and Remedies*, 1889, pp. 29–30.
[29] "Report of the Field Secretary," *Annual Report*, 1890, p. 12.

Another body of broad national scope seeking to bring religion and the social movement together was the Convention of Christian Workers, formed in 1886. City missionaries, many of them followers of the late Jerry McAuley, were responsible. Their leader was the Reverend John C. Collins, a Yale graduate and manager of the Union Gospel Mission in New Haven. At a meeting of Sunday school and mission workers at Hartford in 1885, he suggested that steps be taken to create a national organization.[30] Collins and Colonel George Rogers Clark, a Chicago missionary, were asked to solicit support from all interested persons. "In response," said Collins, "we received words of hearty encouragement and the signatures of about seventy of the most earnest, successful and prominent workers, evangelists, and missionaries throughout the country." After alluding to the fact that previous gatherings of a local nature had accomplished much, the callers hoped that "a general convention . . . would prove helpful" in advancing Christianity. "Our idea of such a convention," they said, "is that it shall be intensely practical. We would have no long philosophical essays or critical discourses, setting forth evils, with which we, as men and women, engaged in hand-to-hand conflict with the power of darkness are already familiar." [31]

The discussions in the first convention at Chicago in June, 1886, resulted in the appointment of a Committee of Seven, headed by R. A. Torrey, of the Church of the Open Door in Minneapolis, which proposed the following broad program of future work: (1) supplying churches with information as to Christian workers, giving information on "evangelistic help" and "work for boys," providing reading rooms for young men and old, children's saving banks and religious classes; (2) employing students of theological schools under capable Christian workers, so as to give them practical experience in cities; (3)

[30] *Christian Union*, Nov. 26, 1892, p. 998.
[31] Convention of Christian Workers in the United States and Canada, *Proceedings*, 1886, pp. 4, 14; *Christian Union*, May 6, 1886, p. 20.

training in missions for those not caring to enter the ministry; (4) advising and counseling women desirous of entering suitable fields of Christian work; (5) coöperating with individual churches wishing to organize missions in neglected neighborhoods; and (6) receiving and disbursing money for these objects and for missions already in existence or to be established in the future.[32] Though Collins's proposal that a special officer be selected to direct mission operations was not adopted, ample provision was made in other ways for supervision.[33]

At the annual conventions, held after 1886, many of the best known religious and philanthropic leaders of the country participated. Outstanding were Graham Taylor, pastor of the Fourth Congregational Church, Hartford; David A. Reed, of Hope Congregational Church, Springfield, Massachusetts; Arthur T. Pierson, of Bethany Presbyterian Church, Philadelphia; Jacob Riis, Josiah Strong and Bishop Frederic Dan Huntington. The prominent women included Mrs. J. K. Birney, of the W.C.T.U.; Miss M. M. McBride, a New York social worker; Mrs. Bernard Whitman, an editor of *Lend a Hand*; Miss Grace H. Dodge; and Miss M. J. MacDonald of Toronto. Most of the delegates, however, were obscure, uneducated people, who, having been saved themselves, desired to save others. This accounts for the clinical nature of the discussions and for the fact that over fifty lines of humanitarian endeavor were represented.[34] Though primarily for exchange of views, the Convention of Christian Workers practised certain types of philanthropic and religious work. In some cities, where meetings were held, the more energetic members exhibited the rescue technique and established missions. More important perhaps were the efforts to give college and theological students opportunities for careers as city missionaries. A committee on students' work

---

[32] *Ibid.*, Sept. 20, 1886, p. 20.
[33] "Secretary's Report," *Proceedings*, 1888, pp. 12–13; *Congregationalist*, Nov. 21, 1895, p. 780.
[34] Graham Taylor, "The Christian Workers' Convention," *ibid.*, Nov. 20, 1889, p. 412.

with the Reverend S. H. Lee as secretary, persuaded over a score of men from Amherst, Williams, Yale, Trinity, Wesleyan and Oberlin to spend their vacations in the missions at New Haven, Hartford and New York.[35]

The chief interest was boys' club work, in promoting which the Convention took the lead in the United States. Collins, who had been active in this field while a student in Yale, persuaded the Convention in 1888 to appoint a committee on Work for Boys, with President Carter of Williams College as chairman. Though the committee failed to raise its contemplated fund of a hundred thousand dollars, it secured worthwhile results with small means. State committees in Connecticut and Massachusetts helped to offset apathy and indifference on the part of churchgoers. By 1891 there were altogether twenty clubs under the auspices of the Convention of Christian Workers with a membership of nearly ten thousand. Designed for boys between the ages of eight and eighteen, the various clubhouses were as a rule spacious, well-equipped, and open for use each evening from seven to nine during the winter months. "Night kindergartens" and "trade schools," they offered games, reading and class work in carpentry, typesetting and drawing. Though sectarian propaganda was avoided, the superintendents during the day tried to exert religious influence among the families of Protestant boys.[36]

That the Convention of Christian Workers commanded a wide hearing cannot be doubted. From a small body in 1886 it comprised before the end of the century over twenty-five hundred active devotees of social Christianity. Their hand-to-hand grapple with "the dreads and horrors of the slums, the depravity of debauchery, the madness of anarchism," [37] impressed observers

[35] *Proceedings*, 1887, p. 11; *ibid.*, 1888, p. 11; *ibid.*, 1889, pp. 222–223, 231; *ibid.*, 1890, p. 184.
[36] *Ibid.*, 1890, p. 21; *ibid.*, 1891, pp. 25–26; *Lend a Hand*, II (March 1890), 174; Raymond Calkins, *Substitutes for the Saloon* (Boston, 1901), pp. 314–320.
[37] Charles M. Southgate, "Fourth Convention of Christian Workers," *Congregationalist*, Oct. 31, 1889, p. 359.

as "Apostolic Christianity restored and worked." [38]   Taylor wrote that the Convention "is a great exhibit of the work and working forces of modern Christianity" and "as nearly ecumenical a gathering of the church in America as is held on this continent." [39]   The *Christian Union* believed that it "is the inspiration of very much of the best missionary work of the time, and makes its influence felt in different ways all over the world." [40]   The stenographic reports of the various meetings, it said, furnished "the best literature on practical Christian work that can be secured." [41]

If the Evangelical Alliance and the Convention of Christian Workers seemed to many to exhaust this field of religious endeavor, others believed that additional organization was necessary. In 1891 Theodore F. Seward, a layman and church musician, formed the Brotherhood of Christian Unity to break down the theological walls keeping Christians from the imperative work of social reform.[42] He planned "to provide, during the evolutionary process through which the churches are passing, a bond of union which shall help toward the ideal of perfect unity." [43]   Seward required members simply to sign a pledge, reading as follows: "For the purpose of uniting with all who desire to serve God and their Fellow-men under the inspiration of the life and teachings of Jesus Christ, I hereby enroll myself as a member of the Brotherhood of Christian Unity." Through lectures and a monthly magazine, *Christian Unity*, Seward popularized the Brotherhood. With a view to establishing local branches, he was wont to pay selected towns a two-week visit. The movement "met with an immediate and widespread approval," especially from the intellectual classes, "orthodox,

[38] *Zion's Herald*, Nov. 16, 1892, p. 364.
[39] *Op. cit.*
[40] Nov. 26, 1892, p. 998.
[41] *Ibid.*, Nov. 29, 1888, p. 618.
[42] "A Brotherhood of Christian Unity," *Christian Union*, June 11, 1891, p. 888.
[43] "A Brotherhood of Christian Unity," *Review of Reviews*, V (February 1892), pp. 45–47.

heterodox and no dox." Josiah Strong believed that the Brotherhood could do among Christians generally what the Evangelical
Alliance attempted among the churches.[44] The Parliament of
Religious at Chicago in 1893 adopted its enrollment pledge as
"a suitable bond with which to begin the federation of the
world on a Christian basis." [45]

An organization analogous to the Brotherhood of Christian
Unity, though more sympathetic to ecclesiasticism, was the
League of Catholic Unity, formed in 1895 by the Reverend
William Chauncey Langdon, long prominent in Protestant
Episcopal social movements. The ground had been fertilized
by a series of sociological studies, entitled "Present Day Papers," published in the *Century* through Langdon's efforts.[46]
Among the contributors were Professor Ely, Bishop Potter and
Washington Gladden. In 1893 the group enlarged to fifty
members who in the following ten years studied the liquor
problem in all its aspects.[47] The earlier studies, which were
scientific in method as well as Christian in purpose and spirit,
made clear the close relationship between church unity and
social life. The time was not far off, said Professor Charles W.
Shields, "when the organization of the Christian denominations
against menacing social evils . . . shall have become a social
as well as an ecclesiastical question, and a question belonging
to the domain of practical rather than sentimental politics." [48]
In this spirit, twenty-one members, seven each from the Congregational, Presbyterian and Episcopal Churches, came to-

[44] Seward, "First Year's History," *Christian Union*, May 7, 1892, p. 897;
Seward, "The Unity of the Spirit," *Outlook*, Oct. 19, 1895, p. 622.

[45] *Encyclopedia of Social Reform*, p. 192.

[46] Vols. XXXIX–XLVIII (November 1889–July 1894).

[47] Frederick H. Wines, *The Liquor Problem in Its Legislative Aspects* (Boston, 1897); John Koren, *Economic Aspects of the Liquor Problem* (Boston,
1899); Raymond Calkins, *Substitutes for the Saloon* (Boston, 1901); John S.
Billings, *Physiological Aspects of the Liquor Problem* (Boston, 1903); Francis
G. Peabody, *The Liquor Problem; A Summary of Investigations Conducted by
the Committee of Fifty, 1893–1903* (Boston, 1905).

[48] "The Social Problem of Church Unity," *Century*, XL (September 1890),
687–688.

gether in the Brotherhood to work up sentiment for a United Church for the United States. They subscribed to the view that a federation of churches would be but "a cluster of class churches, not one church of all classes." "In the New Testament Church," said Professor Shields, "there were no Episcopalian, Presbyterian and Congregationalist denominations, but only congregational, presbyterian and episcopal principles and institutions combined in one organization. That catholic and apostolic church might now return," he believed, "if our congregations would associate in free presbyteries, our presbyteries commit their episcopal functions to bishops and our bishops become confined in the same historic succession, whatever views might be held as to the need or value of that succession." [49]

Liberals as well as evangelicals invoked coöperative action to help solve social problems. If theological dogmatism continued to repel them, they also deplored their own lack of coherence and social sympathy. Hugh O. Pentecost, for example, reflected the new attitude. Forced out of his Congregational pastorate in Newark, New Jersey, by his championship of Henry George and the labor movement, he established Unity Congregation in 1886 and soon after a newspaper, *The Twentieth Century*, both of which hurled defiance at the old order. Pentecost defended agnosticism, which meant to him "the gospel of social revolution by the overthrow of this present industrial system . . . which robs the many for the enrichment of the few." In defending socialism he insisted that environment was of primary importance; if the economic system were changed, "Men's souls would be saved as naturally as apples grow upon apple trees." [50] He scoffed at the Unitarian variety of liberalism since experience taught that, however liberal it may be in thought, "it is quite as intolerant of social heresy as the orthodox." [51]

[49] *Ibid.*, pp. 696–697; *Congregationalist*, June 20, 1895, p. 982.
[50] *The Twentieth Century*, Sept. 29, 1888, pp. 1–4.
[51] *Ibid.*, Jan. 12, 1889, p. 6; *ibid.*, October 1888, pp. 111–112.

Some of the older liberal groups also developed an interest in the sociological approach to religion. Thus, the Free Religious Association, on the verge of collapse in the late seventies, revived and gave precedence to social rather than to intellectual questions. Among Unitarians, the Western Conference in the middle eighties adopted an ethical creed, declaring that anyone who believed character to be the end for which the church should labor "is of and with the Unitarian movement." [52] The great leader in the Conference was Jenkin Lloyd Jones, pastor of All Soul's Church in Chicago, who, having learned "to love trinitarian earnestness more than Unitarian coldness," considered that "the problems of life" had "a more religious bearing than the problems of Biblical criticism or of theological creeds." [53] In *Unity*, his religious newspaper, he sought "the unities of universal religion, the perennial elements in Christendom, Judaism, and all other forms and names that have purified, sweetened and ennobled life." [54] Support also came from the radical groups within American Jewry, who held that Judaism had always been "a religion for this earth and life." Emil G. Hirsch, rabbi of Mt. Sinai Congregation in Chicago, aided the cause after 1890 in his influential paper, the *Reform Advocate*.

The liberal forces did not coalesce, however, until the American Congress of Liberal Religious Societies was formed in 1894. Planned during the World's Fair by such leaders as Jones, Hirsch, Dr. H. W. Thomas of the People's Church, Chicago, and the Reverend W. S. Crowe of Newark, New Jersey, the Congress came into existence in response to the call of six hundred people. The Congress stressed "not independence, but union" — the coöperation of forces "working in the direction of a broader and fuller sense of humanitarian sympathy." [55] In discussing the subject, "The Sociological Basis of Religious

[52] *Congregationalist*, June 3, 1897, p. 801; *Ethical Record*, II (April 1889), 60–61.

[53] *Reform Advocate*, July 13, 1895, p. 329.

[54] *Ethical Record*, II (April 1889), 61.

[55] *Reform Advocate*, June 23, 1894, p. 349; *ibid.*, pp. 346–347.

Union and Work," Professor Albion W. Small of the University of Chicago defended the thesis that all "the forms of religion . . . have a common tendency, varying in degree, but essentially social." [56] The aid of such men as R. Heber Newton, John Faville, Washington Gladden and Professors Ely and John Bascom could have been won only on a sociological platform.[57] Gladden was willing to help because "I want," he said, "to do what I can to promote the cooperation of all who are willing to work for the Kingdom of God." [58]

The liberals practised as well as discussed social reform. Thus the developing work of the Ethical Culture Societies impressed all lovers of humanity. Their program, to which all were invited to subscribe regardless of "theological or philosophical opinions," [59] consisted of conferences between capital and labor, settlement work and a social type of education. The basis for social education was the free kindergarten, established by the New York Society in 1877. This venture, one of the first of its kind in New York, succeeded so well that it was widely imitated. The Society then applied similar methods to older children in a Workingmen's School, at first exclusively for the poor. Aiming to influence the public schools, it taught unsectarian morality, manual training and other forms of industrial preparation.[60] The insistent demands from all sections of the country for teachers nurtured along the new lines symbolized the Society's success. The other Ethical Societies in their educational work followed the example of the New York Society.[61]

The second educational feature of the Societies was the study

[56] First Cong. of Lib. Rel. Soc., *Proceedings*, 1894, pp. 30–33.
[57] W. L. Sheldon, quoted in "The Coming Annual Meeting of the Liberal Congress," *Reform Advocate*, April 27, 1895, p. 157.
[58] *Reform Advocate*, June 9, 1894, p. 283.
[59] Felix Adler, "The Aims of the Ethical Society," *Ethical Record*, II (October 1889), 153.
[60] Caroline T. Haven, "The Workingmen's School," *Altruist Interchange*, II (January 1894), 14.
[61] *Ethical Record*, I (April 1888), 28–29; *ibid.*, I (October 1888), 110.

of social questions. The hesitancy of the seminaries and colleges in cultivating this field led the Union of Ethical Societies in 1889 to appoint a committee of well-known liberals to arrange for a school in autonomous connection with some university. This institution, said Adler, "is intended to serve the highest interest of science and at the same time to send new currents of practical idealism into the life of the common people." [62] It was established, not as originally planned, but as a Summer School with three departments — Religion, Ethics and Economics, headed respectively by Professor C. H. Toy of Harvard, Adler and Professor Henry C. Adams of the University of Michigan. Beginning in 1891, the school held sessions at Plymouth, Massachusetts, and in other New England cities.[63] The comprehensive instruction given can be visualized from some of the published essays. In 1892, for example, the Department of Economics studied the general subject of social progress. One aspect of the discussions was published under the title, *Philanthropy and Social Progress* (New York, 1893). Journalistic efforts supplemented the influence of the Summer School. Besides the publications of individuals and the Societies, the Union issued in 1888 the *Ethical Record*, which two years later was expanded into the famous *International Journal of Ethics*.

A more grandiose scheme to embody the liberal concern for reform was the Union for Practical Progress, launched in the early nineties by B. O. Flower, editor of the *Arena*. An enthusiastic supporter of the American Congress of Liberal Religious Societies, he sought a social theory and technique capable of realizing its program. Convinced that the procedure of reform should correlate the ideals of justice and charity, he saw the solution in the work of the social settlements and the Societies of Ethical Culture. He believed that the obstacles to organiza-

[62] Felix Adler, "The School of Philosophy and Applied Ethics," *ibid.*, II (April 1889), 8.

[63] W. L. Sheldon, *An Ethical Movement*, pp. xii–xiii; *Churchman*, Aug. 6, 1892, p. 157.

tion could be overcome. "The heart hunger of our time," he wrote, "is as significant as it is inspiring" — a fact shown by the inquiries from all sides as to the proper methods of mobilizing the forces of righteousness.[64] He urged that the religious basis of the Unions to be established in the various cities be elastic enough to include all. While delighted with the public reception given the Brotherhood of Christian Unity, he insisted that its name spelled exclusiveness to thousands who failed to grasp the Brotherhood's ideal Christianity. A better platform was that of the Ethical Culture Societies and of the various independent churches.[65]

Unions were formed in many cities, large and small and, through the *Arena*, federated into a National Union which aimed to give the movement a definite and orderly plan of action.[66] According to the Constitution, the purpose was "to unite all moral forces, agencies and persons for concerted, methodical, and persistent endeavor in behalf of the public good and especially for the abolition of unjust social conditions." [67] The Union worked out a plan for mass attacks upon specific evils at particular times. Thus, the local Unions agreed to concentrate each month upon some one phase of the social problem: the sweating system, child labor or municipal corruption. Special efforts were made to enlist the support of churches and clergymen, who were supplied with information and interviewed as to their attitude.[68] In some cases, Union members conducted clerics through slums and factories to acquaint them with conditions. Many ministers in Philadelphia, for example, horrified by the sweat shops and reeking tenements, "went home

[64] "The New Time and How its Advent May be Hastened," *Arena*, IX (April 1894), 685–694.

[65] "Union for Practical Progress," *Arena*, VIII (June 1893), 80–89.

[66] Ella Reeve Ward, "The Union for Practical Progress," *Reform Advocate*, VII (July 7, 1894), 376; see "Union for Practical Progress," *Arena*, vols. IX–XIV (1893–95), for growth of the movement.

[67] W. H. Tolman, *Municipal Reform Movements*, p. 162.

[68] Rev. Walter Vrooman, "First Steps in the Union of Moral Forces," *Arena*, IX (March 1894), 540–544.

to their people with hearts full of earnestness to protest against the tolerance of such a system under the laws of the state." [69] While not disposed to waste time on the older clergy, who in the main were indifferent to social reform, the Union was certain of the younger ones, both orthodox and heterodox.[70]

Several Unions, notably those in Philadelphia and Baltimore, scored enviable records. The Philadelphia Union grew out of the City Conference of Baptist Ministers before whom the Reverend Walter Vrooman early in 1893 urged an organized effort to abolish the slums. The Conference thereupon suggested that each denomination and central body of workingmen select a committee of three to form a central agency "which shall attempt to arrange a program in which the majority of earnest people can unite for aggressive work against the slums." The result was a Central Conference, supported by orthodox and liberal ministerial unions, the Roman Catholic societies and the Knights of Labor. Within a short time it secured a large municipal appropriation for improving slum streets and alleys, and by aiding strikers it removed many of the evils connected with the sweating system. It also established an educational and patriotic club for Russian Jews, a Young Woman's Arena Club, the best of its kind in the City, and endorsed the plan of Rabbi Joseph Krauskoffen for the erection of model tenements. But religious dissension soon forced its dissolution. A prominent Presbyterian divine objected to coöperation with Jews, and the clergy generally feared radicalism, particularly the encouragement of strikes. They withdrew in a stampede, only about twenty out of four hundred and fifty continuing loyal to the Conference. In consequence, the remaining friends of the work reorganized on January 2, 1894, as a Union for Practical Progress.

The Baltimore Union for Doing Good resulted from the

[69] Ella Reeve Ward, *op. cit.*

[70] Thomas E. Will, "The City Union for Practical Progress," *Arena*, X (July 1894), 267.

Reverend Hiram Vrooman's suggestion at a meeting of the Ministerial Union in March, 1893. Three months later the organization was perfected with the consent of at least eighty churches, societies and labor unions under Charles J. Bonaparte as president. In the words of its founder, men "holding all religious belief and unbelief have agreed to bury differences and work shoulder to shoulder against the common enemy." [71] The purpose of the Union was "to promote the good government, health and prosperity of Baltimore; to secure useful and prevent injurious legislation; to correct public scandals and abuses; to restrain vice; and to encourage the coöperation of individuals and existing societies to advance these ends." [72] It concentrated its efforts against child labor, the sweating system and the circulation of obscene literature. Committees drew up several bills, of which those pertaining to child labor and sweating were adopted by the legislature. In the main Flower's bold plan succeeded, for as Minot J. Savage reported the Unions were "appealing to the pulpit with wonderful success," and many people throughout the country were coming to favor their program.[73]

Having asserted the need for coöperation in solving social problems, Christian forces devised organizations to meet special demands. For example, various English movements were reproduced in America. Of these the most important was the Christian Social Union which, by means of active chapters and its excellent magazine, *The Economic Review*, had made its principles widely known.[74] Impressed with its work, the Reverend Robert T. Holland of St. Louis on his return from England in

[71] Hiram Vrooman, "The Organization of Moral Forces," *ibid.*, IX (February 1894), 348.

[72] Tolman, *op. cit.*, p. 163.

[73] "The Present Conflict for a Larger Life," *Arena*, X (August 1894), 304.

[74] These were (1) to claim for the Christian law the ultimate authority to rule social practice; (2) to study in common how to apply the moral truths and principles of Christianity to the social and economic difficulties of the present time; and (3) to present Christ in practical life as the living Master and King, the enemy of wrong and selfishness, the power of righteousness and love.

1890 urged that a similar body be formed in America.[75] A Provisional Executive Committee, appointed by Holland and Bishop Frederic Dan Huntington, organized the Union on April 3, 1891, Huntington becoming president and Professor Ely secretary. At a larger meeting at Baltimore in October, 1892, the Union decided to espouse no definite economic philosophy.[76] As Professor Ely expressed it, the Union "seeks progress, but progress with safety. Its watchword is — progressive conservatism." [77] While membership was restricted to the Protestant Episcopal faith, provision was made for "associates" who might be of any or no definite belief.

The Union depended for growth and influence mainly upon branches established for the study of the social question in connection with parishes and colleges. These were formed at an early date in Alexandria, Boston, Chicago, Omaha, Philadelphia, Pittsburgh and St. Louis, and at Hobart, Kenyon and Wellesley Colleges. Phillips Brooks, President Potter and the Reverend John Williams were responsible for the branches in their respective jurisdictions.[78] The steady increase in the number of Unions, interrupted somewhat by the reorganization in 1893 consequent upon Professor Ely's going to the University of Wisconsin, was resumed under the secretaryship of George Hodges, dean of the Episcopal Theological School of Cambridge. The total membership, varying from five hundred to a thousand, included such well-known figures as Jane Addams, Professor W. J. Ashley, Josephine Shaw Lowell, Robert A. Woods and Mary W. Kingsbury. In popularizing and extending the Union, the Reverend W. D. P. Bliss was scarcely less

[75] Fred W. Speirs, "The Christian Social Union in the United States," *Lend a Hand*, VIII (March 1892), 164; *Publications*, Series A, No. 6, Sept. 1, 1895, p. 3.

[76] *The Bulletin of the Christian Social Union in the United States and Canada*, I (March 1893), No. 1, pp. 2–3.

[77] "The Christian Social Union a Social University," *Churchman*, April 2, 1892, pp. 414–415.

[78] George Hodges, "The Social Union and the Social Conscience," *St. Andrew's Cross*, XI (June 1897), 252; Frank B. Tracy, "Socialism in the Western States," *Forum*, XV (May 1893), 333–334; *The Dawn*, IV (May 1892), 5.

active than in the Christian Socialist Societies. As provisional organizer in 1891, he travelled over America, making sixty-five speeches, instituting five branches and preparing the way for six or seven others. He duplicated this record on a second tour in 1896–97.[79]

Professor Ely suggested that the Christian Social Union be a social university — an educational institution in the broadest sense. He would have it outline courses of reading, prepare and circulate leaflets, translate notable foreign works, publish a monthly bulletin, provide lectures in church schools and seminaries, offer prizes for the best essays on assigned subjects and establish lectureships and professorships. The Union succeeded in carrying out fully the first two parts of this program. The members of the various Unions studied the *Dawn*, Schaffle's *Quintessence of Socialism* and two of Ely's works, *Social Aspects of Christianity* and *Syllabus of Lectures on Socialism*.[80] In the first years of its existence, several pamphlets, including Professor Commons' works, *The Christian Minister and Sociology*, and *Popular Bibliography of Sociology*, were published. After 1893 the program was systematized. A sufficient sum of money having been provided, the Union decided to issue two papers each month, the first, "Series A," to deal with themes bearing upon the "general position and principles of the Christian Social Union," and the second, "Series B," to wrestle with concrete economic matters. Though this plan was not strictly adhered to, the Union by 1900 had issued nearly seventy articles covering a wide range of subjects.[81]

Other features of the Union's contemplated program were less systematically handled. One well-edited issue of a magazine, *The Bulletin of the Christian Social Union in the United*

[79] "Report of Executive Committee," *Publications*, No. 37, May 15, 1897, pp. 22–23.

[80] *Bulletin* . . . , I (March 1893), 3–4.

[81] George Hodges, "C. S. U. Notes for Members," *Publications*, April 1, 1895, appendix; *Publications*, Dec. 15, 1898, No. 56; *ibid.*, Supplement to No. 66, Feb. 15, 1900.

States and Canada, appeared in March, 1893, but for various reasons it could not be continued. The Union in 1897 offered theological students an opportunity to compete for prizes for the best and second best essay on the subject, "The Duty of the Christian Minister in Relation to Social Problems." The winning essay by John Howard Melish, a student at the Episcopal Theological School of Cambridge, appeared in the *Publications* in 1898.[82] The fact that only nine men entered the contest indicated that the church, so far as the seminaries were concerned, was little interested in social questions.[83] In still another way the Union tried to influence colleges and seminaries. In 1899 it provided for three courses of lectures. The one given at the Theological Seminary of Virginia by the Reverend James Yeames, of Arlington, Massachusetts, dealt with the general question of "Social Righteousness," and was printed in the *Publications.*[84]

While the main contribution of the Christian Social Union was educational, it participated somewhat in the practical work of social regeneration. Bliss wrote in 1894 that the Union did not put enough emphasis on action; [85] and four years later the Executive Committee, believing that "study should show some fruit," suggested that members join consumers' leagues and work for the Saturday half-holiday.[86] The Union further advised that all religious printing be done "where the conditions are the fairest," and that "each of the religious and sociological newspapers and magazines . . . publish hereafter in each issue a certificate stating the terms on which the paper is published." "By the adoption of the plan proposed," said the Committee, "the religious press will show that to the Church the principles of the Sermon on the Mount are not merely beautiful abstrac-

[82] No. 51, July 15, 1898, p. 3.
[83] *Churchman,* May 7, 1898, p. 671.
[84] No. 60, April 15, 1899; No. 61, May 15, 1899; No. 68 (Supplement), Feb. 15, 1900, No. 67 (Supplement), March 15, 1900.
[85] *The Dawn,* VI (May 1894), 67; *ibid.,* VI (February 1895), 5.
[86] *Publications,* No. 48, April 15, 1898, pp. 5–6.

tions, but living practical laws." [87] *The Spirit of Missions, St. Andrew's Cross, The Church Militant, The Christian Mirror* (a Congregationalist paper), *My Neighbor, The Trinity Record* and the *Christian Endeavor World* (organ of the Young People's Society of Christian Endeavor) as well as a few dioceses complied with the request.[88]

The Christian Social Union resembled and no doubt influenced several organized movements of native origin. The most important was the American Institute of Christian Sociology, formed at Chautauqua in 1893 to meet the requirements of those unwilling to coöperate with the Episcopal organization.[89] Nevertheless, the objects of the Christian Social Union were adopted at the preliminary meeting at which Herron, Gladden, Bishop John H. Vincent, the Reverend Sidney Strong of Cincinnati, the Reverend James Brand of Oberlin, and Professors Ely and Commons were active. "So apparent is the need," said Commons, "for an interdenominational society of this sort that the plan has received enthusiastic support wherever it has been broached." [90]

Ely was chosen as president, Commons as secretary and Herron as principal of instruction. A Council whose members included William J. Tucker, Philip S. Moxom and Irving Meredith exercised general control. Herron prepared leaflets dealing with local institutes and courses of reading, and visited colleges and seminaries.[91] The "retreats" — meetings for prayer and meditation on the social significance of Christianity — which Herron had started in the summer of 1892 at Iowa (Grinnell) College also popularized the Institute's program. The one of 1894, attended by four hundred "learners," including ministers, college presidents, professors, professional men and others, was

[87] *Ibid.*, No. 44, Dec. 15, 1896, pp. 19–20.
[88] *Ibid.*, No. 48, April 15, 1898, pp. 7–8.
[89] David Kinley, "The Christian Social Union," *Congregationalist*, April 30, 1891, p. 147; *The Dawn*, VI (June 1894), 82–83.
[90] "American Institute of Christian Sociology," *Congregationalist*, July 6, 1893, p. 32.
[91] Irving Meredith, "The American Institute of Christian Sociology," *ibid.*, July 27, 1893, pp. 134–135.

in reality "the first annual session of the American Institute of Christian Sociology." [92]

Besides the activity centering in Grinnell College, the Institute sponsored several conferences in various parts of the country.[93] Of these, the ones held under the auspices of Oberlin College attracted most attention. President W. G. Ballantine, seeing that ministers in the West were more interested in social than in other questions, invited representative leaders to a meeting there on November 14–15, 1894. As a result, the Oberlin Institute of Christian Sociology was organized, with Gladden as president and Z. Swift Holbrook as secretary, and arrangements were made for a Summer School the following year.[94] In compliance with the suggestion of ex-President Benjamin Harrison, the School which assembled June 20, 1895, attempted a comprehensive review of the social question. Clarence Darrow, attorney for the American Railway Union, Robert Bandlow, editor of the *Cleveland Citizen*, Thomas J. Morgan, spokesman for Chicago socialists, Samuel Gompers of the American Federation of Labor and James R. Sovereign of the Knights of Labor, presented labor's case. Ministers, social workers and political economists voiced more conciliatory views. While agreement on a specific program was not attempted, all admitted that old-fashioned *laissez-faire* had had its day and that the church must play a large part in bringing in the new order. The lectures, several of which were published in the *Bibliotheca Sacra*, exerted considerable influence, but the plans for a second School in 1896 did not materialize.[95]

[92] Charles A. Kent, "A School of the Kingdom," *Altruistic Review*, III (August 1894), 54; Archibald H. Bradshaw, "A School of the Kingdom," *ibid.*, p. 57; *Outlook*, May 12, 1894, p. 834; *ibid.*, July 14, 1894, p. 67.

[93] *Ibid.*, Dec. 1, 1894, pp. 931–932; *ibid.*, Oct. 5, 1895, p. 554, *Bibliotheca Sacra*, LIII (October 1896), 755–756; *Charities Review*, VII (November 1897), 793–794; *Congregationalist*, Aug. 22, 1895, p. 280.

[94] *Ibid.*, Nov. 22, 1894, pp. 737–738; *Bibliotheca Sacra*, LII (January 1895), 186–188.

[95] *Ibid.* LII (October, 1895), 773–778; Wilbur F. Crafts, "Labor Men and Christian Thinkers at Oberlin," *Congregationalist*, July 4, 1895, pp. 15–16; J. H. W. Stuckenberg, "Oberlin Institute of Christian Sociology," *Homiletic Review*, XXVIII (Nov. 22, 1894), 737.

Within the denominations themselves, two bodies were formed to bring Christians into harmony with the social movement. The earlier one, the Church Association for the Advancement of the Interests of Labor, was organized in May, 1887, by progressive Episcopalians under the Reverend J. O. S. Huntington's direction.[96] While the Association made good use of its central headquarters in New York City, it depended mainly upon local chapters. A few of these were founded in the early days of the Association, the most important at St. Michael's Church in New York. Under the active leadership of Harrietta A. Keyser, St. Michael's chapter showed what the church might accomplish in social reform. Besides its "social mission" effort,[97] the chapter brought together the several churches of its neighborhood into the West Side Sunday Closing Association, which rendered effective aid in law enforcement.[98] At first confined largely to New York City, the Association by the end of the century was spreading throughout the country. Many additional chapters were created in Eastern and Western cities, and inter-parochial chapters were instituted in Cleveland, Detroit, Milwaukee and St. Paul and in Rome and Utica, New York.[99]

Though mainly interested in organized labor, the Association, on finding that trade-union action was not sufficient, championed governmental intervention: the municipalization of public utilities, the compulsory arbitration of industrial disputes and the purification of politics.[100] In furtherance of these aims the Association appointed three committees: a sweatshop commit-

---

[96] Joseph Reynolds, Jr., "Report on the C.A.I.L. to the General Convention of the Protestant Episcopal Church, 1898," *Hammer and Pen*, II (January 1899), 2; J. O. S. Huntington, "Miners and Ministers," *Churchman*, Sept. 28, 1889, pp. 336–337; E. S. A., "The Endorsement of Labor Organizations," *ibid.*, Aug. 23, 1890, p. 227; Charles Ferguson, "Labor Organizations," *ibid.*, Aug. 30, 1890, pp. 257–258.

[97] *Hammer and Pen*, I (December 1898), 4.

[98] *Ibid.*, II (February 1899), 12; *ibid.*, I (September 1899), 4.

[99] *Ibid.*, II (November 1899), 82; *ibid.*, II (December 1899), 88–90.

[100] *Ibid.*, II (August 1899), 58.

tee, a tenement-house committee and a council on arbitration.[101]
The best work of the Association was done in settling disputes
between capital and labor. In 1893 the Association created a
special Council of Conciliation and Arbitration with Bishop
Potter as president and with a working man and a business man
as associates. In succeeding years, he was able to bring several
important controversies to a happy conclusion.[102] In his work
as a pacifier, Potter refused to be bound by the rule of compro-
mise, but insisted on the concept of justice. The arbiter, he said,
"must consult his highest conscience as to which of the opposing principles makes for the social good, and side with one or
the other of the parties accordingly." [103]

The effort to identify the theatrical profession with organized
religion formed also part of the Association's program, the
point of contact being Sunday labor and the supposed relation
of the theater to the moral health of the community. The demand of the public for immoral plays was held responsible for
a debauched stage. The great peril of our time, said Bishop
Potter, "arises from the commercial greed of those interested in
bringing out such productions. It is not the fault of the actor
and actress." [104] In 1899 the Actor's Union of New York,
headed by F. F. Mackay, and a committee of the C.A.I.L., led
by the Reverend Walter E. Bentley, formed the Actor's Church
Alliance, with Potter as president. The Alliance secured the
services of some two hundred clergymen of various sects as
chaplains. It insisted that the church "help the theatre to
redeem its mission as one of the great ethical forces of society."
"Should not the Kingdom of God," it asked, "be widened until
she ministers, not merely to the devotional and physical in man,
but also to the aesthetical, and so take in his whole being?" [105]

[101] *Ibid.*, I (September 1898), 3–4; *ibid.*, I (December 1898), 4–5.
[102] *Churchman*, May 18, 1895, p. 699; *Hammer and Pen*, II (February 1899),
12; *ibid.*, II (March 1899), 20; *ibid.*, II (March 1899), 22–23; *ibid.*, II (April
1899), 27; *ibid.*, II (May 1899), 39; *ibid.*, II (July 1899), 48; *ibid.*, II (August
1899), 62. [103] *Congregationalist*, May 21, 1896, p. 808.
[104] *Hammer and Pen*, II (August 1899), 58–59; *ibid.*, II (March 1899), 21.
[105] *Ibid.*, II (November 1899), 83.

The second of the denominational bodies interested in expanding Christian social theory was the Brotherhood of the Kingdom, formed by, but not confined to, Baptists. Walter Rauschenbusch, a professor in the Rochester Theological Seminary and well-known for his work in the Baptist Church Congress, was its leader. Practice he had received in his three years' pastorate of a German Baptist church in New York City and theory he had obtained from the advanced social thought of the day — Marx's *Das Kapital*, George's *Progress and Poverty* and Bellamy's *Looking Backward*. In 1892 Rauschenbusch with two friends drew up a declaration known as "The Spirit and Aim of the Brotherhood of the Kingdom," which pledged among other things "obedience to the ethics of Jesus." [106]

The plan meeting with approval, a conference at Philadelphia in December, 1892, perfected an organization. Inasmuch as Christ's purpose to establish a Kingdom of God had been largely forgotten or misunderstood, "the 'Brotherhood' was formed," said Rauschenbusch, to reëstablish this idea in the thought of the church and "to assist in its practical realization in the world." [107] Pained at the divorce between old-fashioned religion and the social movement of the nineteenth century, members of the Brotherhood determined to bring them together. "But our faith," continued Rauschenbusch, "is not yet supported on all sides by knowledge. . . . We must overhaul all the departments of our thought and work out that social Christianity which will be immeasurably more powerful and more valuable to the world than either an unsocial Christianity or an unchristian socialism." [108]

Through its discussions and the social work of its members, the Brotherhood contributed to the realization of its high ideal. Beginning in 1894, it held summer conferences at Marlborough-on-the-Hudson, where "the intellectual and devotional life of

[106] *Rochester Theol. Sem. Bull.*, November 1918, pp. 67–73.
[107] Quoted in W. H. Tolman, *Municipal Reform Movements*, p. 143.
[108] "The Ideals of Social Reformers," *American Journal of Sociology*, II (September 1896), 202–03.

the Christian social movement" was considered on an inclusive platform.[109] In addition to eminent Baptists, non-Baptists such as Ernest Howard Crosby, the leading American disciple of Tolstoi, and the Reverend Charles James Wood of the Protestant Episcopal Church participated in the deliberations. Believing that theory was of little value unless embodied in practice, the members were active in the whole range of social reform — from the establishment of city missions to the organization of civic federations.[110]

With the launching of the Brotherhood of the Kingdom, Protestant organizational activity for the general purpose of joining religion and social reform neared the end. It remained only for the Christian Socialists and the more radical labor reformers to arrive at an understanding. They first rallied around the American Fabian League, organized in 1895 by Bliss, the resourceful Christian Socialist. The Fabians proposed to attain socialism by installments and through private as well as public agencies. "When a democratic government operates a railroad, but allows anybody else to do so, that is voluntary socialism through the state," Bliss explained.[111] He was sure that Fabianism, by showing the worth of public ownership, especially in cities, would in time overcome the popular distrust of enlarged governmental functions. In 1898 the Fabian movement expanded into the Union Reform League. Its president, Paul Tyner, of the Denver Civic Church, made clear that, while the League grew out of the Christian Socialist agitation, it was broader in scope, existing without as well as within the churches. "We appeal to all," he said, "who would see a redeemed humanity, resurrected from the grave of materialism, freed from the shackles of wage-slavery, and resplendent in the recognition of its inherent divinity." [112]

[109] *Outlook*, Aug. 26, 1896, p. 393.

[110] *Annual Report of the Conference*, 1894, pp. 18–42; *ibid.*, 1895, pp. 16–49.

[111] "Voluntary Socialism the Socialism for America," *American Fabian*, I (May–June, 1895), 2–3.

[112] "Religion in Social Reform," *New Time*, III (August 1898), 75–76.

The Fabian plan for concerted action on a semi-religious basis struck a responsive chord, many agreeing with Professor Herron that a "national reform trust" was the great need of the hour.[113] A group of trade unionists, led by George E. McNeill, a member of Bliss's church in Boston, formed a National Economic and Educational League to lend support. At the National Social and Political Conference at Buffalo in July, 1899, the various elements coalesced. Largely attended by Christian Socialists, social workers, labor chiefs and liberal politicians, this meeting was considered the best of its kind up to that time in America. Its "Address to the American People" flayed militarism and plutocracy as destructive of economic liberty without which political liberty was a hollow mockery. In order to help defend academic freedom, the Conference raised a considerable sum for a School of Economic Research and Instruction, to be headed by Edwin D. Mead. At the suggestion of J. R. Buchanan, the labor leader, the members agreed to focus attention on one reform at a time. Non-partisan leagues were to be formed for educating and mobilizing public opinion. A large corps of humanitarian crusaders, with Bliss at their head, formed a Social Reform Union to deal with this phase of the Conference's program.[114]

By coming together in various bodies Protestants widely disseminated religio-social thought during the eighties and nineties. Some of the organizations, notably the Evangelical Alliance, the Convention of Christian Workers, the Congress of Liberal Religious Societies and the Union for Practical Progress, aimed chiefly to interest the churches in the new philanthropy. Other societies such as the Christian Social Union, the Church Association for the Advancement of the Interests of Labor and the Brotherhood of the Kingdom stressed the rela-

---

[113] *Between Caesar and Jesus*, pp. 222, 235.

[114] Eltweed Pomeroy, "The National Social and Political Conference," *Social Forum*, I (August 1899), 82–90; Bliss, "The Social Reform Union," *Arena*, XXII (August 1899), 272–275.

tionship of the church to sociological thinking. But whatever its specific purpose, each association contributed to the socialization of religion. Now that they more thoroughly appreciated the theory of social Christianity, Protestants were ready to enlarge vastly its practice in many forms of humanitarian endeavor.

CHAPTER V

THE SALVATION ARMY IN AMERICA
1880–1900

THE Salvation Army held an important place in the expanding religio-social program of American Protestantism. Introduced shortly after its organization in England in 1878 by William and Catherine Booth, the Army was in the truest sense an outgrowth of the city mission movement. In 1861 Booth and his family had withdrawn from a Wesleyan sect to specialize in evangelism among the degraded dwellers of London's East End. By personal, sympathetic contact with the people they made numerous converts, who refused, however, to join the unfriendly churches. As a result, Booth gradually perfected a military technique which by its discipline provided Christian nurture for members and by its easy adaptation to sensationalism enlisted an ever increasing body of recruits.

Social service soon came to be the distinguishing note of the Army. In the early eighties its leaders began to realize that the pauper poor needed a thoroughgoing reformation in which physical, as well as spiritual and moral, improvement must play a part. After the Trafalgar Riots of 1887 tentative plans were laid for such a program, shelters being opened, meals provided and the registration of the unemployed begun.[1] In his celebrated book, *Darkest England and the Way Out*, published in 1890, Booth pleaded for humanitarian endeavor. Purely spiritual religion appealed in vain to the poor, he said. "You might as well give a tract to a shipwrecked sailor who is battling with the surf which has drowned his comrades and threatens him. He will not listen to you. . . ." He had as little faith in col-

[1] "A New Advance of the Salvation Army," *Unitarian Rev.*, XXXIV (November 1890), 466; Gilbert Simmons, "The Salvation Army and Its Latest Project," *Catholic World*, LII (February 1891), 637.

lectivist social proposals, for they too offered no present help. "The religious cant," he continued, "which rids itself of all the importunity of suffering humanity by drawing unnegotiable bills payable on the other side of the grave is not more impracticable than the Socialistic claptrap which postpones all redress of human sufferings until after the general overturn. . . ." He would give to the three million submerged people in England at least what the cab horse possessed — "shelter for the night, food for its stomach, work allotted to it by which it can earn its corn." [2] Help of this type, along with kind, religious discipline, would, he believed, abolish all involuntary poverty.

Booth elaborated a "Social Scheme" to embody his principles. A series of colonies, as they were called, were expected to lift the degenerate specimen of humanity to complete manhood. The city colony was to give preliminary treatment of a physical and moral kind. Men were to be provided with food and shelter, and set to work in a Salvation Army factory. As soon as the individual had acquired the basic elements of good character — willingness to work and freedom from the more repulsive habits — he was to be placed in a rural colony where the second stage of renovation would begin. In this place, in an industrial-farm village conducted on a coöperative plan, habits of self-reliance and resourcefulness were to be cultivated so that the patient could be depended upon to earn his own living. When this was accomplished, the restored man would be sent to an overseas colony, which would allot suitable lands. The Scheme could be carried out, in whole or in part, as circumstances allowed. The plan appealed to many friends of the poor as a systematic and highly humane type of social reform likely to eliminate the worst features of poverty.

Since the Army's program developed inside, and seemed to acquiesce in, a highly stratified society, it was certain to encounter difficulty in the United States where the tradition of democratic equality flourished. Yet the Army in America dated

[2] Pages 20, 45, 80.

almost from the year of its formation in England, where it made an immediate impression upon the large class of English immigrant wage-earners. The Amos Shirley family, recent arrivals from England, began meetings in 1879 in the industrial sections of Philadelphia, and, discovering great opportunities for future growth, they appealed to Booth, saying "you must come over and help us." Accordingly, Commissioner George S. Railton with seven women assistants, "Hallelujah lasses," landed at Castle Garden in 1880, and promptly claimed "America for Jesus." Philadelphia, a city which allowed free street preaching, was selected as headquarters. During the seven months of his stay Railton established in various cities twelve Army corps and other agencies, including the official newspaper, the *War Cry*. The recall of Railton, a man of great ability, threw the organization into complete confusion for five years. His successor, Thomas E. Moore, proving inefficient, especially in financial management, General Booth replaced him with Major Frank Smith. But Moore resisted recall, seized the posts and proclaimed the American Army, a name which thus stigmatized the regular one as "English." Though Smith emerged victorious, much harm was done to a cause which had as yet little to commend it.[3]

Internal dissension, however, was a less serious obstacle than American public opinion, which looked upon the Army as vulgar and ridiculous. When Railton began services in a New York saloon, the churches were horrified, a prominent minister calling the place "the most disreputable den in the United States, in the worst slum of the city!" The *Christian Union*, for all its liberalism, did not think that the city authorities should grant Railton's request for street-preaching privileges. It was true, it admitted, that Christ "bids his servants to go out in the highways and hedges to compel the poor, the halt and the blind

---

[3] For its early history in America, see Thomas F. G. Coates, *The Prophet of the Poor: The Life Story of General Booth*, pp. 121–124; and Maud B. Booth, *Beneath Two Flags*, pp. 205–208.

to come in to the feast, but he does not bid them spread the feast in the highways nor under the hedges." [4] Some saw not only sensationalism but evil in the Army. The Reverend James M. Buckley, editor of the *Christian Advocate*, spoke of it in abusive terms as late as 1891, when he declared that the worst characters of both sexes entered it to carry out "schemes of iniquity." [5] Objection was raised, also, to its alleged absolutism, regarded by many as strikingly similar to that of the Society of Jesus. This, said one writer, "is utterly abhorrent to the democratic instincts of our people" and would prevent the growth of the movement in the United States. [6] Even more important was the view, voiced by a New York minister, that the Army "was thoroughly un-American, and could not succeed because there were no defined classes." [7] A symposium in the *Independent* on General Booth's Social Scheme revealed little sympathy, the opinion being that no group in this country corresponded to the one aimed at in England. [8]

Two influences, however, enabled the Army after the middle eighties to advance rapidly in America. One was the development of a new and virile leadership. After 1886 the Booth family assumed command. The ablest guidance was found in the son and the son-in-law of General Booth, namely, Ballington Booth and F. L. Booth-Tucker. The former along with his wife, Maud B. Booth, came to America in 1886 after several years' experience in the slums of East London, and the latter ten years later after a brilliant record in India. Ballington

---

[4] March 24, 1880, p. 267. One woman felt, in reference to a telegraphic report from the field, "Sunday glorious smash; 13 in fountain; died hard hallelujah!" "that in accustoming men's ears to such rough and ready dealings with the most sacred of subjects the Army leaders are sacrificing too much to their desire for sensation!" Agnes Maude Macher, "Red Cross Knights — A Nineteenth Century Crusade," *Andover Rev.*, II (August 1884), 209.

[5] *The War Cry*, Aug. 15, 1891, p. 9.

[6] C. P. Osborne, "The Salvation Army," *The New Englander*, n.s. VI (July 1883), 429.

[7] Quoted in *Christian Union*, July 12, 1888, p. 51.

[8] "General Booth's Plan: Can It Be Applied to the Outcasts of New York?" Dec. 11, 1890, pp. 1741–42.

Booth was untiring in his efforts to disarm American prejudice. He pointed out, for example, that while the Army dealt with the submerged tenth, it held the democratic tradition in high esteem. "Our movement," he said, "is especially raised to help those who are the lowest fallen, the most depraved and the most neglected. In carrying out this aggressive mission, we do not, as has been said, create evil in the world, nor do we curb any man's freedom, nor do we interfere with any man's social happiness. On the contrary, we restore all these to those who through moral slavedom have lost them." [9] The fact that he held meetings in well-to-do congregations showed his antipathy to class appeal.[10] Realizing the hold of the churches on the middle class, Booth urged converts of the Army to join them and *vice versa*. By the end of his commandership a large group of Salvationists had done so [11] — a trend continued under Booth-Tucker. General Booth himself lent the influence of his personality, explaining and defending the Army's program in the course of three protracted visits in 1886, 1894 and 1899.

But the increasing desire of Protestants to harmonize religion and social reform was the more important factor in the advance of the Army. Its contention that at least three million people in America were at all times on the border of pauperism [12] and that the "churches have lapsed into social clubs" [13] was too obvious for successful denial. Change in clerical opinion toward the Army began as early as 1886. A large gathering of New York ministers in December, 1886, pleased with General Booth's explanation of his purposes, resolved "that the Salvation Army is worthy of the sympathy of all the Christian Churches in New York and the United States." This meeting, said the *War Cry*,

---

[9] *War Cry*, Aug. 13, 1887, p. 8.
[10] *New York Tribune*, March 31, 1895, p. 29.
[11] *Ibid.*, Nov. 17, 1894, p. 4.
[12] F. L. Booth-Tucker, *Social Relief Work in the Salvation Army in the United States*, pp. 8–9.
[13] *War Cry*, Aug. 27, 1887, p. 4.

was "unsurpassed" for "its favorable recognition of the Salvation Army and its work." [14] Between this date and Booth's second visit in 1894 sentiment deepened in its favor. General Booth "comes here," said the *Independent*, "to find that the Salvation Army has quickly won recognition from the churches in the United States." [15] At a huge reception in Carnegie Hall, New York, Josiah Strong expressed the feeling of religious leaders when he declared that he had been "converted to the brass drum and the cymbal. General Booth is the only British General in more than one hundred years whose commission has conferred upon him any authority in the United States." [16]

Representative Protestants agreed that the Army had succeeded in doing what the churches did not or could not do.[17] This fact led them to approve its sensational methods. It may be, as the Reverend J. E. Roberts of Kansas City surmised, that the Army's ways "are the inevitable reaction from our methods in which passion is quenched by the exactions of our hypercritical refinement, and the spirit and power of religion are sacrificed to the vain-glorious pride of decorum." [18] The amazing result of the Army's campaign, wrote A. Mackay-Smith, "is due to one great and yet very simple discovery . . . that in carrying the Gospel to souls one degree above the bestial you must use their language, express your feelings as they express theirs. . . ." [19] "The methods of the Army may be deemed peculiar," admitted Chauncey M. Depew, "but the recesses of the human mind are a thousand times more peculiar." [20] Professor Briggs refuted the charge that the Army was a dangerous competitor of the churches, by pointing out that it was of a

[14] *Ibid.*, Jan. 1, 1887, p. 7.
[15] Quoted in *War Cry*, Nov. 10, 1894, p. 12.
[16] *New York Tribune*, Oct. 24, 1894, p. 4; also *War Cry*, Nov. 4, 1894, p. 4.
[17] For statements, see Ballington Booth, *From Ocean to Ocean*, pp. 113–116; R. Ogden, "The Salvation Army and the Churches," *Nation*, July 7, 1892, pp. 4–5; *War Cry*, Oct. 24, 1891, p. 8.
[18] Ballington Booth, *op. cit.*, p. 6.
[19] *War Cry*, March 14, 1891, p. 3.
[20] *New York Tribune*, Oct. 24, 1894, p. 4.

different type, being simply "a religious order of the nineteenth century" [21] — an interpretation accepted by Joseph
Cook who believed that it was in no sense "a new sect. The
people whom it leads into the religious life it urges to join the
evangelical churches." [22]

For the cultivated members of society, who sympathized with
the Army without being willing to "enlist" as soldiers, the
Army organized an Auxiliary League. All agreeing to pay a
membership fee of five dollars, to receive a pin or badge and to
defend the Army when criticized in their presence were eligible.
A "society" enthusiasm, beginning in 1891 in New York City,
projected the work of the League into public notice.[23] A journalist who attended a grand "encampment" for New York in
1892 reported that "Little by little evidence has come out that
what is known as the Auxiliary League of the Salvation Army
has been winning members among church people whose social
position is as high as their reputation for philanthropy." [24]

Maud B. Booth was a great personality in extending the
League, adding, for example, some seven hundred members during a single visit to the Pacific Coast. A special organization,
headed by Adjutant Edith Marshall, a refined and educated
woman, was even more effective in securing recruits.[25] The
Army also utilized the press, establishing in 1892, *The Conqueror*, an attractive monthly magazine, to do "in the Fifth
Avenues of our land" what the *War Cry* was doing in the
slums.[26] With nearly four thousand members in 1895, the
League made large yearly accessions to the end of the century,
having staunch supporters in all denominations "as well as

[21] "The Salvation Army," *No. Amer. Rev.*, CLIX (December 1894), 700–704.
[22] "General Booth and the Salvation Army," *Our Day*, XV (September 1895),
121; for a similar view, see *Lend a Hand*, XIV (March 1895), 163–69.
[23] Maud B. Booth, *Beneath Two Flags*, p. 214; *War Cry*, May 7, 1892, p. 8;
ibid., Dec. 10, 1892, p. 15.
[24] R. Ogden, *op. cit.*, p. 4.
[25] *The Conqueror*, V (January 1896), 44; *War Cry*, Oct. 15, 1892, p. 8; *New
York Tribune*, March 12, 1894, p. 5; *ibid.*, Nov. 18, 1894, p. 13.
[26] *The Conqueror*, I (February 1892), 12–13.

among friends of the poor who have no strong [religious] views." [27]

Having won popular approval, the Army gained those legal privileges necessary for properly performing its work. One of these was liberty to hold out-door services of a noisy type. While never wholly free from mob action and discriminatory ordinances with respect to street marching, the Army gradually won "the liberty of every city." [28] As early as 1888 the Presbyterian Ministerial Association of San Francisco, recognizing the Army "as comrades in the war against sin and Satan," demanded with success "that the liberty guaranteed by the Constitution and laws be secured to them." [29] The request of a Boston mass meeting in 1890 that Salvationists be given the "right to march the streets of Boston" bore fruit the following year.[30] When a judicial decision in New York City charging Booth-Tucker with keeping "a certain common, ill-governed, disorderly house" became known, resentment flared up throughout the country.[31] But the development of the Army showed best its growth in public esteem. By 1900 it had in America seven hundred corps, with over twenty thousand privates commanded by nearly three thousand officers, which held over eleven thousand weekly meetings attended by over two million people. To this religious strength was added a hundred and eighty-seven social institutions for the benefit of the poor.[32] Josiah Strong's statement that "the Christianity of the Army is thoroughly philanthropic, and its philanthropy is thoroughly Christian" was fully justified.[33]

Philanthropic endeavor, particularly the Social Scheme, was

[27] Ibid., VI (January 1897), 23.
[28] Harbor Lights, III (March 1900), 72.
[29] War Cry, July 7, 1888, p. 12.
[30] Ibid., March 29, 1890, p. 8; ibid., Oct. 24, 1891, p. 9.
[31] Ibid., June 12, 1897, pp. 3–5; ibid., June 19, 1897, p. 8. For protest against the arbitrary action of Philadelphia police, see War Cry, Aug. 19, 1899, p. 8; ibid., Aug. 26, 1899, p. 9; ibid., Sept. 30, 1899, p. 4.
[32] "Brief Record of a Remarkable Advance," War Cry, Dec. 25, 1900, p. 2.
[33] War Cry, Dec. 25, 1900, p. 2.

the Army's notable contribution to America as well as to England. The foundation was laid by the Slum Brigade — a form of service bringing Salvationists into intimate touch with the slums. Even sensationalism had no attractions for the lowest elements of the submerged tenth; but the people fully appreciated the women residing among them and offering humane as well as spiritual aid. Having developed this plan in England some years before the rise of Toynbee Hall and the social settlements, Mrs. Ballington Booth urged its appropriateness to American cities with their polyglot slum populations. Prejudice, however, delayed action until 1889 when Mrs. Booth organized the first Slum Brigade in New York City. Only as she and her assistants discarded Army uniform and literature were they accepted by the people of the Water Street tenements. Time, however, along with the winsome personality of Emma J. Boun, a Brigadier General of the Army, transformed the attitude of New York slum-dwellers from indifference to enthusiasm.[34] From the metropolis the movement spread to other cities until by 1901 there were twenty-four slum posts or settlements in the United States.[35]

The Slum Brigade performed a three-fold task: visitation and relief; the conduct of religious services in halls and saloons; and the creation of sentiment against vice. The first was the most important since it created in the city a measure of the old sympathy between people so helpful in village communities. The "daily work in the homes of the people, watching over the sick and dying, and loving service in trying hours," said Adjutant Ida Turpin, "have given to the Salvation Army a weight and influence that no amount of charitable gifts of food and money would ever have done." [36] Visitation prepared the way

[34] Maud B. Booth, *Beneath Two Flags*, pp. 115–116; same author, "Salvation Army Work in the Slums," *Scribner's Magazine*, XVII (January 1895), 102–106; *New York Tribune*, Dec. 4, 1894, p. 13; *ibid.*, Oct. 9, 1895, p. 7; *War Cry*, Dec. 15, 1894, p. 1.
[35] *Ibid.*, Dec. 25, 1900, p. 2.
[36] "Salvation Work on Cherry Hill," *The Conqueror*, IV (October 1895), 470.

for formal religious meetings, which were always in charge of women, often girls of tender years. While these doughty "lasses" were at first subjected to insult, they won their way through sheer persistence. If, as often happened, they were ordered out of saloons, they would invariably return, and to the owner's question, "Did I not tell you not to come here any more?" they would reply, "Yes, sir! But I have come to see whether you have changed your mind!" [37] The Slum Brigade endeavor revealed that conditions in many other cities were almost as bad as in New York, where Mrs. Booth found "a state of dirt, poverty and misery" quite equal to anything she had "seen or heard in the city of London." In Boston, the Athens of America, as in some other places, the "Slum Angels" had to spend a large part of their time fighting vermin.[38]

The experience of the Slum Brigade suggested several forms of social service. For children whose parents were unable to care for them, the Slum Brigade of New York established in 1893 a day nursery on Cherry Street — the first of its kind in the down-town section of the city. Rescue work for prostitutes was also closely associated with the Slum Brigade. "We look forward to a time," said Mrs. Booth in 1891, "when we can do for this city [New York] . . . what has been done in the large cities of the Old World." [39] Public sympathy enabled the Army to open its first Home in Cleveland in March, 1892, and a second three months later in New York City.[40] Aid in supplying experienced workers came from International Headquarters in London. By 1900 seventeen Rescue Homes, to whose management a hundred officers devoted full time, had been established in a dozen or more cities from coast to coast.[41] The Auxiliary League was chiefly responsible for this development. The Rescue Home in Boston, opened in 1892, resulted from an

---

[37] F. L. Booth-Tucker, *Social Relief Work of the Salvation Army in the United States*, pp. 18–20.
[38] Maud B. Booth, "Salvation Army Work in the Slums," *loc. cit.*, pp. 109–111.
[39] *Beneath Two Flags*, p. 220.
[40] *War Cry*, June 25, 1892, p. 7.   [41] *Ibid.*, Sept. 7, 1900, p. 4.

Auxiliary meeting at Park Street Church.[42] In 1893, in a plea for money with which to support the New York agency, Mrs. Booth explained to a dignified audience, "all well-dressed and prosperous looking," that ninety-nine out of every hundred women leading the abandoned life were doing so not from choice but from necessity.[43] Slum Sewing Battalions, whose members were generally the wives of clergymen, also aided this and related activities of the Slum Brigade.[44]

The end of the century found the Army extending and perfecting its slum and rescue service. The Cherry Tree Home, built in 1897, and located first at Fordham, New York, then at Rutherford, New Jersey, and finally at Fort Amity Colony in Colorado, provided for the orphan child.[45] This and another established in San Francisco on a similar plan were purely charitable, not self-supporting as were most Salvation Army agencies. A Slum Maternity Nursing system, organized in 1897 with a view to placing a nurse in every post, was a second innovation. In the following year a training home — The Pines — was opened at Fordham. Prominent physicians of New York not only heartily endorsed its curricula and gave courses, but also aided in actual work among the poor. The school, wrote *Harbor Lights*, "is being quickly recognized as one of the fixed institutions in New York City." [46]

With religious and slum work in operation, the Army was ready for the Social Scheme as outlined in General Booth's book. Only the bare foundations were laid by Ballington Booth, leaving its further development to Booth-Tucker, who assumed control of the Army in February, 1896. He insisted that it be carried out in its entirety. The district and farm colonies, for example, were necessary. The city institution

[42] *Ibid.*, April 9, 1892, p. 7.

[43] *New York Tribune*, March 1, 1893, p. 5; *ibid.*, March 9, 1894, p. 2; Alice Lewis, "To Our Auxiliary Friends," *Harbor Lights*, II (December 1899), 367.

[44] *War Cry*, Oct. 15, 1892, p. 8; *ibid.*, May 9, 1891, p. 10.

[45] *The Conqueror*, VI (March 1897), 73–74; *War Cry*, Aug. 27, 1898, p. 11; *ibid.*, Oct. 22, 1900, p. 6.   [46] I (February 1898), 53.

might relieve poverty, mitigate its evils, and even permanently reform individuals, but it could not cure the evils which surrounded the submerged classes. Colonization fully applied would turn the genuine "hobo" into a "homebo," or at least into a "hopebo." The fifty million dollars spent year in and year out in American cities for mere alleviation would send a half-million people yearly to agricultural colonies. The Social Scheme would "place Waste Labor on Waste Land by means of Waste Capital, thus combining this Trinity of Waste, the separation of which means the destruction of each, the coöperation of which means the prosperity of all." [47] This became known as the Booth-Tucker "Pauper Policy."

The Army carried out his comprehensive plan. The city colony, first in point of time and of extent, had its beginnings in a Food and Shelter Depot, established in December, 1891, by Ballington Booth at Downing and Bedford Streets in New York. The second depot was founded in 1893 in Buffalo, where for years the Army had had a vigorous corps in close proximity to the slum district. An appeal to the two hundred Auxiliaries of the city, along with the support of several churches, furnished funds for the agency. These depots charged users a nominal sum in order to relieve the financial strain on the Army and to avoid pauperizing the persons benefited.[48] From the totally destitute the depots exacted a simple kind of work. For the slightly better group of men a Lodging House or Salvation Army Hotel was started by Ballington Booth, though for a time failure resulted. Under Booth-Tucker these forms of service made more progress than any other since unemployment became increasingly more tragic in American life.[49] The Army

[47] F. L. Booth-Tucker, "The Social Work of the Salvation Army," *War Cry*, Aug. 21, 1897, p. 9.

[48] *The Conqueror*, I (February 1892), 11–12; Major R. E. Holz, "The Ark — Buffalo's Food and Shelter Depot," *War Cry*, Aug. 26, 1893, p. 4; *ibid.*, Jan. 25, 1896, p. 4; *The Conqueror*, V (February 1896). p. 81.

[49] R. E. Holz, "Social Summary for 1898," *Harbor Lights*, II (February 1899), 53.

reported that of the men sheltered by it in New York City eighty per cent would work if given the opportunity. So great was the need on the part of homeless men that the Army in 1900 was providing over one and a quarter million meals each year.[50]

In supporting these shelters the Army also had in view preventive objects. The higher-class hotels, designed for clerks, shopkeepers and better paid artisans gave superior accommodations for a small outlay. They also served an uplift function for those redeemed from the lowest depths. A student, investigating substitutes for the saloon, believed that the Salvationists "have hit upon more that is practical, and are really doing more to solve the social problem than many others more highly educated, who are so learnedly discussing it." [51] The institutions for women were almost entirely of this type. The Flower Home in San Francisco and the Benedict Home in Boston, given by Washington Benedict, were among the best of them. Designed for homeless women dependent upon odd jobs for a living, and for poorly paid girls in industrial and mercantile pursuits, they were only partially successful since many did not relish residence in a place managed by an organization so prominent in rescue and slum work. The majority of the seventy-three depots, run by the Army at the beginning of 1901 for both sexes, were of a rescue character.[52]

Through its depots the Army, while not unmindful of social reform, was mainly interested in repairing the damage done by a defective industrial system. Securing employment was another step in the same direction. Through its own instrumentalities — industrial depots, wood yards and salvage brigades — it gave work to those unable to meet the nominal charges of

[50] F. L. Booth-Tucker, *Social Relief Work of the Salvation Army in the United States*, p. 22.

[51] Royal Loren Melandy, "Social Functions of the Saloons in Chicago," *The Commons*, V (November 1900), No. 52, p. 7.

[52] F. L. Booth-Tucker, *Social Relief Work of the Salvation Army in the United States*, pp. 11–12.

the shelters and hotels. By 1900 there were twenty-four of these agencies.[53] They were overshadowed, however, by the work of the four central labor bureaus, established to bring employer and employee together. Since state laws enacted to outlaw fakers in this field required high license fees, the Army was somewhat handicapped. It overcame this obstacle in great part, however, by using its organization as a labor exchange. The social secretary in 1897 partitioned the country into divisions, each under command of an officer. These were parcelled out into districts, which, in turn, were separated into sections. The local corps was, of course, the lowest unit, in each of which a person was commissioned by headquarters as labor sergeant. At the top was placed Captain G. A. Manwaring, who as head of the Social Labor Bureau of Boston had rendered distinguished service. By means of this system sixty thousand men in 1900 were enabled to obtain jobs.[54]

Despite the inherent difficulties of colonization, the Army made considerable progress. The intermediate colony, for which the thousands of unused acres on the outskirts of cities provided ample opportunity, was developed in several places somewhat after the pattern of the Pingree Potato Patch Plan in Detroit.[55] The distant colony met with decidedly more success. During his tour of inspection in 1897 with a view to locating sites in the West, Booth-Tucker was offered lands in varying amounts and at almost all prices. Sentiment first crystallized in California, where as an outcome of his address before the San Francisco Chamber of Commerce a committee of fifteen leading citizens was appointed to coöperate with the Army. This Citizens' Colonization Society planned to assign carefully

[53] R. E. Holz, "Social Summary for 1898," *Harbor Lights*, II (February, 1899), 54; "Brief Record of a Remarkable Advance," *War Cry*, Dec. 25, 1900, p. 2.

[54] Staff-Captain McFee, "The Salvation Army Labor Bureau System," *Harbor Lights*, I (January, 1898), 33; Booth-Tucker, *Social Relief Work of the Salvation Army in the United States*, p. 24.

[55] *The Conqueror*, VI (April 1897), 89.

selected families to small tracts of land, equipped for agriculture, the plots to be purchased from gifts and loans and repaid by a weekly rent. At its annual convention in 1897 the Army endorsed the plan and arranged for a mass meeting in Carnegie Hall. Ample support from several sources enabled the Society to purchase five hundred acres in Monterey County, the colony at first being called Soledad and then Fort Romie.[56]

Though attention centered on Fort Romie, a colony in Colorado, called Fort Amity, was established in January, 1898, a few weeks before the one in California. Its site in the fertile Arkansas Valley had been selected by Booth-Tucker the previous year. Meanwhile, plans were laid for a third colony, which in the summer of 1898 was put into operation on 285 acres of land, located a few miles east of Cleveland. It was named Fort Herrick, for its chief sponsor, Myron T. Herrick, of the Savings Bank of Cleveland and later Ambassador to France.[57] The three colonies with two hundred inhabitants were successful from the first, justifying Booth-Tucker's belief that "in the Colonization Plan lies the solution of the Social Problem."[58] The only obstacle to continued expansion was lack of capital. To raise money a Pass-it-on-League was formed, each member of which paid twenty-five cents toward a five-hundred-dollar fund necessary to send out a family of five. After ten years each fund would be at the disposal of a similar group. The device, said *Harbor Lights*, was to be "a permanent and far-reaching philanthropy."[59]

The Social Scheme did not by any means exhaust the Army's humanitarian interest. It was alert to nearly every need of the poor. In the extremely cold periods of winter the Army threw open its well-heated halls to the people denied all comforts in

[56] F. L. Booth-Tucker, "Farm Colonies of the Salvation Army," *loc. cit.*, p. 756.

[57] *New York Tribune*, Aug. 28, 1897, p. 5; *ibid.*, May 30, 1898, p. 9; *War Cry*, Sept. 17, 1898, p. 9.

[58] *Ibid.*, Jan. 21, 1899, p. 5.

[59] III (October 1900), 309.

the terrible rookeries which passed for homes in Christian America. In Detroit alone, in one severe period, it distributed two hundred thousand dollars in food and clothing to seven thousand families. So appreciative were the tenement dwellers that they often refused the hospitality of the public stations and armories. "We have plenty of room," said New York officials in 1899, "but the people have gone to Booth-Tucker's show." [60] While its general policy was to charge for its services, on two occasions, Thanksgiving and Christmas, the Army invited the poor to its table "without money and without price." In New York City, for example, the Army secured Madison Square Garden to give these feasts a fitting solemnity. This practice was warmly approved by all except the Charity Organization Societies. For these, however, Salvationists had only righteous contempt. "They will have to learn," said the *War Cry*, "that harsh measures which treat poverty as a crime will not be tolerated by the American public." [61] In sweltering summer months the Army was on hand with fresh-air corps, steamboat excursions and cheap ice.

Other forms of social service included a Missing Friends and Inquiry Department, a Legal Department in charge of a "poor man's lawyer," a First Aid to the Injured Society and a Life Insurance Department. The work of these agencies, all set up after 1897, is largely self-explanatory. The first and last were perhaps the most important. The Missing Friends and Inquiry Department restored to relatives a large percentage of cases. The insurance scheme involved an arrangement by which a well-established company reduced rates, made Salvationists its agents and gave the Army a commission on all business secured, thus enabling most laborers to take advantage of it. [62]

Finding that several racial and immigrant groups needed

[60] F. L. Booth-Tucker, *Social Relief Work of the Salvation Army in the United States*, pp. 25–28.

[61] Feb. 20, 1897, p. 8.

[62] *Harbor Lights*, I (January 1898), 30–32; *ibid.*, III (April 1900), 125; *War Cry*, March 10, 1900, p. 16.

special attention, the Army provided separate corps for Scandinavians, Germans, Italians, Chinese and Negroes. The first Swedish corps, formed in Brooklyn in 1887, was followed by others the next year in Minneapolis and St. Paul. The strength of the Army in Scandinavian countries was mainly responsible for the sixty corps established in America by 1900. The impetus given by the visit in 1892 of Commissioner Hanna Ouchterlong, the Mother of the Salvation Army in Scandinavia, was of great aid, as was also the service offered by several adjutants who came as organizers.[63] German work was started in 1892 in Buffalo under the leadership of Lieutenant R. E. Holz, who had done so much to develop the Army, especially on its social side, in that city. Since the weakness of the Army in Germany, as contrasted with Sweden, did not allow the importation of organizers to America, progress was slow, with only twenty-one corps formed by 1898. Among the Italians only one corps could be gathered.[64] A Foreign Department, or Home Missionary Department, created in 1898 with R. E. Holz as secretary, consolidated activity among foreigners. The concern for Negroes was prompted by the fact that their churches were also affected by class distinctions in industrial centers, and, therefore, failed to reach large numbers. Sensing this situation, the Army in 1896 moved to meet it with hearty encouragement from Booker T. Washington.[65]

The Army organized along age as well as racial lines. A Junior War, so called, trained youth for lives of piety and social service. The Junior corps, though resembling Sunday schools, placed far more emphasis on early conversions. To prepare children for membership and to break down parental objection, a "Band of Love," giving to unconverted boys and girls "useful information on mechanical and industrial matters, or instruc-

[63] *Harbor Lights*, I (June 1898), 179; *ibid.*, I (November 1898), 325.

[64] Mary A. Scherer, "The German Work," *ibid.*, I (March 1898), 91; Ensign Jaeger, "The German American War," *The Conqueror*, V (August 1896), 357–358; *War Cry*, Feb. 1, 1898, p. 8; *Harbor Lights*, II (September 1899), 284.

[65] *The Conqueror*, V (October 1896), 474–475.

tion in music or painting," was formed. By this and other means nearly four hundred Junior corps had been organized by 1899.[66] These furthered the interest of the Army in that they served as training schools for officers, the lack of which had become the most serious obstacle to expansion. Corps Cadet Brigades, of which there were five hundred by 1900, enrolled those planning to make Army officerships their life work. The Army prepared Juniors for slum social service by setting up in New York a Slum Training Home and Children's Day Nursery.[67]

Though increasingly successful, the Army was harassed by secessionist movements, the most serious resulting in the Volunteers of America. When ordered to "farewell" in January, 1896, Ballington Booth and his wife refused to return to England for another assignment.[68] Dissatisfied in various ways with the administration of the Salvation Army, they resolved "to give our abilities, our time, our lives, to something that shall win over the middle or artisan class in this country to the cause of Christ." [69] In organization, the Volunteers paralleled the mother body, but recognized, as Booth said, the "American people, American institutions, American rights, and above all the American Constitution." [70] The emphasis on the patriotic note prompted an Auxiliary to write "that the American flag is playing a more prominent part in the new movement than is the banner of Christ." [71] Likewise the new army stressed friendly relations with the churches. Symbolic of this were Booth's ordination in 1896 by Bishop Fallows of Chicago as a presbyter of "the Church of God in General" and the provision that

---

[66] Brigadier Miles, "Saving Young America," *War Cry*, June 3, 1899, pp. 2–3; *Harbor Lights*, III (June 1900), 184–186.

[67] *Ibid.*, II (November 1899), 357.

[68] For details of this conflict, see *War Cry*, May 2, 1896, pp. 2–3; *ibid.*, Feb. 1, 1896, p. 8; *New York Tribune*, Feb. 26, 1896, p. 2; *ibid.*, Feb. 22, 1896, p. 1; *ibid.*, Feb. 25, 1896, pp. 1–2.

[69] *Outlook*, March 14, 1896, p. 480.

[70] *New York Tribune*, April 20, 1896, p. 12.

[71] Charles G. Pease, "The New Salvation Army," *ibid.*, March 20, 1896, p. 14.

each post consider itself subordinate to some particular church in its community.[72]

The bond of sympathy between the Volunteers and the churches was prompted in large part by their common belief that the slum dwellers should not be preferred to the higher class of workingmen. "There is room," said the *Outlook*, "for both the Salvation Army and the Volunteers — the one working primarily in the slums, the other among non-church goers of a self-respecting type."[73] On the social side the offshoot developed two specialties — prison and temperance work. An expert in the care of discharged prisoners, Mrs. Booth provided a temporary home for them and an employment bureau to protect them against blackmailers. The second annual congress of the Volunteers in November, 1897, officially voted to make the reform of inebriates a special field of endeavor — "as important a feature as the prison work."[74]

As for the Army, it rode out the storms of dissension and schism, the while gaining added strength for the burdensome tasks of the new century. Because of its sympathy with the human wreckage of an industrial civilization, its efficiency as a relief organization and its singular success in harmonizing universal with national aspirations, the Army was assured of a brilliant future in the United States. As the "Personal God of the Slums," the Salvation Army sought out the degraded and wretched poor, being, as the English Cardinal Manning said, the "only considerable body of Christians who had a passion for sinners as such." But indirectly all gradations of the poor benefited, for the Army's example of heroic self-sacrifice encouraged Protestant Christianity to redouble its efforts for the social salvation of all men.

[72] *Outlook*, Oct. 3, 1896, pp. 618–619; *New York Tribune*, Dec. 8, 1898, p. 10.
[73] May 2, 1896, p. 822.
[74] *New York Tribune*, Nov. 30, 1897, p. 5.

CHAPTER VI

THE INSTITUTIONAL CHURCH MOVEMENT

DURING the eighties and nineties the brotherly spirit which the Salvation Army so thoroughly applied cast its spell over all organized religion. Most Protestant bodies, including those which earlier had frowned upon social service or deemed it of minor importance, now accepted it as a definite part of their religious mission. "Too long," they agreed, "has Rome been allowed a practical monopoly of the humanitarian agencies of religion." [1]

The adjective "institutional" was commonly employed to describe the numerous churches and missions which were expanding their functions to cover the entire life of man. Though the term is of uncertain origin, it was credited by most people to William Jewett Tucker, the well-known Andover professor. Some devoted friends of religion objected to it as awkward and misleading, for they felt it cloaked the fact that the new agencies were expressions of a free, vital spirit at war with the inertia and mechanism of religious "institutions."

Although public attention centered on a few great congregations, all phases of city missionary activity were, in effect, institutional. Take, for example, the scores of missions established in every industrial area by the men in the Convention of Christian Workers. Largely modeled on Jerry McAuley's Water Street Mission, these missions, though basically rescue institutions, developed in many instances elaborate educational and philanthropic features. The Convention's secretary, John C. Collins, used social agencies at his Union Gospel Mission in New Haven to help make the "mass of pauperized humanity self-respecting, self-supporting, upright God-fearing citizens." [2]

[1] Cincinnati Conf., Meth. Epis. Church, *Minutes*, 1889, p. 89.
[2] "Ministry to the Poor," *New Englander*, n.s. II (March 1877), 169–183.

In Chicago, Colonel and Mrs. George Rogers Clark had organized in 1877 the Pacific Garden Mission, thought to be "the most successful mission of its kind in this country." It looked after all classes in its neighborhood, though, of course, the every-night gospel meeting was its most important function. A corps of five paid and fifty unpaid workers gave it an excellent system of house-to-house visitation by means of which it discovered and ameliorated social needs. This mission proved the model for a score of similar ventures in Chicago.[3]

Colonel H. H. Hadley, a convert of McAuley's mission, also helped to realize the objectives of the Convention of Christian Workers. By organizing in 1888 a rescue mission for St. Bartholomew's Church in New York, he introduced an influential congregation to progressive methods of church work. Besides, he had to his credit about sixty other missions in various parts of the country, many of which grew into strong, permanent agencies.[4] The Convention of Christian Workers was directly responsible for a few missions. Thus, in the course of its meeting in Buffalo in 1889, it set up the Christian Workers Rescue Mission which soon became a refuge for homeless men on the plan of the Salvation Army.[5]

The Christian Industrial Alliance, founded in the early nineties in New York City, similarly imitated the men's homes of the Salvation Army. It was best known, however, for its preparation of cheap food, having the first "people's" restaurant in the city.[6] In Louisville, Kentucky, Stephen P. Holcombe, an ex-gambler, succeeded so well with a small rescue station that influential citizens provided him with a spacious structure in which to engage in social work of far-reaching scope. In Washington,

---

[3] James M. Campbell, "Progressive Methods of Church Work," *Christian Union*, Feb. 27, 1892, pp. 414–15; Conv. of Christian Workers, *Proceedings*, 1886, pp. 27, 97; *ibid.*, 1887, p. 41; *ibid.*, 1890, pp. 244–245.

[4] *Ibid.*, 1890, pp. 250–251; *ibid.*, 1891, pp. 83–84, 161–62; *ibid.*, 1892, pp. 409–411, 418–419.

[5] *Ibid.*, 1890, pp. 89–90.

[6] *Ibid.*, 1892, pp. 265–266; *Our Day*, XVI (March 1896), 173–174; *Churchman*, Nov. 9, 1895, p. 579.

D. C., the Central Union Mission, dating from 1884, established preaching stations in various parts of the city and several departments of philanthropic activity: police station and house-to-house visitation, free lodging, feeding of transients and the securing of employment. The Bedford Street Mission in the slums of Philadelphia was highly praised for its ministrations to children.[7] By the end of the century Boston was expanding along the lines of its pioneer North End Mission. "The rescue work of Boston," said the Reverend Addison P. Foster in 1892, "is assuming large proportions. Within a few years there has sprung up in different parts of the city a number of these missions, some for men exclusively, some for women only, and some for both." [8] One of the first of these was the Eliot Christian Mission, formed in 1887 by a group under the influence of Ballington and Maud Booth. Others followed: the Women's Mission, the Portland Street Mission, the Pitts Street Mission and the Kneeling Street Mission.[9]

The missionary and tract societies also significantly contributed to socialized religious effort. The New York City Mission and Tract Society, for example, boldly pioneered in every important branch of Christian philanthropy. Alive to the new need, the Society's executive committee in 1880 suggested that "the proper development of the work calls imperatively for enlarged accommodations in many of the chapels. . . ." To help implement this "new departure," Morris K. Jesup, the Society's president, gave sixty thousand dollars for a Church of Christ for the People, dedicated the following year as the DeWitt

[7] Conv. of Christian Workers, *Proceedings*, 1886, p. 65; *ibid.*, 1890, pp. 234–235; *ibid.*, 1892, pp. 172–173.

[8] *Ibid.*, pp. 59–60.

[9] Some employers sponsored socialized missions for the express purpose of improving the moral and economic status of their employees. John B. Stetson of Philadelphia and the Armour brothers of Chicago were among the manufacturers interested in this type of humane helpfulness. The latter lavished over a million dollars on their mission, which grew into the Armour Institute, an excellent trade school. Moseley H. Williams, "The New Era of Church Work in Philadelphia," *Open Church*, I (July 1897), 110–111; Charles H. Henderson, "Social Work of Chicago Churches," *ibid.*, II (April 1898), 267–270.

Memorial. In this way the Society hoped to silence the complaint of lower New York "that the large and fine churches have been moved up-town, leaving here but poor, badly ventilated barns." [10] A similar church grew out of Carmel Chapel, located at 134 Bowery in the notorious Fourteenth Ward. When its pastor, the Reverend John Dooly, reported that a "union" enterprise was needed in the region, William E. Dodge responded by giving a hundred forty thousand dollars for a Broome Street Tabernacle. Olivet Chapel, generously financed by the A. K. Ely family, also expanded into a people's church.[11] These edifices marked the real beginning of an heroic effort on the part of courageous Christians to stem the tide of church removals below Fourteenth Street. The New York City Mission and Tract Society, contended A. F. Schauffler, its secretary, is the only Protestant organization on strictly missionary ground "which is building new churches and manning them with a corps of competent workers." [12]

The three churches gradually perfected far-reaching social programs. DeWitt Memorial succeeded in building up a following among tenement dwellers of the self-respecting type. Sensing that the dole associated religion with pauperism, the church's first pastor, James Marshall, abolished it, and referred needy cases to the appropriate charitable society. But his successor, the Reverend William T. Elsing, realized that people compelled to work at starvation wages needed constructive help. He thereupon organized a series of mutual benefit societies. To satisfy the desire for popular reading, particularly of American history, he collected a large library, obtaining the funds from stereopticon lectures delivered in London and Paris. High-class concerts and addresses on subjects of health and first-aid completed the service. Personal visitation, made possible by a large

---

[10] *Report*, 1880, p. 17; *ibid.*, 1881, p. 27; see also Lewis E. Jackson, "City Evangelism," *Christian at Work*, Dec. 2, 1880, p. 978.

[11] *Report*, 1880, pp. 11–12; *ibid.*, 1890, p. 20.

[12] *Ibid.*, 1895, pp. 16–17.

corps of lay assistants, yielded gratifying spiritual results despite constant shifts in the population.[13]

Broome Street Tabernacle, under Dooly's guidance, gathered a congregational from nine nationalities. There were four secular features: a well selected library, a cooking school, a gymnasium and certain privileges in the way of lectures and instructive entertainments. Though tenement conditions necessitated careful attention to social welfare, the Tabernacle stressed distinctly religious service. By 1889 it conducted twenty-one Sunday-school classes, a missionary association and several young people's societies. Located near the cheap lodging houses which surrounded Chatham Square and lined the Bowery and Park Row, the congregation formed the Lodging House Missionary Society, with fifteen men and eighteen women workers, for the conduct of gospel meetings. At Olivet Church, a kitchen garden was expanded in 1885 into a department of household economy.[14]

The Society's method of handling the foreign-born became an object lesson for other groups. It consisted in organizing for Germans, Italians and Jews special churches in charge of ministers speaking the appropriate language, and the services were held in the edifices of the regular congregations with a view to as speedy Americanization as possible. Though the Reverend Theodore Leonhard successfully managed the Germans, the Reverend Antonio Arreghi's efforts were the more significant. Beginning in 1879, he developed an Italian Evangelical Church which presently became the largest of its kind in the world. Being "the first in the field," this congregation turned the attention of Protestants to an immigrant group which had been too often viewed with distrust. Converts formed similar churches in representative cities, an example followed by other religious organizations, including the great denominations. While the large mass of Jews welcomed only the philan-

---

[13] *Ibid.*, 1882, pp. 47–61; *ibid.*, 1895, pp. 43, 47.
[14] *Ibid.*, 1885, pp. 51–52; *ibid.*, 1890, pp. 92–93.

thropic and non-sectarian work of the Society, a few embraced Christianity — as evidenced by the fact that the Society erected a home in 1891 for converted Hebrews who experienced difficulty in winning recognition from Gentiles with respect to employment and social intercourse.[15]

Direct ecclesiastical effort did not exhaust the social interests of the New York City Mission and Tract Society. By establishing a workingmen's club in 1878, the Society exemplified the Christian method of social reform. "What this club . . . wishes to do," explained William J. Tucker, then pastor of Madison Avenue Presbyterian Church, "is to unite men by a closer bond than any which holds them together at the present day, or rather to show them more clearly how close the union really is. It is not desired to change the relative position of men, to make the rich poor and the poor rich but to teach them the nature of their mutual relations and the duties which it involves."[16] The Women's Branch, dating from 1867, was responsible for several worthwhile philanthropies. Its Christian Workers Home, given in 1881 by the Jesup family, trained missionary nurses for the tenements. Its home at Hill Hope provided summer vacations for young working girls, and three day nurseries pioneered in that phase of social service. Moreover, there were penny provident banks, a "helping hand," a home department for Bible study, a home for the aged and invalid, a "white rose" mission for the colored people and aid for first offenders in courts and prisons.[17]

Many socialized missions aimed at only the more notorious urban evils, particularly the ubiquitous saloon. A few reformers, believing with the Reverend William S. Rainsford that "in a great and crowded city . . . drinking is a necessary evil,"

---

[15] *Ibid.*, 1891, pp. 73–77; *ibid.*, 1895, pp. 45–51.

[16] "The Churches and Socialism," *Amer. Socialist* (Oneida, New York), I (June 6, 1878), 17; Lewis E. Jackson, "Concerning Workingmen," *Christian at Work*, June 6, 1878, p. 461.

[17] "Women's Branch," *Report*, 1881, pp. 81–82; *ibid.*, 1891, pp. 151–157; *ibid.*, 1898, pp. 68–97; *Altruistic Interchange*, II (April 1894), 6–10.

hoped for little more than improved saloon management.[18] A large majority of Christians, however, saw larger possibilities, contending that most people patronized saloons more for their clublike features than for their intoxicants. These temperance advocates therefore favored substitutes for the saloon — "places of resort which shall be pleasant but not perilous." [19] The Right Reverend Samuel Fallows, of the Reformed Episcopal Church, was acclaimed for his non-intoxicating "bishop's beer," which he sold in his Chicago "Home Saloon." [20] Impressed by the success of the English coffee houses, the Boston Episcopal Church Temperance Society opened a half-dozen similar institutions which resembled saloons in everything except the liquor. After 1885 the Society's New York branch engaged in aggressive rescue work and at the century's turn established a spacious, well-equipped coffee house.[21] Frequently, in nearly every part of the land, ministers set up liquorless saloons on their own initiative or helped like-minded reformers.

The Woman's Christian Temperance Union, the strongest battalion in the temperance army, found a place for the socialized mission among its multitudinous activities. The Union soon discovered the futility of purely religious propaganda. "Those who had been won to the pledge, and over whom we had wept and prayed," confessed a prominent leader, "fell again and again, and as a result were arrested and imprisoned." [22] Accordingly, the Union sent missionaries into the jails, prisons and almshouses to reclaim the backsliders. On learning that these institutions neglected women, the Union in 1879 began furnishing police matrons — a practice which rapidly expanded and in

[18] *Our Day*, X (July 1892), 537; Prot. Episcopal Church Cong., *Essays, Debates and Proceedings*, 1893, pp. 17–18.

[19] Gen. Assembly, Presby. Church, *Minutes*, 1898, p. 104.

[20] *Homiletic Rev.*, XXX (September 1895), 282–83.

[21] Church Temperance Soc., *Report*, 1882, pp. 27–28; *ibid.*, 1887, pp. 34–35; *ibid.*, 1899, p. 60.

[22] Mrs. J. K. Birney, "Department of Prison, Jail, Police and Almshouse Work," *Lend a Hand*, II (June 1887), 409.

time secured state support.[23] In order to keep its wards out of penal institutions, the Union founded several rescue missions, beginning in 1883 with the Benedict Home in Des Moines, Iowa. The Bethesda Mission of Chicago, the most noted of these missions, provided for both men and women a lodging house and restaurant and for children a kitchen garden, a kindergarten and a dispensary.[24]

Though rescue loomed large in the Union's program, it was less important than preventive philanthropy. Thus kitchen garden and kindergarten training, dating from the early eighties, helped to counteract the saloon by preparing youth for a better home life. In this educational endeavor the Union not only coöperated with church organizations, but also established its own schools, having by 1886 a score or more under its sole control. Since science had shown the influence of heredity in perpetuating crime, poverty and drunkenness, it also created and instituted an elaborate lecture system to disseminate information. The Medical Temperance Association, formed by and working alongside the W.C.T.U., published the *Medical Temperance Quarterly*, for persons who were unschooled in physiology and hygiene. To demonstrate the truth of its conviction that intoxicants had no medicinal value, the Union opened in 1886 at Chicago the National Temperance Hospital, followed by a few others elsewhere during the ensuing years.[25]

Institutional missions made up only part of the W.C.T.U. program. White Ribboners sponsored every plan which seemed likely to promote a more wholesome family life — the sound basis of national sobriety. Besides prohibition and woman suffrage, the Union believed that labor reform was essential. The more we study the causes, said Frances E. Willard, "the

---

[23] Mrs. J. K. Birney, "Police Matrons," *ibid.*, II (August 1887), 471–475; W.C.T.U., *Report*, 1895, p. 259.

[24] Frances E. Willard, "A Day Among Chicago Philanthropists," *Chautauquan*, VII (March 1887), 348–349.

[25] W.C.T.U., *Report*, 1886, pp. 125–126; *ibid.*, 1888, pp. 254–255; *ibid.*, 1893, pp. 263–265.

more certainly we find that justice, not charity, must be the watchword of the future." [26] She supported the new political economy and the Christian Socialist movement, the ideals of which she believed "might be slowly but steadily wrought out." [27] But pending this desirable revolution in the social system, the Union's leaders would continue to "do everything" in the way of charity and social service for the victims of intemperance.[28]

Similar attitudes held sway in the social purity movement. Its greatest leader was Charles Nelson Crittenden, a New York business man and prominent figure in the Convention of Christian Workers, who gave the last thirty years of his life to the work. His Florence All-night Mission, established in 1883 in memory of his daughter, bestowed upon abandoned women many spiritual and material benefits. So many seemed permanently reformed during the first years' operation that Crittenden and his helpers decided to launch a national crusade. After inspecting similar missions in Europe, Crittenden became a "merchant evangelist," travelling throughout America making speeches and organizing over fifty institutions by the end of the century. Though a few communities proved indifferent, even hostile, religious folk as a rule warmly welcomed him, especially the W.C.T.U. which placed several rescue homes under his management. The founding in 1895 of the National Florence Mission Association also aided the movement. Its first convention in 1897 led not only to additional homes but to greater efficiency, especially with respect to the grading of inmates.[29]

[26] *Ibid.*, 1888, p. 50.

[27] "The Coming Brotherhood," *Arena*, VI (August 1892), 321–322.

[28] Mary A. Livermore, "Woman's Work in Moral Reforms," *Chautauquan*, VII (November 1896), 269–272; Willard, *Do Everything* (Chicago, 1895), pp. 130–144.

[29] Florence Crittenden Mission, *Report*, 1887, pp. 7–8; *ibid.*, 1899, p. 7; Mary G. Charlton Edholm, *Traffic in Girls and the Florence Crittenden Missions* (Chicago, 1893), p. 20, *passim*; *Fourteen Years' Work among Street Girls as Conducted by the National Florence Crittenden Mission* (Washington, 1897), esp. pp. 12–13.

Though all promoters of social purity favored the rescue mission, they did not ignore the other means of reform. Thus the American Purity Alliance directed its energies mainly against the licensing of prostitution. It would also rescue the victims of immorality. "But even more important," said Aaron M. Powell, its president, "is the preventive educational purity work among the young and the older, which shall ultimately make rescue work no longer a necessity." [30] To this end, two distinctly Christian organizations were formed. The first, the White Cross Society, originating in 1883 in the Church of England, associated men for the purpose of bringing public opinion to sanction the same moral standard for both sexes. The Reverend B. F. DeCosta formed the first American branch at his Episcopal Church of St. John the Evangelist in New York. In numerous congregations, but more generally in colleges and Young Men's Christian Associations, these societies advanced their cause through a wide variety of reforms, industrial, social and educational.[31] Unlike the White Cross, the National Christian League for the Promotion of Social Purity, started in New York in 1886 by Mrs. Elizabeth B. Grannis, enlisted both men and women in coöperative efforts to extirpate the social evil. In line with its contention that it was not merely for the rescue of the fallen, the League established an industrial and woman's club home and several young people's clubs for social culture.[32]

The W.C.T.U. aided with a Department for the Promotion of Social Purity which, under Frances E. Willard's immediate direction, sponsored preventive, reformatory and legal measures. Its *Social Purity Series*, issued in 1887, attained a large circulation. Even more important were its mothers' meetings, both in and out of the churches, before which lecturers presented the desired information. So effective was this form of

[30] Nat. Purity Cong., 1895, *Papers, Addresses and Portraits*, p. 6.
[31] B. F. DeCosta, *Manual of the White Cross* (New York, 1887), pp. 1–14.
[32] *Annual Meeting*, 1893, pp. 9–16; *ibid.*, 1899, p. 9.

propaganda that in 1895 the department started a monthly periodical, *The Mothers' Friend,* to systemize moral instruction. Favoring state action in this as in other spheres of philanthropy, the Union organized vigilance committees which helped to strengthen the laws against impurity in literature and art. Similarly, the Union successfully struggled to raise the age of consent in the many states.[33]

Though producing fruitful results, neither the general nor the special missions had enough resources to carry humanitarian endeavor beyond the pioneering stages. Further advance would have been impossible had not hundreds of congregations with their greater permanence, wealth and influence joined the movement. Among the outstanding institutional churches, St. George's and St. Bartholomew's, both in New York City, typified the new trend within the Episcopalian fold. The strategic importance of the former stemmed in part from the changed direction of its activities and in part from the personality of its leader. Located on the East Side, at Sturtevant Square, it had once been a flourishing church of the fashionable type; but, as in the case of so many other houses of worship, the coming into its neighborhood of a boarding-house and tenement-house population, largely German, had by 1880 dispersed its wealthy clientele. Only a few people, headed by J. Pierpont Morgan, remained to keep up an unequal struggle for existence in an environment hostile in temper and lacking in "aesthetic charm." [34]

Unwilling for sentimental reasons to join the up-town movement, the vestry was ready for new pastoral leadership, even if it involved radical plans of reorganization. The man selected as rector, the Reverend W. S. Rainsford, had gained from wide experience an accurate knowledge of urban religious problems. Born in Dublin in 1850 of a rather distinguished clerical family, he had participated as a young man in the religio-social work

[33] *Report,* 1886, p. 75; *ibid.,* 1889, pp. 263–264; *ibid.,* 1894, pp. 455–457.
[34] "Modern Churches," *Church Work,* vol. IV (May 1893), No. 7.

of East London. Coming to the United States in 1876, he had assisted the Reverend Stephen H. Tyng, Jr., at Holy Trinity Church and conducted missions throughout the country.[35] When called to St. George's he was assistant minister of St. James' Church in Toronto, the largest in the Dominion. After informing the St. George's vestry that, if chosen, he wanted "a church of the people, a truly democratic church," he insisted that the pews be free, that all committees be abolished (the new ones to be appointed by him), and that an annual fund of ten thousand dollars be given for a period of three years for evangelistic work. "Dead silence followed," said Rainsford of his unprecedented ultimatum. "I saw Mr. Morgan look round that circle of tense faces. Then he looked full at me and said one word, 'done.' "[36]

Undeterred by obstacles or opposition, Rainsford pushed his program with all the strength at his command. From the family of Charles Tracy, a late warden, he secured two hundred thousand dollars for a parish house. From this center, on East Sixteenth Street, there developed every agency of the new philanthropy.[37] Club life strikingly similar to that of the later social settlements helped to improve the environment in a part of the city where "every condition adverse to true manhood and womanhood is accentuated."[38] Industrial education, particularly in its trade features, came in for special attention. "Our whole idea of education," he told his congregation in 1893, "needs to be raised and developed. The public schools of New York are lamentably behind the times; and what the church should do is to set an example of a higher standard for growing boys and girls . . . until . . . at last our Boards of Education gain light on educational matters seemingly at present denied

[35] W. S. Rainsford, *A Preacher's Story of His Work*, pp. 1–91.
[36] *Story of a Varied Life*, pp. 201, 286.
[37] *Ibid.*, pp. 218, 235–241, 305; George W. Shinn, *King's Handbook of Notable Episcopal Churches*, p. 139; *Christian Union*, June 24, 1886, p. 20; *ibid.*, Aug. 27, 1885, p. 25.
[38] "Modern Churches," *loc. cit.*

them." [39] Especially organized and expertly taught, the industrial work at St. George's was soon the best of its kind in New York. One of the teachers, Arthur Hamerschlag, a graduate of Auchmuty's Trade School, succeeded so well that Andrew Carnegie later picked him to head the women's division of his Institute of Technology.

The stress on industrial education illustrated Rainsford's idea that church work should be closely related to social reform. Since the congregation could not do everything, she should concentrate on imperative needs. "That having been done," he said, "let her step from under and let her take up some new need, some new reform." [40] Rainsford also insisted on trained helpers, clerical and lay. A deaconess home, supported by the church, provided a corps of women assistants. In John Reichart, an immigrant from Germany, he secured an excellent administrator. For assistant clergy, Rainsford drew upon experienced ministers — one an ex-Methodist and another a High Churchman of Canada — who on adopting the methods of the Salvation Army had been ejected from their churches. These were able to squeeze the "seminarism" out of young men from the theological schools, twenty-six of whom Rainsford employed during his career. A clergy house, in which they lived in common, forced them to forego fashionable churches, large salaries and early marriages and to secure instead a real acquaintance with practical religion.

By all outward signs St. George's succeeded brilliantly. In the years from 1883 to 1899 the congregation expended over two million dollars on religious and philanthropic objects and

[39] *Story of a Varied Life*, pp. 251–254; "What Can We Do for the Poor," *Forum*, XI (April 1891), 115–121.
[40] *Story of a Varied Life*, p. 225. Rainsford laid down three rules for the guidance of the church in social work: (1) it should select its points of attack and education wisely; (2) it should be positive rather than negative, that is, illustrate a good thing as well as attack an evil thing; and (3) it should select its agencies with a view to the education of the community and when that was accomplished, it should turn them over to other organizations. *Ibid.*, pp. 230–231.

increased in membership from less than two hundred to over four thousand, one third of them German born. These results were secured, however, in the face of serious drawbacks. The failure which threatened from the constant withdrawal of people to up-town sections was averted only by a large endowment fund which by 1897 amounted to some two hundred thousand dollars. The chief obstacle was the stiff opposition to Rainsford's social gospel. Charles A. Dana, editor of the *New York Sun*, summarized conservative opinion when he wrote that Rainsford "is a shallow, harumscarum thinker, and is a conspicuous representative of a school of unwise and mischievous social agitators." [41] Within the parish itself, influential members like Admiral A. T. Mahan found his humanitarian preaching so distasteful that they withdrew. Morgan and others, while rejoicing in Rainsford's ability to accomplish things, opposed a representative vestry, and but for his determination and iron will would have wrecked the whole plan for a people's church. [42]

At St. Bartholomew's, also a fashionable church in central Manhattan, the theory of social reform was minimized, but its practice became more extensive perhaps than in any other congregation in America. Deciding on a change of policy in 1888, the parish chose as leader the Reverend David H. Greer, of Providence, who soon demonstrated as much ability in administration as he had shown eloquence in preaching. The parish house, located in East Forty-second Street, was completed in 1891. Costing four hundred thousand dollars, the bulk supplied by Cornelius Vanderbilt and his mother, and having a floor space of three and a half acres, it was the most elaborate of its kind in the world. In view of the idea of its founders "that it should be devoted to humanitarian as well as religious objects," there was nothing "ecclesiastical about the architecture." [43] Here during the following ten years nearly

---

[41] *Ibid.*, p. 306.   [42] *Ibid.*, pp. 258–259, 279–286.
[43] George J. Manson, "Progressive Methods of Church Work," *Christian Union*, Nov. 28, 1891, p. 1946.

eleven million dollars was expended, an average annual outlay exceeding that of "many an American College and University." [44] So large and varied a work required for its description a year-book of over three hundred and fifty pages. For its oversight, a staff of five assistant clergy and several lay workers and instructors was employed. Activity at the parish house was supplemented by a girls' club boarding house, a working girls' summer home and a children's home. [45]

On the religious side, the church specialized in caring for Oriental peoples, being equipped for ministration in three languages: Armenian, Syriac and Turkish. In social service it was distinguished for its excellent medical and surgical clinic, which held over twenty thousand consultations and wrote over ten thousand prescriptions each year. An employment bureau secured positions at the rate of about fifteen hundred a year. Its Loan Association provided money in sums from fifty cents to one hundred dollars at low rates of interest to self-respecting people in temporary difficulty. [46]

If institutional churches among Congregationalists were as a rule less elaborate than many Episcopal ones, they were quite as influential. The Fourth Church of Hartford, Connecticut, located near a wage-earning population, attracted only forty-five worshipers in 1880; the congregation had little support among either the wealthy or the poor. When Graham Taylor became its pastor that year, he found it "to have more of a history than a hope." [47] Responding to his "democratic evangelism," the church in 1884 appointed a city missionary, Henry J. Gillette, who, with "a real love for the unlovely," visited and relieved families in their homes and befriended the inmates of jails and police stations. [48] The church was so successful with

[44] Herbert Baxter Adams, *The Church and Popular Education*, pp. 27–28; St. Bartholomew's Church, *Year Book*, 1897, pp. 333–335.

[45] *Ibid.*, pp. 11–12, *passim*.

[46] *Ibid.*

[47] *Pioneering on Social Frontiers*, pp. 362–371.

[48] *Congregationalist*, April 20, 1893, pp. 619–620.

the outcasts of society — the drunkard, the gambler and the criminal — that fastidious folk called it the church for ex-convicts. For men of this class, an ex-gambler, an ex-drunkard and an ex-clergyman's wife, Mrs. Horace Bushnell, provided funds for a social center. Within ten years the church added nearly three hundred families to its membership.[49] Besides setting an example for other churches, the congregation prepared Graham Taylor for a brilliant career as seminary professor and settlement leader.

In somewhat the same manner as Taylor, the Reverend Oscar Carlton McCulloch deeply influenced the social movement through a Congregational pastorate. Born at Fremont, Ohio, in 1843, McCulloch had been in early life a traveling salesman. Deciding finally upon the ministry, he entered the Chicago Theological Seminary, where practice in the city missions taught him the intimate relation between physical and spiritual conditions. After a short stay at Sheboygan, Wisconsin, he took charge in 1877 of Plymouth Church in Indianapolis, a congregation which had been steadily declining. McCulloch first rid it of its Calvinistic creed, listing the objects of the church in a new constitution as: "public worship of God, weekly renewal of religious sympathies and affections, mutual acquaintance and assistance, and the alleviation by physical and spiritual means of poverty, ignorance, misery, vice and crime." This abandonment of theological tenets endeared the Church to many former adherents of all faiths who under McCulloch's leadership became the "Church of the Divine Fragments." [50]

Though the church dispensed poor relief under McCulloch's expert guidance, it stressed intellectual development. "I would make this church a People's College," said McCulloch at an early date. "What Peter Cooper did in a large way, we must

[49] Charles S. Mills, "The Institutional Church," *Bibliotheca Sacra*, XLIX (July 1892), 458–459.
[50] George Willis Cooke, "The Institutional Church," *New England Magazine*, XVI (August 1896), 650–651.

undertake in a small way." The Plymouth Institute, opened in 1884 upon the model of the Cooper Institute of New York, the Boston Young Men's Union, the Women's Industrial Union of Boston and the Chicago Athenaeum, partially realized his dream. Designed as a place "in which the young could improve themselves on all sides of their nature and a place where workingmen could find the means of culture adapted to their needs," [51] the Institute provided a cheerful reading room and library open day and evening and organized classes in all the common branches. Able speakers gave series of lectures each winter on subjects of the highest importance.[52] These accomplishments led a magazine editor to say that Plymouth Church "is known by thoughtful people through this whole nation by the success with which it has attacked the most difficult problems of human need." [53] For his leadership of the church and in the Charity Organization Society movement McCulloch was hailed on his death in 1891 as a foremost representative of the new philanthropy.

Another widely known Congregationalist institutional church was Berkeley Temple of Boston, an outgrowth of Berkeley Street Congregational Church. The Temple was strategically placed with respect to social groups, standing, in the words of a contemporary, "at the intersection of avenues, one of which leads immediately to the homes of wealth and social predominance, another of which opens right up on scenes of vice and misery and still another is connected with the dwelling places of that immense class of people who are most likely of all to be overlooked in any scheme of religious activity, those who go their way and lead their life without attracting attention to themselves by any outward sign." [54] In 1888 a yearly sum of twenty thousand dollars, guaranteed by the Massachusetts

[51] *Ibid.*, 648–649.
[52] *Christian Union*, Dec. 24, 1885, p. 25.
[53] *Lend a Hand*, VIII (January 1892), 38–39.
[54] M. C. Ayers, "The Work of Berkeley Temple," *Christian Union*, Dec. 6, 1888, p. 653.

Home Missionary Society and by several individuals, among them Daniel S. Ford, editor of the *Youth's Companion*, permitted the Church to experiment along new lines. Charles A. Dickinson, after Francis E. Clark the most active figure in the Christian Endeavor Movement, was chosen pastor.[55]

In a neighborhood of some six thousand Protestant non-church goers, many of them young men and women living in boarding houses, the church found a Young Men's Institute and a "Dorcastry" of great value. These agencies necessarily stressed entertainment and classes, though the former engaged in rescue work and established at Westminster, Vermont, a home for redeeming drunkards.[56] While facetiously called "the Church of Young America," Berkeley Temple was not restricted to youth, having in 1892 about five hundred families in its membership.[57] Less equipped than many churches of its class, the Temple excelled in its personnel. R. B. Tobey and W. S. Kelsey were assistant pastors, the former, an expert in relief administration and a man of untiring zeal, ardent sympathy and rare modesty. Lucy Wheelock, a woman of national repute, directed the kindergartens, and S. Brainerd Pratt, a Bible collector, C. N. Allen, an eminent violinist, and Mrs. L. W. Schneider, long a missionary in Constantinople, served as teachers and workers. But the strong individuality of its helpers did not interfere with organization. "The extent to which division of labor is pushed," wrote Edmund K. Alden, "would gratify a pronounced bureaucrat." [58] It was in connection with Berkeley Temple that Professor W. J. Tucker first used the word "institutional."

As one further example of Congregational undertakings, the Jersey City Tabernacle, in the worst section of a drab and unprogressive city, was socialized by John L. Scudder, the son

[55] *Home Missionary*, LXI (July 1888), 112; *Golden Rule*, Dec. 8, 1887, p. 4.
[56] *Christianity Practically Applied*, I, 26–29.
[57] "Berkeley Temple," *Congregationalist*, May 4, 1893, pp. 699–700.
[58] "Berkeley Temple of Today," *Christian Union*, Jan. 9, 1892, p. 78.

of missionaries to India. His assistant, the Reverend J. Lester Wells, had scored a modest success with institutional methods in neighboring Newark. Combining buoyant enthusiasm with spiritual consecration, the two made "a team which it would not be easy to match." [59] Though active in social reform in its wider aspects, the Tabernacle's unique feature was the People's Palace, established in 1891 and, like its London model, offering a bewildering variety of recreational and athletic benefits. Scudder described the Palace "as a bold ecclesiastical leap into the arena of sin" and as "the outward manifestation of a purpose to fight Satan on his own ground and with his own weapons." In words at once pungent and unequivocal, he defended this "ruinous but most godly competition," [60] telling the Convention of Christian Workers, for example, that the "novelty of a custom is no argument against its adoption." [61] William E. Dodge called the Palace "practical Christianity guided by common sense"; Bishop Vincent viewed it as "a wise Christian scheme"; and Terence V. Powderly, of the Knights of Labor, said that any institution "that aims at bettering the condition of the masses will always receive my endorsement." [62] Though run at a cost as low as four thousand dollars a year, the church depended in part for support from the outside.[63]

If Presbyterians at first were less ready to establish institutional churches than their Congregational brethren, they had outgrown their conservatism before the end of the century. Bethany Presbyterian Church in Philadelphia, founded as a Sunday school in 1859 by John Wanamaker and never seriously affected by the fashionable virus, steadily gained in humanitarian emphasis. Greater progress in this direction resulted from the pastorates of Arthur T. Pierson and J. Wilbur Chapman.

[59] "Jersey City Tabernacle," *Congregationalist*, April 27, 1893, pp. 659–660.
[60] "The People's Palace of Jersey City," *Charities Rev.*, I (December 1890), 90–91.
[61] *Proceedings*, 1890, pp. 261–262.
[62] "The People's Palace," *Zion's Herald*, Nov. 25, 1891, p. 369.
[63] *Christian Union*, Dec. 12, 1891, pp. 1178–1179.

Having as a youth helped to found the Y.M.C.A. of New York City, Pierson had spent his mature years in ineffectual protests against undemocratic churches. Beginning at Bethany in 1883, he increased the lay force, perfected evangelistic and social agencies and lifted a heavy debt — a work continued by his successor.[64] At Bethany House, the parish house, the congregation operated a day nursery, kindergartens, diet kitchens, an employment bureau, a workingmen's club and a dispensary. To philanthropic interest education was added when the parishioners established Bethany College. Developing alongside the church, the college decided to become independent at the end of the century, reorganizing as the John Wanamaker Institute.[65]

Unlike Bethany, most Presbyterian churches entered the institutional stage by abruptly abandoning traditional methods. Thus the Madison Avenue Presbyterian Church of New York City, faced in the early nineties with the alternative of moving or changing its program, decided to follow in the footsteps of its neighbor, St. George's Church, and "become positively and aggressively a people's church." Its pastor, the influential Charles L. Thompson, believing that the ecclesiastical system fostered the separation of classes, insisted that the church should aim at "not merely salvation for eternity, but salvation of the whole man for the regeneration of society." [66] To this end he established philanthropic agencies at the mother church and at its Goodwill Chapel, where the Reverend E. L. Chichester served as assistant. A men's league, a ladies' benevolent association, which conducted a penny provident fund and a cooking school, and a free library were among the social adjuncts. Despite predictions of failure, the congregation met the usual tests of success, raising yearly huge sums for missionary

[64] Herbert Adams Gibbons, *John Wanamaker*, I, 181–194; D. L. Pierson, *A Spiritual Warrior*, pp. 22–40, 132–64, 167–207; *Golden Rule*, July 27, 1893, pp. 877–880.

[65] J. Wilbur Chapman, "Bethany Church of Philadelphia," *Chautauquan*, XII (January 1891), 470–473.

[66] "A New Departure," *Christian Union*, Dec. 5, 1891, p. 1100.

purposes and establishing religious relations with a large number of people, many of whom became members.[67]

In Philadelphia and New York, Baptists also founded representative institutional churches. In the former emerged the most famous of these, Grace Church, whose pastor, Russell H. Conwell, was after Rainsford the most colorful of the new leaders. Born in Massachusetts and educated at Yale, Conwell, after his release from the Northern army, devoted successful years to law, journalism, lecturing and real-estate speculation. Finding at last his vocation, he accepted in 1882, shortly after ordination, the charge in Philadelphia. Deciding that a teaching, healing and preaching church, after the manner of Christ, would improve his miserably poor congregation, he opened several reading rooms as a step toward the desired goal. But real progress awaited the erection of a new edifice, the Baptist Temple, completed in 1890 at a cost of some two hundred fifty thousand dollars. Only by the utmost sacrifice on the part of the membership and by Conwell's resort to a sensationalism which in other cases he avoided, could the money be raised.[68]

By means of the Temple, which from the street presented "the appearance of an institution of some kind rather than of a church," Grace Church gathered the largest Protestant congregation in the United States and developed a "wider system of ministeries" than could "be found anywhere else in America." [69] Hundreds of voluntary and paid workers manned societies for the benefit of both old and young, and formed athletic, literary and benevolent organizations of every variety. To perform the teaching function of Christ, Temple College grew from inconspicuous beginnings in 1884 to a fully accred-

[67] Charles L. Thompson, *The Church Ideal, A Sermon* (New York, 1896), pp. 18–24.
[68] Agnes R. Burr, *Russell H. Conwell and His Work*, pp. 32–65, *passim*; *Outlook*, Feb. 22, 1896, p. 349.
[69] Edmund K. Alden, "The Temple, Philadelphia," *Christian Union*, March 18, 1893, 508–509; Moseley H. Williams, "The New Era of Church Work in Philadelphia," *Open Church*, I (July 1897), 111.

ited institution by the end of the century, with special provision for students from the wage-earning class. Samaritan Hospital was established in 1892 to reproduce Christ's concern for the sick. A training school for nurses, a dispensary and a well-organized plan of district nursing aided its work, in which sectarian considerations had no part.[70]

In New York, the Judson Memorial, located on the south side of Washington Square, resulted from the efforts of Edward Judson, son of the great missionary to Burma, Adoniram Judson. Becoming dissatisfied with his conventional career, first as a professor in Madison University and then as pastor of a fashionable church in Orange, New Jersey, he accepted in 1880 a charge at Berean Baptist Church in lower New York.[71] His labors successful, he appealed to Baptists throughout the country for a memorial edifice to his father, to be located "in the borderland between the rich and the poor, expressive of the truth that makes us one in Jesus Christ."[72] Four hundred fifty thousand dollars were subscribed and the structure was dedicated in 1893. In it Judson was able to conduct a "work as many sided as it is admirable." The clubs amply provided for the floating class "that are neither very poor nor altogether comfortable." As an institution of "organized kindness" it covered the whole field of spiritual and social interests.[73]

Methodists were not behind other evangelical groups in establishing similar churches. One of the first was Wesley Chapel of Cincinnati. The oldest Methodist house of worship in the city, it declared in 1891 that a "down-town church like Wesley Chapel can only succeed by being an institution of all-round salvation. It ought to be honeycombed with educational,

[70] Washington Gladden, *The Christian Pastor and the Working Church*, pp. 403–404.

[71] Alfred H. Moment, *The New York Down Town Presbyterian Churches*, p. 14; *Independent*, Jan. 4, 1882, p. 17.

[72] *Christian Union*, March 21, 1889, p. 392; *ibid.*, Feb. 4, 1893, p. 232.

[73] Edward Judson, *The Institutional Church. A Primer in Pastoral Theology* (Handbook for Practical Workers in Church and Philanthropy, edited by S. M. Jackson), p. 180.

musical and industrial work and appliances, doing their part in the work along with the sermon, the Sunday school and the prayer meeting. It must work as Christ did, healing and helping the temporal condition of man along with its ordinary spiritual work." [74] Led by the Reverend J. W. Magruder, the congregation enlarged its functions, having by 1895 a kindergarten, a day nursery, a young ladies' benevolent society, a bureau of justice in which four lawyers gave their services to the poor, a building association in which people were taught to save toward a home, and a visitation society. "The work," reported the *Outlook*, "is said to have but just begun but to us it seems already far advanced." [75]

More conspicuous was the transformation of Central Methodist Church in New York City (corner of Seventh Avenue and Fourteenth Street) into the Metropolitan Temple under the leadership of a recently arrived young Englishman, the Reverend S. Parkes Cadman. Since Methodist churches in the neighborhood disbanded and consolidated with the Temple, adequate equipment was possible. A large ministerial and lay force enabled the new enterprise to hold fifty services each week as well as to increase the membership within five years from a hundred and fifty to eleven hundred. Every "legitimate method of reaching men" [76] was pressed into service. Choral societies, a reading room, an athletic association, an employment bureau, young people's organizations, a kindergarten, a Froebel normal institute, a sewing school and millinery and dressmaking classes were some of the agencies employed.[77]

While the liberal denominations were more inclined than the orthodox ones to perform philanthropic service in coöperation with the secular social movement, they also welcomed the institutional church. Among Unitarians, for example, the conversion after 1882 of the Fourth Unitarian Church of Chicago into All

---

[74] *Zion's Herald*, May 27, 1891, p. 164.
[75] "An Institutional Church in Cincinnati," Nov. 2, 1895, p. 358.
[76] *Zion's Herald*, Jan. 5, 1898, pp. 17–18.
[77] *Forward*, I (December 1900), 6–7; *New York Tribune*, Dec. 1, 1897, p. 11.

Souls' Church symbolized a broader viewpoint. Having failed in its old form, the congregation gradually revived under the strenuous Jenkin Lloyd Jones as pastor and with the aid of its sister churches of the same faith in the city. Members subscribed to a "Bond of Union" in which they joined together "in the interests of Morality and Religion, as interpreted by the growing thoughts and purest lives of humanity, hoping thereby to bear one another's burdens, and promote Truth, Righteousness and Love in the World." [78] In his first sermon, "The Ideal Church," Jones pledged that there would be no "ownership of private boxes where the pride of caste may enter the last hope of democracy to set up its galling distinctions in the very home of religion." The church would require "not a little money, but a great deal," he warned, "because it will cover a large area of life's interests." [79]

On the plan of the early Unitarian churches, social, charitable, missionary and educational sections were formed, each under a superintendent. Since it performed its extensive philanthropic service in coöperation with outside bodies, particularly with Hull House, the congregation stressed education, with a kindergarten, manual training, mechanical drawing and a day lectureship for young people as special features. Study classes in philosophy and literature, taught by Jones, evoked great interest. Thus organized, the membership increased from sixty families in 1884 to two hundred fifty in 1892. Early in the new century the church became the Abraham Institute of Chicago.[80]

Universalists also felt that their denomination should do something outstanding in philanthropy and city evangelization. Thus the Shawmut Universalist Church of Boston, urged by its progressive pastor, George L. Perin, and one of its lay members, Irving C. Tomlinson, long an active social worker of the city,

---

[78] All Souls' Church, *Tenth Annual*, 1893, p. 7.
[79] Jenkin Lloyd Jones, "Ten Years' Ministry in Chicago," *ibid.*, pp. 72–73.
[80] *Tenth Annual*, 1893, pp. 9–10, 16–17, 31–35, 44–46.

voted on May 30, 1894, to become the institutional Every Day Church of Boston. Aid, not "only generous" but "spontaneous," came from Universalist congregations throughout New England. Since the edifice was not equipped for social duty, a large sixteen-room house at No. 401 Shawmut Avenue was acquired. The Reverend Florence E. Kollock, active in reform movements, proved as assistant minister a splendid organizer. A young people's Christian union provided entertainment and carried on flower mission and summer work. A boys' club, a kindergarten and a day nursery were other features. University extension courses were given in the Old Testament, English History and Practical Economics. When the Church in 1896 extended its activities to industrial and commercial education, its adhesion to applied Christianity was complete.[81]

The numerous humanitarian missions and churches, which contributed so effectively to the urban expansion of Protestantism, necessitated an instrument of coördination. The Open or Institutional Church League, formed in 1894 at a conference in the Madison Square Presbtyerian Church of New York, focused attention on the changing course of organized religion. "The time seems ripe," the leaders said, "for an organized advance along the lines of practical church work. A number of churches, having experimented for several years with some of the new methods, have reached results which encourage us to believe that the burning question, 'How to reach the masses,' is practically solved. What we now need is coöperation and aggressive action on the part of these churches."

Excepting for the Protestant Episcopal Church, the great divisions of Protestantism were represented in the Conference somewhat in proportion to their activity in the movement. William E. Dodge, Josiah Strong and Frank Russell spoke for the Evangelical Alliance. Charles A. Dickinson of Berkeley Temple, a caller of the meeting, Charles M. Southgate of

---

[81] *Year Book*, 1896, pp. 11, 13–14, *passim*.

Pilgrim Congregational Church, Worcester, John L. Scudder of
Jersey City, and Howard Bliss, assistant pastor at Plymouth
Church, Brooklyn, were among those of the Congregational
faith. Charles L. Thompson, the host of the gathering, Samuel
V. Holmes, of Westminster Presbyterian Church in Buffalo and
W. M. Paden of the Holland Memorial Church in Philadelphia
appeared for the Presbyterians as did F. M. North of New
York and George P. Mains of Brooklyn for the Methodists.
From Baptist centers came J. C. Thoms of the Mariner's Tem-
ple, New York, James M. Bruce, assistant pastor at Judson
Memorial, and John L. Campbell of the Lexington Avenue
Church. The Reverend George W. Cooke, of Follen Church,
Lexington, Massachusetts, was a Unitarian participant.[82]

In its platform the League tried to define the functions of the
institutional church. As the agent of Christ, it "aims to provide
the material environment through which his spirit may be
practically expressed. As his representative in the world, it
seeks to represent him physically, intellectually, socially and
spiritually to the age in which it exists." Repudiating "so far
as possible the distinction between the religious and the secular," it would sanctify "all days and all means to the great end
of saving the world for Christ."[83] In the statement, "ministration to all men and to all of the man," the League endorsed
the kind of church which sought the welfare of men as individuals and in their social relations.[84] The League insisted that
the spirit of ministration rather than any specific method of
expressing that spirit was fundamental in the institutional
church, but stated that "it stands for open church doors every
day and all the day, free seats, a plurality of Christian workers,
the personal activity of all church members, a ministry to all
the community through educational, reformatory and philanthropic channels, to the end that men may be won to Christ and
His service, that the church may be brought back to the sim-

[82] Open or Institutional Church League, *Preliminary Conference*, pp. 5–6.
[83] "Platform," *ibid.*, p. 14.   [84] *Outlook*, Oct. 21, 1896, pp. 793–794.

plicity and comprehensiveness of its primitive life, until it can be said of every community, 'The Kingdom of Heaven is within you,' and Christ is all and in all." [85]

The Open or Institutional Church League was a potent factor in multiplying institutional churches. Its clear-cut statements as to their nature and function did much to induce congregations to adopt the broader conception of religion. In its first three presidents, Thompson, Dickinson, and North, and in its large number of other officers, which included such figures as William E. Dodge and Josiah Strong, the League had a leadership which inspired general confidence.[86] Its basic influence was exerted in its series of annual conventions in such cities as Boston, Philadelphia, Hartford and Chicago.[87] The League aided the movement also through its correspondence and publication. To direct these an executive office was established in New York City, in 1895, headed by the Reverend E. B. Sanford as corresponding secretary. After April, 1897, Sanford edited the *Open Church*, a monthly paper dealing with every aspect of the modern church problem. The *Open Church* was particularly significant for its excellent descriptions of the new institutions which had sprung up in the chief cities. In this way, Christians for the first time obtained an adequate picture of the changing religious scheme.

Thus by 1900 the institutional church had assumed an important place in American life. Its influence is hard to measure quantitatively. The one contemporary leader, Russell H. Conwell, who attempted to do so, reported at the end of the century a hundred seventy-three institutional churches.[88] He admitted, however, that some may have escaped his attention. Obviously, this estimate can be accepted only if the term "institutional" is restricted to churches engaged in a well-rounded social service

---

[85] "Platform," *loc. cit.*

[86] J. W. Stuckenberg, "Social Study and Social Work," *Homiletic Rev.,* XXXIII (March 1897), 276.

[87] *Outlook*, Oct. 21, 1896, pp. 793–794; *The Commons*, V (September 1900), 20.

[88] "The Church of the Future," *Our Day*, XIX (July 1899), 205.

and if missions and many other agencies are excluded. Nor are sweeping statements about the comparative interest of the denominations in the movement justifiable. All that can be truthfully said is that the Protestant Episcopal and the Congregational groups seemed to be more active than the others. In practically all cities, Episcopal churches in strategic locations added parish houses to their ecclesiastical architecture.[89] Likewise, Congregationalists, in all parts of the country, adopted the institutional form with great enthusiasm. The *Congregationalist* remarked that it "is consonant with the energy and vitality of Congregationalism to push out as a pioneer into untried fields."[90] But the preëminence of these sects in this aspect of religio-social effort did not imply, as will be seen, their equal strength in other branches.

As to the significance of the movement, one may generalize more confidently. The growing alienation of labor in the urban-industrial crisis after 1880 saddened and perplexed many ministers and lay folk. As they agonized over the problem, they decided upon progressive methods of church work, feeling that no persons were beyond religion's reach if Christians would devote time and money to the task of influencing them. In a broader sense, the institutional church was the religious phase of the increasing determination to implement under urban conditions the inherited ideals of humanitarian democracy. Like the social settlements, the new churches superbly embodied the principles of the new education and the new charity. In the interests of greater adaptability, many institutional churches and missions discarded all ecclesiastical formality and became Christian social settlements in fact and sometimes in name.[91] Whatever technique it from time to time employed, the institutional church movement was but a means to the great end of

[89] For its vast range, see George W. Shinn, *King's Handbook of Notable Episcopal Churches in the United States* (Boston, 1889).

[90] "The Institutional Church Up to Date," May 4, 1893, p. 689.

[91] Anson P. Atterbury, "The Church Settlement," *Open Church*, I (October 1897), 161–173.

Christianizing society. Often, of course, the churches confused ends and means, either attempting to make philanthropy do the work of social justice or substituting one or both of these for genuine spiritual power. But the great leaders at least kept the real meaning of the movement in the foreground.

CHAPTER VII

COOPERATIVE PHASES OF THE INSTITUTIONAL CHURCH MOVEMENT

Though many institutional churches relied upon their own initiative and resources, others enjoyed a large measure of outside direction and guidance. The denominational and non-sectarian coöperative bodies supported humanitarian churches and missions. Progressive Protestants had long urged associated effort as the only effective way of enabling the churches to remain in the poorer sections of the city. Some form of general oversight was all the more necessary after 1885 when improved urban transportation, especially the trolley car, accelerated the exodus of the middle classes and their houses of worship from the industrial to the suburban areas. In order to save, and also to restore, the down-town church, every important denomination consolidated its scattered forces by means of city missionary societies. These local coördinating organizations received aid from the various denominational national assemblies and agencies. Likewise city and inter city non-sectarian groups applied the same principle to Protestantism at large.

The Methodists most clearly typified this approach to the city problem, for most of their institutional churches and social settlements grew out of extension societies for consolidating their denomination in urban communities. During the last two decades of the century, they founded nearly fifty of these societies and federated them in city evangelization unions. In so doing they were following the example of English Wesleyans, whose Forward Movement comprised a large Church Extension Fund for the erection of commodious houses of worship in slum sections and a Wesleyan Methodist Mission for philanthropic activity.[1] After endorsing the church extension society in

[1] *Aggressive Methodism*, III (November 1891), 6–10.

1888,[2] the American bishops repeatedly recurred to the matter, declaring in 1896, for example, that "Methodism in our cities should be slow to abandon what are called down-town populations because of changes from native to foreign, and rich to poor. The greater the change the more need of our remaining. Combine the plants, if need be; adapt them and the services to the new surroundings but remain and save the people."[3] Progressive Methodist opinion favored the institutional church as the only remedy.[4]

The Societies in New York, Boston, Brooklyn, Baltimore, Cincinnati and Chicago were typical. Though those in New York and Boston dated from 1866, they were relatively inactive till the late eighties. The remaining ones were formed much later, mostly in the nineties. All of them emphasized church extension. The New York City Church Extension and Missionary Society aided all New York Methodist churches established after 1871 as well as those weakened by shifts in population. Its forty-five enterprises, on which it expended over two and a half million dollars by 1900, were mostly in the region below Fourteenth Street [5] — a fact justifying the *Outlook's* statement that at least one denomination had not deserted the down-town sections.[6] The Boston Society after its reorganization in 1891 specialized in church building and mission work, and the newly founded Baltimore and Brooklyn Societies proposed to build churches and chapels for those unreached by older ones.[7] The Cincinnati Society, organized in 1888, aimed to unify the city's Methodism "by rendering financial assistance to the needy

[2] General Conference, *Journal*, 1888, pp. 57–59.
[3] *Ibid.*, 1896, p. 60.
[4] George P. Mains, "The Church and the City," *Methodist Review*, LXXVI (March 1894), 221–237; P. H. Swift, "The Problem of Religious Life in the City," *ibid.*, LXXXII (May 1900), 414.
[5] *Christian City*, XI (October 1899), 172–184; *ibid.*, XII (December 1900), 97–143.
[6] L (Oct. 13, 1894), 595.
[7] Gen. Conf., *Journal*, 1896, p. 690; *Zion's Herald*, Nov. 24, 1897, p. 750; *Christian City*, VI (June 1894), 3.

churches and drawing from the more prosperous ones workers
for the mission Sunday schools and Gospel meetings." [8] It succeeded so well that in 1896 the Church invited it "to take the
responsibility of deciding in what new field it is desirable to
undertake city mission work." [9] The Chicago society scored
the most brilliant record. Incorporated in 1885 as the Chicago
Home Missionary and Church Extension Society, it was generously supported by prominent lay folk and ably led, first by
Luke Hitchcock and then by "the incomparable Rev. A. D.
Traveller." By 1900 the Society had raised over a million
dollars for a hundred churches which comprised at least a third
of the Methodist membership of the city. All this was accomplished in face of opposition from shining lights in the Church
who preferred cathedrals to small houses of worship.[10]

Besides the church extension and city mission society, Methodists developed other consolidating bodies. Thus, the Social
Union of New York, formed in 1887 to "bring together the
ministers and laymen" of all the churches for the prosecution
of movements necessitating concurrent action, was extensively
copied all over the country.[11] The various societies promoted
their joint interests through the National City Evangelization
Union of the Methodist Episcopal Church, formed during
a convention at Cleveland of the General Missionary Society.[12] At its first meeting in March, 1892, the Union memorial-
ized the Church for approval. On granting the request, the
General Conference urged the Union to set up "local organizations" in all places having five or more charges "for the purpose
of affording financial aid to needy churches, organizing new
enterprises and conducting religious work among the religiously

---

[8] J. R. Clark, "Address," City Evangelization Union, *Proceedings*, 1892, pp. 35–36.

[9] Gen. Conf., *Journal*, 1896, p. 695.

[10] Stephen J. Herben, "Methodism in Chicago," *Zion's Herald*, June 5, 1895, pp. 354–355; *Christian City*, X (December 1898), 730.

[11] New York Conference, *Minutes*, 1888, p. 61.

[12] *Christian City*, VIII (January 1896), 4–5.

destitute." [13] The Union exerted great influence through its yearly conventions in the large cities. Early presidents included the Reverend D. H. Carroll of Baltimore, Hudson Samson of Pittsburgh, Horace Hitchcock of Detroit and Dr. John E. James of Philadelphia. The well known institutional church leaders, George P. Mains of Brooklyn and Frank Mason North of New York, served as corresponding secretaries. The actual founder of the Union, Horace Benton, a drug manufacturer of Cleveland, aided it at every turn.[14]

The Union's leaders insisted that an effective church-extension movement must include social reform. The alleviation of human misery, North pointed out, falls within the scope of the Gospel since the problem of poverty "lies very close to the problem of sin." In its urban form, poverty was not that delicate suffering portrayed by Mary E. Wilkins in her New England stories, but "a crowding, brutalizing, crushing horror which makes one sneer at civilization and wonder if God has forgotten to be just." It was within the power of the church "to recast the life of the wretched poor of our great cities" since many social evils were "curable by law" and since false social teaching could be "rebuked and overthrown." [15] The Reverend P. S. Merrill of Buffalo at the Union's seventh convention said that if "you would save the people, who are in squalor, poverty and degradation, exchange their tenements for homes. And to do that you must put your finger on legislation and wealth and the more highly developed and refined citizenship of the commonwealth. If you wish to prevent the perpetuation of slum life, you may as well understand that it will not be done altogether by direct evangelization." [16]

In its various conventions the Union evaluated the agencies of the new philanthropy, particularly the social settlements. All

[13] *Journal*, 1892, pp. 460–461.
[14] *Christian City*, VI (April 1894), 5; *ibid.* (May 1894), 11.
[15] *Zion's Herald*, Feb. 1, 1893, p. 36.
[16] *Zion's Herald*, Nov. 24, 1897, p. 753.

speakers agreed that the congregations by means of the humanitarian parish house could attain greater success with the poor. The third convention issued an "Address to the Methodist Episcopal Church in the Cities of the United States," urging members to establish immediately at least one institutional church in every city.[17] The various local societies echoed the program of the national Union. In 1891 the New York Society sponsored the lectures of the English Wesleyan, the Reverend Hugh Price Hughes, on social Christianity. In the same year, before a great mass meeting in Carnegie Hall held to promote city evangelization, Bowles Colgate, the Society's president, urged that the time had come to consider whether "perhaps radical changes in our methods are not necessary," and if we should not take "a leaf from the book of our friends of the Protestant Episcopal Church in this city and man our churches and mission stations more largely and more strongly than we have done." [18] In its excellent periodicals, *Aggressive Methodism*, established in 1889, and *The Christian City*, which supplanted it, the New York Society aided the whole American Methodist Forward Movement. Other cities also displayed interest. The Baltimore and Kansas City Societies took note of the fact in 1894 that while genuine homes predominated in their respective cities the tenement evil was growing: a fact underscoring the need for social Christianity.[19]

The New York Society established several institutional churches. As North wrote in 1897, the Society during previous years had begun addressing itself "not alone to the founding and supporting of churches and Sunday schools, but to the larger ministry which social conditions are forcing upon it." [20]

---

[17] *Aggressive Methodism*, V (December 1893), 5.

[18] *Ibid.*, III (November 1891), 5, 12.

[19] Benjamin P. White, "Aggressive Movements in Kansas City," *Christian City*, VI (April 1894), 3; W. W. Davis, "City Missionary and Church Extension Work in Baltimore," *ibid.* (June 1894), 3.

[20] "The New Era of Church Work in New York," *ibid.*, IX (January 1897), 20–24.

For example, the Allen Street Memorial, once a flourishing family church, had failed by 1890 because of the Jewish invasion of its neighborhood. Reëstablished as a mission on Rivington Street, it attained success again when institutionalized by the Reverend Horace W. Byrnes and his associates.[21] The Eleventh Street and the Asbury Methodist congregations, faced with similar problems, were likewise transformed under Ernest L. Fox and James S. Stone respectively as leaders.[22] Somewhat later the Asbury Church combined with Washington Square Church to make possible a more extensive service. Two churches in New York, Calvary and the Cornell Memorial, though independent of the Society, enjoyed its aid on changing to the new type in the early nineties.[23] Besides helping these churches, the Society sponsored miscellaneous social agencies,[24] a fact prompting the *Outlook* to remark that "the City Mission Society of the Methodist Church is in itself a great institutional church, with twenty-three different branches." [25]

In similar fashion societies elsewhere participated in social reform. The Boston Society's most "interesting features" were its "philanthropic and charitable ministries." [26] Among these was the Morgan Chapel, which with Unitarian assistance developed into a splendidly equipped institutional church.[27] The Philadelphia Society, besides its social agencies at several churches, converted the Old Fifth Street Church into a People's Temple.[28] In the early nineties the Society in Baltimore ex-

---

[21] "Allen Street Memorial," *ibid.*, XI (February 1899), 36–37.

[22] *Christian City*, XII (March 1900), 75–76; *ibid.*, VI (November 1894), 6–7; *ibid.*, XII (October 1900), 144–150; George J. Manson, "How Rich and Poor Meet Together at Asbury Church," *Christian Union*, April 8, 1893, pp. 865–866.

[23] William Baldwin, "The Gospel of Ministration in a Methodist Episcopal Church," *Christian City*, VIII (February 1896), 5–6; "Cornell Memorial Church," *ibid.*, X (April 1898), 453–459.

[24] "Summer Work," *ibid.*, XI (August 1899), 142–143.

[25] *The Outlook*, July 11, 1896, p. 65.

[26] New England Meth. Epis. Church, *Annual Conf.*, 1897, p. 73.

[27] E. J. Helms, "Morgan Chapel," *Christian City*, XI (February 1899), 60–65.

[28] Moseley H. Williams, "The New Era of Church Work in Philadelphia," *Open Church*, I (April 1897), 73; *ibid.* (July 1897), 121.

panded the activities of the Patterson Memorial Church and the Eutaw Street Church.[29] The Forward Movement in Detroit began in 1893 under William F. Sheridan, a graduate of the Boston University School of Theology. After opening a Mission Hall on Gratiat Avenue to foster a four-fold work, he institutionalized a down-town house of worship on the resignation of its pastor to accept the presidency of Lawrence College.[30] Harry F. Ward commenced his distinguished career by socializing the Wabash Avenue Church of Chicago in 1895.[31] In all their work, the various Methodist societies wisely approached the immigrant peoples through missionaries acquainted with their languages and customs.

For the purpose of accelerating the social program, the church-extension societies expected active support from the official Church. While Methodists were raising large sums for progressive church work, the General Missionary Society was ignoring the city in favor of the frontier and the foreign fields. "Does it not seem," asked *Zion's Herald*, "as if the leaders of our Israel had failed to interpret the heart and purpose of our people with respect to the city problem?"[32] Finally in 1900 the General Conference took the matter in hand, ordering the General Missionary Society to coöperate with the city societies, requiring presiding elders to shoulder responsibility for social service and abolishing the time limit on urban pastorates. This legislation "will prove not only that the purpose of the church includes the evangelization of the cities," said the National City Evangelization Union, "but it will stimulate the proper organization of the forces in the various cities that they may properly be associated with so important a forward movement."[33]

[29] W. Sheers, "The Election to Service," *Christian City*, XII (April 1900), 81–82; *Zion's Herald*, Nov. 24, 1897, pp. 750–751.
[30] W. F. Sheridan, "Detroit's Forward Movement," *Christian City*, VI (February 1894), 10; *ibid.* (September 1894), 11.
[31] *Christian City*, VII (October 1895), 7.
[32] "City Evangelization," Dec. 23, 1896, p. 828.
[33] *Christian City*, XII (April 1900), 86.

Like Methodism, the largest Protestant denomination, the lesser ones applied the consolidating idea in their religious work. The Dutch Reformed Church in New York was coöperative in theory, its official name being the (Collegiate) Reformed Protestant Dutch Church of the City of New York. In practice, however, it was a religio-social club, only one of its three churches and three chapels having remained in the working-class districts. But in its *Year-Book*, beginning in 1880, the Church aimed "to emphasize the fact that the different congregations under the care of the consistory are but parts of the same church, members of one body, pervaded by a common life and having a common interest." The Consistory determined also "to hold at least some of the ground below Fourteenth Street." When in 1887 the old Middle Church on Fourth Street and Lafayette Place failed as a family house of worship, a new edifice rose in the same region. Completed in 1892, this Second Avenue and Seventh Street building was a beautiful Gothic free church and parish house. The latter, said the *Year-Book*, contains "an abundance of rooms, and all modern appliances for church work." With its reading room, gymnasium and other agencies it afforded "special opportunities for instruction, recreation and physical training." [34]

The up-town churches and chapels gradually elaborated programs of social service. Although the Fifth Avenue Church at Twenty-ninth Street was but little affected, the work of the one at Forty-eighth Street assumed large proportions. Its Society for Christian Work in 1885 started a boy's club on West Fifty-first Street, which succeeded in taming the unruly youngsters of the neighborhood. The pastor, Edward B. Coe, justified this philanthropic venture on the ground that, "whatever leads to a better understanding of the duties of life, and a better preparation for discharge of its responsibilities makes ready for the

[34] *Year-Book of the (Collegiate) Reformed Protestant Dutch Church of the City of New York*, 1881, p. 1; *ibid.*, 1892, p. 101; *ibid.*, 1893, pp. 32, 37, 127–147.

reception of higher truth." [35] Vermilye Chapel, organized in 1891 alongside the club, realized his expectation. In order to make the Chapel a more effective social center, the mother congregation leased a large building from the Ladies Helping Hand Association. Social activities at the three chapels were no less extensive. The Seventh Avenue Chapel — Grace Reformed Church after 1885 — launched its program in 1882 by organizing a young peoples' society and a kitchen garden. The DeWitt Chapel started a kitchen garden in 1878, fresh-air aid in 1881 and a kindergarten and gymnastics in 1892. The work at Knox Memorial Chapel practically duplicated that at the others. A unique feature was a Loan Relief Association formed to "develop and foster a spirit of industry and independence in the place of the too prevalent willingness to depend upon charity." [36] On receiving from the Consistory in 1898 a new building on the model of the beautiful Middle Church, Knox Memorial became a truly institutional church.[37] Another structure, provided in 1891 for upper New York, was not content to be merely a family church, creating a "mission committee" for service at Vermilye Chapel.[38]

The Unitarian group confined its associated effort to the city of its main strength. By means of the Boston Fraternity of Churches, organized in Channing's day, Unitarians supported five mission chapels, carried on Sunday school work and distributed alms and relief.[39] But by the middle eighties the Fraternity could see no point in insisting on religious instruction "when there is no possibility of producing any good results." While the foreign-born population was particularly indifferent to religion, the masses generally were "eagerly striving to better their condition," said the executive committee, "without stopping to consider whether their methods are going to improve

[35] *Ibid.*, 1888, pp. 46–47.
[36] *Ibid.*, 1883, p. 48.
[37] *Ibid.*, 1899, pp. 830–833.
[38] *Ibid.*, 1892, pp. 110–116.
[39] Ellen M. Tower, "The North End Union," *Bostonian*, II (July 1895), 393.

their condition or not, — seeking rather it would seem to overturn and destroy than to build up." For this reason the Fraternity entered upon social service "to keep the popular sentiment pure and wholesome rather than to let it degenerate into corruption and vulgarity."[40]

At least three of its chapels became institutional churches and social centers. Having failed by religious means to reach the Catholics and Jews of its neighborhood, the Parmenter Street Chapel under Fred Chandler's leadership decided in 1889 to seek "in other directions to exert at least a generally civilizing and uplifting influence."[41] The agencies used included a loan fund, clubs for boys and girls, a kindergarten, a dressmaking department and lectures and concerts. In 1892 the Reverend John Tunis changed Unity Chapel into the Church of the Savior. Assisted by his wife, he established a series of clubs, and secured the services of a district nurse. During the same year the North End Chapel, also realizing the futility of the traditional approach, reorganized as the North End Union. In charge of a lawyer, S. F. Hubbard, the Union planned "to make a social home for young men, to stimulate a better intellectual life, to promote good citizenship and to lend a hand wherever needed." As a social settlement, it was recognized as a permanent factor for the improvement of the North End. "It is regarded," it was said, "as a coöperative agent by the police department, the public schools and the reform organizations."[42] Edwin D. Mead and his clerical friends, Brooke Hereford, Edward A. Horton and S. W. Brooke, were largely responsible for the Fraternity's enlarged program.

Although coöperation within the Congregational, Presbyterian and Baptist Churches was not stressed as much as in the Methodist and the smaller bodies, it was nevertheless important. By means of earnest, intelligent discussions and through various committees on city evangelization, Congregationalists took the

[40] *Report*, 1890, pp. 4–5.
[41] *Ibid.*, 1891, p. 4.
[42] *Ibid.*, 1892, p. 13; *ibid.*, 1896, p. 8.

first steps toward adjusting their working forces to the institutional church movement.[43] Thus the State Association of Massachusetts endorsed the people's church as "a timely and characteristic expression of the one spirit of God in Christ," approved its methods "as susceptible of real and effective spiritual purpose" and welcomed them "among the agencies which the Church of Christ may legitimately use in the great work of city evangelization."[44] In view of the fact that isolated congregations went "after the rich to the neglect of the poor,"[45] the urban churches turned to the incorporated city missionary society, having by 1900 active organizations in a score of the larger cities. The Chicago City Missionary Society, formed in 1883 under the direction of the Reverend E. P. Goodwin and Dr. Samuel Ives Curtiss "to promote religion and morality in Chicago and vicinity," pioneered the way. Within twenty years the Society had spent seven million dollars and added over sixty churches, giving about equal attention to the down-town and suburban sections. The coming of the Chicago Society, said Henry A. Stimson, ushered in "an aggressive Christianity and a genuine Christian brotherhood applied to its own home territory."[46] The National Council in 1889 advised "the formation of such societies in all cities where they do not exist."[47]

The various societies aided nearly every type of modern church work. The Chicago Society, for example, emphasized industrial education as well as church extension. The Boston Society, the oldest city mission organization among the Congregationalists, practiced the new philanthropy while continuing its old specialties of house-to-house visitation and poor relief. In several cases, the societies assisted the institutional churches. In Hartford, Connecticut, the Pastors' Mission, as the Society was called, helped the Fourth Church, its action

---

[43] National Council, *Minutes*, 1892, pp. 240–253; *ibid.*, 1895, pp. 2, 108–114.
[44] *Minutes*, 1895, pp. 19–20, 113–114.
[45] National Council, *Minutes*, 1886, pp. 223–225.
[46] "Report on City Evangelization," *ibid.*, 1898, pp. 290–292.
[47] *Minutes*, 1889, p. 295.

being "another example on a smaller scale," said Graham Taylor, "of the success of associated evangelistic effort from a church center."[48] In St. Paul, Minnesota, the Congregational Union, representing ten churches, provided money and workers for the parish house of the People's Church which had been founded in 1885 by the Reverend Samuel G. Smith as an independent venture.[49]

The national agencies of the denomination, the American Home Missionary Society and the American Congregational Union, moved into line with the new mission policy. The former, an organization for frontier missions, decided in its "new departure" of 1883 that aid to city churches was "a wise expenditure of home missionary money."[50] For a time it considered the advisability of appointing a secretary for work in cities, but finally concluded that a better policy would be to subsidize the local churches through their city missionary societies.[51] In this way the Society was giving to cities a third of its total receipts by 1895.[52] A special fund, donated in 1885 by Samuel W. Sweet, a Boston Unitarian, provided a considerable source of income.

A similar change took place in the American Congregational Union, a church building body, which before 1886 had refused to give more to a city than to a rural church, notwithstanding the cost differential. But in that year a committee of the National Council urged realistic action and the raising of two hundred thousand dollars for urban houses of worship. Of the one hundred and fifty thousand dollars secured in 1887, a large part was bestowed as gifts and the remainder, eighty-six thousand dollars, kept as a National Council Church Fund.

[48] "Do We Need Churches or Missions, or Both, in City Evangelization?" Convention of Christian Workers, *Proceedings*, 1887, p. 202.

[49] *Congregationalist*, Dec. 17, 1891, p. 439.

[50] Walter M. Barrows, "New Aspects of Our Home Work," *Home Missionary*, LVI (August 1883), 156; Joseph B. Clark, "The Historic Policy and the New Work of the American Home Missionary Society," *ibid.*, LVIII (July 1885), 80.

[51] *Home Missionary*, LX (July 1887), 85–86.

[52] National Council, *Minutes*, 1895, p. 178.

The changing trend in these general institutions was expected to redound to the city missionary society which the National Council of 1889 endorsed as "the best intermediary between the American Home Missionary Society, or the American Congregational Union, and the field." [53]

Coöperative effort among Presbyterians resembled that among their Congregational brethren. As social problems became acute, Presbyterians expected the presbyteries to become in fact what they were in theory — city mission societies. The Synod of New York reported in 1880 that the need was "so distinct and important that we see no way of reaching it but by the Presbytery itself. It will need explanation to understand all that is demanded, organization and superintendence, and no small amount of money to carry the work forward." [54] Within a few years, in all the larger cities, many presbyteries, aided in some cases by Presbyterian Alliances and Social Unions, followed these suggestions. In Philadelphia one outcome was Beacon Presbyterian Church, located in the Kensington manufacturing section. The church-extension committee of the Presbytery in 1885 commissioned its chairman, the Reverend Francis L. Robbins, to establish a mission, which soon developed into a church to minister "not only to the spiritual, but also to the physical and intellectual needs of the common people." [55] It exemplified nearly every aspect of the new philanthropy, one of its special features being Beacon College, similar in plan to the neighboring Bethany College. By appealing to the membership for increased interest and by granting money from the Board of Home Missions to the presbyteries, the Presbyterian Church as a whole promoted the city missionary movement.[56] To the same purpose was the journal, *The Church at Home and Abroad*, authorized in 1886 by the General Assembly. Edited by the Reverend Henry A. Nelson, the magazine

---

[53] *Ibid.*, 1889, p. 295.   [54] *Minutes*, 1880, p. 14.
[55] *Golden Rule*, Jan. 27, 1887, p. 9.
[56] General Assembly, *Minutes*, 1887, pp. 71–72; *ibid.*, 1891, p. 274.

dealt not only with sectarian matters but "with other benevolent interests in which, though Christian rather than denominational, members of the Presbyterian Church in many parts of the country, notably in great cities, are so largely engaged." [57]

The coöperative movement among the Baptists proved considerably stronger than among the Presbyterians. In the meetings of the Baptist Congress [58] and the American Baptist Home Missionary Society, leading members thoroughly discussed urban religious problems, agreeing that the institutional church was desperately necessary. Before the latter body Johnston Myers, pastor of a Cincinnati institutional church, showed from his extensive correspondence with city Baptists that from using conventional methods the down-town churches were dying. "A man," he said, "may preach the pure Gospel in such a way as to lose even his deacons." [59] Likewise Baptists realized that the whole denominational brotherhood in each city must assume responsibility for churches and missions in the industrial areas.[60] To this end, city missionary societies arose, there being at least thirty by 1895. About twenty of these were efficient agencies, eight of them with salaried superintendents giving full time to the work. Yearly receipts for religious purposes totalled a hundred and fifty thousand dollars, half of which was raised from the societies in Boston, New York, Brooklyn and Philadelphia. The various societies supported altogether a hundred and fifty missions. Some of the earlier societies had not been truly missionary. Thus, the New York City Mission had lent money to weak churches only on mortgage, in this way forcing them to become aristocratic congregations as quickly as possible. But in the early nineties the Mission overthrew this "self-perpetuating junto," this "unrecognized episcopacy," for a policy of church extension on human-

[57] *Ibid.*, 1887, pp. 59–68.
[58] "Enlarged Church Work in Cities," *Discussions*, 1890, pp. 131–167.
[59] "City Missions," *Minutes*, 1895, pp. 10–12.
[60] "The Down-Town Church," *Watchman*, Nov. 7, 1894, p. 4.

itarian lines, typifying, no doubt, the changing attitudes of societies elsewhere.[61]

Baptists were fairly successful in associating their coöperative endeavor with institutional church work. The Boston Society wisely kept the congregations "where the needy multitudes can reach them." [62] Its Committee on Christian Work, appointed in 1882 with Daniel S. Ford as chairman, raised in the following fifteen years seventy thousand dollars, in addition to the large gifts of Ford himself, for the support of weak houses of worship.[63] At least five Baptist churches developed a high order of social service, sponsoring lectures for working people, literary unions and classes in many subjects and setting up employment bureaus, dispensaries and food and fuel depots.[64] The Ruggles Street Church was noteworthy. Though covering the entire philanthropic field, it stressed trade education, the "evangel of handicraft," since the poverty of its clientele was due largely to lack of skill.[65] The course of the Boston Society, "if followed by other similar bodies, and by more of our churches," said the Reverend Albert G. Lawson, "would go very far toward putting an end to the labor troubles." [66] Several cities did try to follow the Boston example. The Baptist City Mission of New York, for example, supported the well-known Mariner's Temple, at which, besides religious exercises in three languages, Baptist folk extended relief, kindergarten, day-nursery and industrial service. The Mission carried on a threefold program — "the evangelistic, the educational and the institutional." [67]

[61] Leighton Williams, *Enlarged Church Work in Cities* (New York, 1890), pp. 6–8.

[62] *Watchman*, March 17, 1898, p. 12.   [63] *Ibid.*, March 21, 1895, p. 4.

[64] Daniel E. Owen, "Free Reading Rooms Among the Boston Baptist Churches," *Golden Rule*, Nov. 28, 1889, p. 141.

[65] Everett D. Burr, "Methods of an Open and Institutional Church," *Open Church*, I (April 1898), 96–99; William T. Ellis, "The New Era of Church Work," *ibid.* (January 1898), 205–213.

[66] "The Labor Question," Baptist Cong., *Discussions*, 1886, p. 58.

[67] *Annual Report*, 1898–99, p. 20.

Though all the Baptist city missionary societies needed outside support and oversight, the American Baptist Home Missionary Society was committed historically to frontier work, holding that "aid in behalf of immigrant populations in cities and towns where there are strong churches is incidental." [68] But it altered its attitude as social strife threatened the nation's unity. Following the Anarchist outbreak in Chicago, the Society observed that, if it should decide "that broader and more effective measures should be used to strengthen our work within its bounds, it would only be doing what the brethren of other names are planning to do on a most liberal and comprehensive scale." [69] After further consideration over several years, the Society finally acted, reporting in 1898 that it had entered into relations with the Baptist City Mission of Chicago on a plan to be extended presently to the leading cities of the country.[70]

As they consolidated their agencies for social service, the three denominations, Congregational, Presbyterian and Baptist, trained ministers in the various foreign languages for the immigrant peoples. While the regular ministry sufficed for the children of immigrants, it exerted no appreciable influence over the older folk.[71] "In order to reach any powerful body of foreign people, *in a large way*," agreed a Congregational missionary, "there must be a native ministry springing from among the people themselves." [72] To this end the Congregationalists, in the "new departure" of their American Home Missionary Society in 1883, created three departments, each with a superintendent, to deal with Germans, Scandinavians and Slavs. In George E. Albrecht, W. W. Montgomery and Henry A. Schauffler the Society found able preachers and administrators,

[68] *Proceedings*, 1878, pp. 37–38.
[69] *Ibid.*, 1887, pp. 55–56.
[70] *Ibid.*, 1898, pp. 133–34; *ibid.*, 1900, p. 154.
[71] "Immigrant Populations," Gen. Assembly of the Presby. Church in the U.S.A., *Minutes*, 1889, pp. 44–45.
[72] George E. Albrecht, "Address," *Home Missionary*, LXIII (August 1885), 145–146.

equipped by association or training to adjust their respective groups to American religious conditions.[73] By means of a Bible Readers' School working along social-settlement lines among the Slavs of Cleveland, Schauffler recruited converts and trained them for the seminaries.[74] Similarly, the Reverend E. A. Adams developed a great institutional mission among the Poles of Chicago. Through these and more conventional methods the Congregationalists gathered by the end of the century a hundred and thirty-three German, ninety Swedish, twenty Danish-Norwegian and sixteen Slavic churches.[75] As a result of constant study and agitation, the Presbyterians secured over a hundred and fifty German churches, clustered in Brooklyn, Philadelphia and Cincinnati, nearly fifty congregations among the Scotch and Scotch-Irish of New England, a dozen or more among the Bohemians, who have a certain affinity for the Reformed faith, and a few among other nationalities.[76] Baptists also encouraged foreign-speaking churches, particularly among the Germans and the Scandinavians.

The regular seminaries trained the majority of ministers for the immigrant churches. Thus, Congregationalists provided courses and professors at Chicago Seminary for the Germans and Scandinavians in 1882 and 1884 respectively, and for the Slavs at Oberlin in 1885.[77] So ample were these facilities that by 1900 a body of clergymen ready to meet all calls for independent or assistant pastorates had come into existence. In

---

[73] National Council, *Minutes*, 1886, p. 121; *Home Missionary*, LXIII (March 1891), 482–483; *ibid.*, LXI (December 1888), 364–365.

[74] A. Schauffler, "The School for Bohemian Bible Readers," *ibid.*, LXII (March 1891), 501; National Council, *Minutes*, 1886, pp. 122–123; *ibid.*, 1892, pp. 251–252.

[75] A. Schauffler, "The Foreign Element in American Civilization," National Council, *Minutes*, 1901, p. 289.

[76] Gen. Assembly, *Minutes*, 1888, pp. 220–221; *ibid.*, 1903, p. 108.

[77] National Council, *Minutes*, 1886, pp. 271–276; *ibid.*, 1889, p. 131; *ibid.*, 1892, pp. 133–135; W. W. Montgomery, "The Work Among the Scandinavians," *Home Missionary*, LVIII (March 1886), 402; "An Important Conference," *ibid.*, LIX (June 1886), 40–41.

1895 the Congregational Home Missionary Society wrote that the once "greatest desideratum, — trained Congregational pastors, — to supply these churches of foreign tongues, is now supplied in a degree almost beyond our power of use, through the Oberlin and Chicago Theological Seminaries, whose well-equipped graduates stand ready to enlarge the field of our missionary service wherever the means are at the command of this society to employ them." [78] Baptists gave their instruction also in the old seminaries, having a German department at Rochester, a Scandinavian one at Chicago and a French division in Newton Theological Institution.[79] Presbyterians, however, established for the Germans two separate theological schools, one at Dubuque, Iowa, and another at Newark, New Jersey. The Congregationalists also had one independent agency: the French Protestant College at Lowell, Massachusetts, organized by the Reverend C. E. Ameron.[80]

Though Episcopalians had established many city missionary societies in the early urban period, some of them had ceased to function by the middle eighties. This applied to the Episcopal City Mission of Boston, for example, which in 1888 reorganized with the Reverend F. B. Allen as superintendent. In the following years the Mission engaged in prison, hospital and immigrant service, besides helping Charles H. Brent and his assistants at St. Stephen's Church with their social settlement. A second step in the unification of Episcopal forces was the centering of control over church building and related matters in the hands of bishops. Believing that the "poor of a great city, the outcast and stranger, the criminal and the pauper, should be preëminently his parishioners," Bishop Potter took charge of the New York Episcopal City Mission and its activities after

[78] National Council, *Minutes*, 1895, p. 197.

[79] "Annual Report of the Board," Am. Bapt. Home Mission. Soc., *Proceedings*, 1882, p. 58; *ibid.*, 1884, p. 44.

[80] *Home Missionary*, LX (July 1887), 103–104; C. E. Ameron, "French Evangelization," *ibid.*, 1900, pp. 72–73.

1885.[81] Another invigorating and unifying influence was the Parochial Mission, the Episcopal equivalent of the "revival" among evangelical bodies. Thus, in 1885, a large number of churches, after a two years' preparation, held the celebrated Advent Mission which reached many thousands of people in New York City.[82] The Reverend Henry Y. Satterlee believed that the Mission afforded him and his associates enough spiritual power to expand the institutional program of Calvary Church. To one of his helpers, he wrote that, above "all other things I feel that our united prayers, first in the Advent Mission and then in the continuation of those meetings for intercessory prayer which we held Sunday after Sunday, have been the seed of faith which under God has produced such a blessed result." [83]

Quite as influential as the Advent Mission [84] were the score or more of church clubs in as many cities for the discussion of religio-social problems. The New York Club, formed in the late eighties and described as "the Church's right hand in rescue work and city evangelization," would abandon the "technical modes of salvation . . . until we can get something done for the material help of the people." [85] Its five hundred members, fearing that America was going the way of eighteenth-century France, insisted that Episcopalians unite to secure social reforms ranging from house-to-house visitation to the abolition of child labor. While relying chiefly upon the parish houses,

[81] Prot. Epis. Church, New York, *Journal*, 1885, p. 128; *ibid.*, 1886, p. 53; *ibid.*, 1897, pp. 138–139; *ibid.*, 1900, pp. 72–73.

[82] "General Mission in New York City" (manuscript).

[83] "Letter to Dr. W. C. Rives, July 5, 1886, Relative to Social Work at Galilee Mission," quoted in C. H. Brent, *A Master Builder, Henry Y. Satterlee*, pp. 103–104.

[84] In order to conserve and extend the influence of the Advent Mission, Episcopalians formed the Parochial Mission Society with Satterlee as first chairman. One of the Society's chief interests was responsibility for several Church Army posts practicing religion along Salvation Army lines. See Montague Chamberlain, *The Church Army*; H. H. Hadley, "What Is the United States Church Army?" *Christian City*, IX (February 1897), 61–62; Church Army in New Haven, *Report*, 1898, pp. 2 ff.

[85] *Churchman*, May 21, 1892, p. 648.

the Club also favored independent effort as often the only way to reach people who were prejudiced against ecclesiastical institutions.[86] Mainly for this reason, the Club in 1891 established the East Side House, one of the first great social settlements in America.[87] Though the other clubs did not engage in social work so extensively, they all were alike otherwise, even in name, except in Pittsburgh, where the designation, Laymen's Missionary League, was used. Founded in 1889 to promote religion and charity, this League rendered invaluable aid by means of its lay readers, evangelists, Sunday School superintendents, physicians and social workers.[88] Beginning in 1893, the various clubs shared experiences in annual conferences.

With these Episcopalian ventures, denominational consolidation for social reform was virtually at an end. Though the many unifying trends vastly expanded progressive church work, additional social service was clearly possible if only the denominations and Christians generally would coöperate. In several cities, notably in Philadelphia, New York and Buffalo, Christians were ready seriously to experiment with the plans recently formulated by the Evangelical Alliance and similar bodies. In the City of Brotherly Love, the Presbyterian Social Union, with the aid of the institutional First Presbyterian Church, formed in 1895 the Christian League of Philadelphia.[89] An Outlook Committee, headed by George Griffiths to investigate social-settlement work, reported that the problem lay beyond the reach of any one denomination, and accordingly suggested a league of all evangelical bodies. As a remedy for urban ills, the founders of the League favored the simultaneous application of

[86] *Churchman*, Feb. 6, 1892, pp. 158–159; *ibid.*, April 9, 1892, pp. 448–450; *ibid.*, Feb. 9, 1895, pp. 199–200.

[87] Prot. Epis. Church, New York, *Journal*, 1891, p. 125; "East Side Work in This City," *Churchman*, Dec. 24, 1892, pp. 848–849.

[88] Cortlandt Whitehead, "The Laymen's Missionary League of Pittsburgh," *ibid.*, Oct. 17, 1896, pp. 467–468; "Laymen in the Episcopal Church," *Outlook*, Oct. 24, 1896, p. 732.

[89] *Lend a Hand*, XIV (April 1895), 251–262; *ibid.*, XIV (June 1895), 465–467; *Open Church*, I (April 1897), 53–56.

the Gospel and the civil law. They, therefore, advised that humanitarian churches and missions be established, and that pressure be exerted on the city government to destroy the slums and to erect model tenements.

The League, with a board of directors representing fifteen denominations, directed its fire at the so-called "coast" region, for a century synonymous with everything evil in urban life. An area of reeking tenements, the "coast" teemed with notorious dives like the "Sparrows Nest," the "Bloody Pit," the "Lovers' Retreat" and other aptly named haunts of entertainment; but they could not withstand the pitiless exposure of the League. In another district close by Independence Hall, the League with strong public support brought about destruction of unfit and the erection of model tenements. Pressure on the city government completed what implacable criticism had commenced.[90] The work of the League, said the sociologist, Stuckenberg, showed not only "what opportunities are open for Christian effort in neglected fields," but also that there was "no necessity for the slums." [91]

In New York, the Federation of East Side Workers, formed in June, 1894, under the leadership of John B. Devins, pastor of Hope Chapel, was of broader scope, including Catholics and Jews as well as Protestants. Convinced by his relief work in the severe winter of 1893–94 that joint action of religious and charitable bodies was imperative, Devins welded the temporary participants in the East Side Relief Workers Committee into an effective organization covering a fourth of the city.[92] The Federation, composed of the pastor, priest or rabbi and an additional member from each church, and the president and one accredited representative from each philanthropic society, was,

---

[90] Charles H. Bond, "The Christian League of Philadelphia," *Open Church*, I (October 1897), 191–195.

[91] *Homiletic Rev.*, XXX (November 1895), 450; *ibid.* (April 1896), 365–366.

[92] E. C. Ray, *John Bancroft Devins* (New York, 1912), pp. 81–86; John B. Devins, "The Federation of East Side Workers," *Altruist Interchange*, IV (October 1896), 11–12.

said Devins, "an honest effort . . . to coöperate along lines upon which there is a general agreement, that time and money may be saved, fraud checked and the people of the coming generation be better fitted to cope with the problems which will confront them." [93] Committees were formed to deal with a wide range of subjects: benevolence, education, labor, small parks, street cleaning, building, sanitation and lectures. While making no effort to create church union, the Federation promoted a better understanding among religious groups, secured an improved administration of charity and influenced legislation. The *Outlook* in 1897 advised that its scheme be extended to the whole city.[94]

More public attention, perhaps, centered on the "Buffalo Plan," a scheme for poor relief originating in the progressive work of the Charity Organization Society and of several institutional churches. Convinced that the churches should supervise the people of their neighborhood just as the politicians looked after the voters, the Society's chairman, Maria Love, drew up a plan in 1895 for parcelling out the city among the congregations. In the meantime the First Presbyterian and the Westminster Presbyterian churches had established social settlements to relieve all the poor within their respective areas. Thereupon the Charity Organization Society prepared a set of principles which, without impairing the spiritual or philanthropic independence of the churches, enabled them to coöperate for social service.[95] It was suggested that

In certain districts the care of children would possibly lead, with the growth of the work, to the establishing of kindergartens, of kitchen gardens, of sewing schools, of carpenter shops and of public playgrounds. Some knowledge of the ways of the men might lead to the establishment of bright, attractive coffee houses, with billiard tables which would ultimately cover the neighboring saloon.

[93] "The Federation of East Side Workers," *loc. cit.*
[94] Quoted in Ray, *op. cit.*, pp. 84–85.
[95] *Charities Review*, IV (June 1895), 460–461; *ibid.*, V (February 1896), 215–218.

Personal intercourse with the women would disclose their ignorance of household economy, and lead to their availing themselves of the privileges offered by the Women's Union, in classes of cooking, laundry work and general household work, and lead, too, to some effort to make the home clean, comfortable and attractive.

By 1901, over a hundred churches, representing the Protestant, Catholic and Jewish faiths, had accepted districts.[96] Though Wilbur F. Crafts's suggestion that "these churches add to their separate work in charity, a united preventive work for social reform," [97] was followed only in part, the congregations greatly improved the character of the poor. Thus, one church in a year's time reduced the number of families on the poor books from a hundred and thirty-four to eight as a result of "lessons of self-help rather than substitution of church money for city money." [98] By means of district conferences, sponsored by the Charity Organization Society, the churches gradually eliminated faulty methods of giving, more and more adopting as their own the principles of organized charity. Frederick Almy, the Society's secretary, highly pleased with the educational value of the plan, declared that, if "the sum total of the charity of the city is improved, we do not care if we, the Charity Organization Society, are not recognized as the only *illuminati*." [99]

These examples of successful coöperation foreshadowed the late-century Federation of Churches movement. This began in 1895 when nearly a hundred and fifty churches and charitable foundations came together in the New York Federation of Churches and Christian Workers — "one of the most practical

[96] *Federation*, II (April 1902), 99; *Charities Review*, VIII (March 1898), 7–8; *ibid.*, VI (March 1897), 83–84.
[97] "The Philanthropic Mission of the Church," *Our Day*, XVI (August 1896), 427.
[98] Quoted in Gladden, *The Christian Minister and the Working Church*, pp. 470–471.
[99] "Church Districts in Charity Work," *Charities Review*, VIII (May 1898), 127–128; see *Churchman*, Jan. 27, 1900, p. 98, for the influence of the "Buffalo Plan" in promoting social settlements.

forms of Christian union," said the *Outlook*, "which has yet been devised."[100] At a meeting of the Alumni Club of Union Theological Seminary in March, 1895, J. Winthrop Hegeman, an Episcopal clergyman, suggested the federation in the course of an address on "What Are the Churches Going to Do About It?" The churches upon whom rested the responsibility of "doing the constructive work of city civilization" were "not accomplishing their social mission," he charged, because of disunion, churchism and individualism.[101] A committee representing eight denominations drafted a plan during the following year. In the work of religious and sociological investigation preceding definitive action, Hegeman received help from Walter Laidlaw, who had made a brilliant record as president of a branch Evangelical Alliance and as pastor of the institutional Vermilye Chapel in New York City.[102]

Statistical study with a view to appropriate action was basic in the Federation's work. In the words of its Council, it was "an interdenominational instrument for sociological investigation in the city of New York, contributing the directive information it accumulates to the churches of the districts investigated, to the various denominational church extension committees, and to the charitable organizations of the city."[103] It planned, said Hegeman, to "furnish the churches a scientific basis for accomplishing their social mission."[104] By 1900 the Federation had canvassed five important regions, four in New York and one in Brooklyn, for information on church attendance, schools, libraries, social agencies and general conditions as to labor and economic life. The studies revealed that social life in most parts of the city was unsatisfactory. One amazing discovery was that the most crowded place in New York was

[100] "Practical Christian Union," Feb. 19, 1897, p. 514.
[101] Thomas Dixon, *The Failure of Protestantism in New York*, 140–144.
[102] "Historic Sketch — A Decade of Federation," *Federation*, III (November 1905), 2–5.   [103] *Ibid.*, pp. 3–4.
[104] "The Federation of Churches and Christian Workers in New York City," *Homiletic Review*, XXV (April 1898), 376; *Federation*, III (June 1903), 1–22.

not on the East Side but on the West Side in the Nineteenth Assembly District. In one block — eight hundred by two hundred feet — were found three thousand five hundred people: a congestion much greater than the "densest of London." By showing that Sunday and child labor widely prevailed, the five surveys suggested the need for social reform in this important field also. Besides creating public opinion for better legislation, especially for adequate tenement regulation, the investigations encouraged private agencies to supply urgent needs. Thus the first study led to the founding of two churches, two social settlements, two circulating libraries, a public park and several kindergartens. The second study brought similar institutions to the Negroes living in squalor in their districts.[105]

The Federation desired above all else, however, to establish a coöperative parish system on the lines suggested by President James McCosh of Princeton and others. To this end, the reports showed that the Protestant congregations, as compared with the Roman Catholic Church, were ineffective. Thus, in one region where Protestants were relatively strong and Catholics relatively weak, the latter were nearly eighty-eight per cent efficient in attaching their people to homes of worship, while the former were only a little over fifty per cent efficient.[106] As for the Sunday schools, a smaller proportion of children attended them than attended the public schools. "A house-to-house canvass by the church," concluded the Federation, "is necessary to give the highest educational efficiency to the house-to-house canvass by the State." [107] After failing in two attempts to provide religious oversight for selected districts, the Federation in June, 1900, put into operation a successful house-to-house visitation system for the whole Fourteenth Assembly District. Within five years the plan reduced Protestant families without a church home from forty-eight to twenty-eight per

---

[105] "Seven Years of Social Exploration," *Federation*, III (June 1903), 1–22.

[106] "First Sociological Canvass," p. 54, quoted in "Federation and Evangelistic Work in Cities," *Federation*, VI (April 1906), 93.

[107] "Third Sociological Canvass," *Report D.*, pp. 25–72.

cent as well as setting an example for other parts of the city.[108]
As the century closed, many cities were either following the
example of New York or transforming their previous coöperative plans into federations. In several cases, the old Evangelical
Alliances changed into Federations. Thus the Alliance in Boston
and vicinity declared in its *Report* for 1900 that it was tending
"toward a work for the neglected classes of Boston, similar to
the work in progress in New York." [109] The Federation in
Pittsburgh, in some respects the most successful one outside
New York, stemmed from the pioneer labors of George Hodges,
rector of Calvary Episcopal Church, and of Morgan M. Sheedy,
pastor of a neighboring Roman Catholic church. Their welding
together in 1893 of nearly all the churches in the East End for
social reform and house-to-house visitation was, as Washington
Gladden said, "a demonstration of Christian unity worth more
than weeks of talk in union meetings." [110] On these foundations
the Pennsylvania State Evangelical Alliance in 1899 persuaded
over a hundred and forty Pittsburgh congregations to enter a
Federation of Churches. Its quarterly meetings discussed such
questions as "House-to-House Visitation," "Associated Charities," "Sabbath Observance," the "Half-Holiday Movement,"
"Model Tenements" and "Sweat Shops." Besides effective
action towards a rest day for labor, the Federation helped to
bring about tenement-house reform through public and private
means.[111]

The Associated Churches of Cambridge, Massachusetts,
formed in 1898, was also the work largely of Hodges, now dean
of the Episcopal Theological School. The organization was "an
attempt," he explained, "to use the Christian churches in Cambridge to lift the general level of the city's life." [112] Though it

[108] "Fourteenth Assembly District," *Federation*, I (June 1900), 25, 29, 31.
[109] Walter Laidlaw, "Church Federation in the Old World and New," *Federation*, II (April 1902), 91.
[110] *The Christian Pastor and the Working Church*, p. 258.
[111] William Charles Webb, "Federation in Pennsylvania," *Hartford Seminary
Record*, X (May 1900), 207–208; *Churchman*, May 5, 1900, p. 532.
[112] *Charities Review*, VIII (February 1899), 536.

was not church union by any means, as the *Churchman* said, "it was nevertheless a good beginning. It is an approach to this great matter from a side which is at present attractive to a great many people — the social side. It is a union for better social service." [113] The Connecticut Bible Society, alarmed at the large percentage of nominal Protestants who failed to attend church, proved a capital influence in the forming of the Federations of New Haven, Hartford, Winsted and New Britain.[114] The instructions given by the New Haven Federation to its workers epitomized the aim of these bodies: "Our purpose is not primarily to build up individual churches or denominations, but . . . to show the real spirit of the modern church, through a loving ministry to the social and moral needs of men in His name and for His sake." [115]

A national federation greatly contributed to the later progress of the movement. During the nineties the Non-Conformists of England formed the National Council of the Evangelical Free Churches for the better "application of the law of Christ in every relation of human life." [116] With this object lesson before them, the Congregationalists in 1896 called for a similar organization in this country. "Nothing so near the spirit of apostolic times," said Charles L. Thompson, "has yet been proposed." [117] In its convention of 1900 the National City Evangelization Union of the Methodist Episcopal Church resolved that we "desire to renew the expression of our profound interest in the current movements toward the federation of churches and Christian workers." [118] Earlier in the year the New York Fed-

---

[113] Dec. 17, 1898, pp. 883–884.

[114] Henry B. Roberts, "The Connecticut Bible Society and Church Federation," *Hartford Seminary Record*, X (May 1900), pp. 218–220; Watson L. Phillips, "Federation in New Haven," *ibid.*, pp. 208–214; Newell M. Calhoun, "Federation in Winsted," *ibid.*, pp. 214–215.

[115] Phillips, *op. cit.*, p. 212.

[116] Arthur L. Gillette, "Church Federation in England," *Hartford Seminary Record*, X (May 1900), 188–195.

[117] "A Federation of Churches," *Independent*, May 21, 1896, p. 677.

[118] *Federation*, I (January 1901), 9.

eration and the Open or Institutional Church League had assembled a representative conference which in turn appointed an executive committee: (1) to assist in the formation of additional local and state federations; (2) to report to the next Conference a plan for a basis of membership in the Conference; (3) to foster intercommunication between local federations and to supply them with needed information; and (4) to institute plans to obtain sufficient financial support. The outcome at the Second Conference in February, 1901, was the National Federation of Churches and Christian Workers — an organization which within a few years evolved into the Federation of the Churches of Christ in America.

By 1900 Protestants were nearing the limits of coöperation. Through concerted effort they had to a large degree consolidated their forces, both as denominations and as Christians apart from the denominations, to maintain churches and missions in the more strategic and needy urban areas. Using institutional methods alongside these churches and missions, Protestants were now applying social Christianity, the principles of which they had already widely diffused in the American Christian Commission, the Evangelical Alliance, the Convention of Christian Workers and similar bodies. Though most of the leading denominations and some of the lesser ones made use of the city mission and church extension-society, only the Methodists formed a national coördinating agency — the City Evangelization Union. A desire to influence the religiously indifferent and socially maladjusted immigrant had been mainly responsible for the progressive church work of the denominations in their organized capacities. They achieved only partial success, for relatively few immigrants joined the Protestant churches. But the newcomers so gladly availed themselves of the enormous material and cultural benefits at their disposal that Protestant social service must be ranked high among the factors which prevented social revolution in the final decades of the century.

CHAPTER VIII

THE AUXILIARY FORMS OF PROTESTANT SOCIAL SERVICE

THE institutional church by no means monopolized Protestant endeavor in the social field. Though superb expressions of Christian brotherhood, the many humanitarian churches and missions did not utilize all the great reservoirs of social potential. New sources of strength awaiting development were the latent energies of women and youth. While every institutional church made use of these groups in its welfare work, they were capable of far greater service if fully trained and organized. Moreover, the influence of religion could be greatly extended through special efforts in their behalf. In order better to employ and provide for women and youth emerged the auxiliary forms of Protestant social service, notably the young people's societies, the brotherhoods, the sisterhoods and the deaconess associations. Like the institutional church itself, these societies evidenced and in turn enlivened the great religious awakening of the late nineteenth century.

These implications were clearly present in the growing popularity of the accredited woman church worker. Though distrust of the "sister" or "deaconess" did not entirely subside, nearly a hundred and fifty well-equipped deaconess institutions arose between 1885 and 1900. Under the circumstances, this was amazing progress, reflecting as nothing else did the impact of the social crisis upon conventional modes of religious behavior. Many ministers specialized in deaconess work and hundreds of Protestants discussed it in religious assemblies, all agreeing that the demand for the deaconess "is like the need for religion, as natural and persistent as the sorrows of the world." [1] Deacon-

[1] "Deaconesses — Why Not?" *Christian At Work*, May 12, 1881, p. 437.

esses, it was pointed out, were needed in the local churches. "Much of the work that ought to be but cannot be done by the pastor could be done most effectively by deaconesses," wrote the Reverend George W. Wenner of the Lutheran Church. "They could supply much of the help that is now derived from secular and humanitarian sources." [2] The churches must officially recognize the movement, its friends explained, for otherwise women entering the calling lost self-respect and social standing. In view of the new needs, most Protestants laid aside the old argument that an order of deaconesses would be a "deliberate establishment of a Protestant sisterhood of charity." The female diaconate, as one minister wrote, "savors of Romanism only in so far as Romanism savors of the New Testament" — admittedly "a very safe guide for all who would serve God acceptably." If Catholics had unwarrantedly modified it, Protestants had just as unwarrantedly ignored it.[3]

Now that the deaconess idea was acquiring the proper credentials, the leading denominations prepared to carry it into effect. The German-American religious bodies were the first seriously to consider the movement. In the hope of putting an end to the wretched nursing at the German Lutheran Hospital in Philadelphia, the directors called upon the Kaiserswerth Institutions in Germany for help. Though these had no deaconesses to spare, a small independent community of German deaconesses arrived in 1884, their labors soon producing excellent results. John D. Lankenan, son-in-law of F. M. Drexel, the merchant, gave in memory of his wife a half-million dollars for improving the hospital and an equal sum for a Deaconess Home.[4] This auspicious beginning influenced Lutherans elsewhere to experi-

---

[2] "Woman's Ministry in the Church," *Luth. Quart. Rev.*, XXVI (October 1896), 475–476.

[3] L. H. Jordan, "The Ministry of the Deaconess," *Presby. Rev.*, X (October 1889), 627–631.

[4] Jane M. Bancroft, *Deaconesses in Europe and Their Lessons for America*, pp. 207–211; A. Cordes, "Deaconesses," *Luth. Quart. Rev.*, XXII (April 1892), 179.

ment along similar lines. Thus, the Reverend E. A. Fogel-stroem opened the Immanuel Deaconess Institute of Omaha, Nebraska, in 1890 in charge of a Philadelphia trained deaconess. By 1900 the Lutherans in the General Council had established five additional homes, whose residents engaged in hospital nursing or in parish social service as their inclination dictated. Desiring to have deaconess activity include all social endeavor, these Lutherans affiliated nearly all their charities with the central Deaconess Homes in Philadelphia and Milwaukee. The Lutherans of the General Synod in 1885 appointed a committee with Wenner as chairman to study the subject. The outcome was a Board of Deaconesses which, after sending young women to Europe for several years, founded a training school of its own, the Lutheran Deaconess Home and Training School of Baltimore. Likewise, the Evangelical Synod of North America, commonly called "Missouri," formed the Evangelical Deaconess Home of St. Louis and the Tabitha Institute of Lincoln, Nebraska. As in Europe, the Lutherans in America united after 1895 in the Lutheran Diaconate Conference whose yearly proceedings, conducted in English, helped to unify and extend the movement.[5]

The other branches of German Protestantism lent support. In the Reformed Church the Reverend J. H. C. Roentgen, an immigrant and near-relative of the great Austrian physicist, was largely responsible for two institutions of the Kaiserswerth type. He also exerted great influence upon all German Protestants in the United States, who by combining their efforts were able to launch a dozen or more institutions. While the "Missouri" ministers assumed the initiative, all denominations participated: Lutheran, Reformed, Methodist, Baptist and Presbyterian. The first of these undenominational agencies was the German Deaconess Home and Hospital of Cincinnati, formed in 1888.

---

[5] E. A. Fogelstroem, *Evangelical Deaconess Work the Great Need of America* (Omaha, 1889); *Annual Cyclopedia*, 1895, p. 429; Bancroft, *op. cit.*, pp. 268–270.

With a society of patrons, a women's auxiliary, a board of managers, a corresponding secretary and a journal, it was a model for the others which followed in such cities as Dayton, Evansville, Indianapolis, Buffalo and Chicago. Frank F. Henning, a German Methodist friend of Dwight L. Moody, financed the Home Bethesda in Chicago; and the Reverend Carl Mueller, won to the deaconess cause by a visit to Kaiserswerth, presided at the founding of the Homes in Dayton and in several other Mid-Western cities. The Protestant Diaconate Conference, dating from October, 1894, represented German Protestants. Apart from advancing common interests, it was active in persuading the smaller institutions to affiliate with the larger ones—a goal partially realized. The Reverend Charles Golder, a former president, declared in 1903 that the "conference has not been without its influence upon the development of the Deaconess work in America." [6]

Though the German Protestant churches established several deaconess institutions, one American denomination, the Methodist, far outdistanced them. With seventy-three deaconess homes by 1900, the Methodist Episcopal Church had nearly as many as all other denominations combined.[7] The agitation, begun by Bishop J. M. Thoburn before the Central Ohio Conference in 1886, led the General Conference two years later to draw up a plan for deaconess work. Women wishing to engage in it were to abandon other pursuits and "to devote themselves in a general way to such forms of Christian labor as may be suited to their abilities." While the Conference favored the German semi-monastic establishment, "no vow shall be exacted from any deaconess, and any one of their number shall be at liberty to relinquish her position as a deaconess at any time." The annual conference boards were not to certificate women un-

[6] *History of the Deaconess Movement in the Christian Church*, pp. 274–302, 468–471.
[7] "Swift Progress of the Deaconess Work," *Christian City*, XII (May 1900), 102–103.

less they "shall have served a probation of two years of continuous service, and shall be over twenty-five years of age." The Conference further voted that "each deaconess shall be under the direction of the pastor of the church with which she is connected. When associated together in a Home all the members of the Home shall be subordinated to, and directed by the superintendent placed in charge." [8] These statements evidenced the Church's desire to introduce the German deaconess system, as Bishop Simpson and Mrs. Wittenmeyer had earlier urged.

Coming at one of the peaks of social unrest, this official endorsement evoked paeans of praise from progressive Methodists. "The vast possibilities that it involves," said the Cincinnati Conference, "are beyond our present conceptions. . . . We have been so engrossed with the distinctively spiritual part of our mission that we have largely left the humanities of religion to others." [9] Promptly the annual conferences formed deaconess boards. In order to gain and to share experience, Methodists discussed deaconess work after 1888 in yearly conventions. The chief outcome was a Plan for Securing Uniformity in the Deaconess Movement, which the homes gladly accepted. The Deaconess Society of the Methodist Episcopal Church also served the ends of unification. Since the annual conferences exercised direct authority over the new service, several agencies remained under their immediate control. Thus, the Elizabeth Gamble Deaconess Home of Cincinnati, founded at a public meeting in November, 1888, took orders from the Conference Board of Deaconesses. The Home in Cleveland, secured in 1889 by Horace Benton as a gift from a prominent minister and his wife, was placed in charge of the North German, the North Ohio and the East Ohio Conferences.[10] A few small donations led the New England Conference in the same year to recommend "the founding of a Deaconess Home and Training School

[8] Gen. Conf., *Journal*, 1888, pp. 435–446.
[9] *Minutes*, 1889, p. 89.
[10] East Ohio Conf., *Minutes*, 1889, pp. 20, 30–31.

for Boston and its suburbs at an early day." Interested Methodists carried the suggestion into effect and added a hospital a few years later.[11]

But the Woman's Home Missionary Society, dating from 1881, was mainly responsible for the Methodist deaconess homes. Although the Society was chiefly interested in Negroes and the other "peculiar" populations of the South and Southwest, its efforts in their behalf included social development as well as evangelism. By means of Industrial or Domestic Economy Homes the Society elevated the Negro and gained priceless experience in preparation for urban social work. "Why not," asked the secretary in 1887, "make mission churches centers of all saving influences, where may be found schools in which children may be trained in moral and in useful occupations, young women taught . . . industries, agencies where employment may be secured, and above all places where any who come would meet with loving sympathy?"[12] In furtherance of this aim, the Society in 1885 set up a Department of Local Work which soon expanded into a Bureau of Local Missionary Work. Many Methodists learned of the new departure from a three-year course of reading on the plan of the Chautauqua Literary and Scientific Circles, and from the Society's organ, the *Woman's Home Missions*, whose circulation by 1892 totalled fifteen thousand.

Within a few years the Bureau of Local Missionary Work had nearly a half-hundred city missions, several of which developed into excellent social centers. The model one was the Glenn Home, which opened in Cincinnati in 1890 and carried on its work in a four-story structure with an adequate corps of resident workers, some of whom served as pastoral assistants, some as house-to-house visitors and others as teachers in industrial and Sabbath schools. Additional features included a kinder-

[11] Golder, *op. cit.*, pp. 370–72.
[12] Mrs. R. S. Rust, "The Woman's Home Missionary Society," *Methodist Review*, LXIX (September 1887), 653–678.

garten and a school of domestic science. Quite similar was the E. E. Marcy Home in Chicago, with its kitchen garden, kinder-gartens, sewing and cooking schools and classes in dressmaking, sloyd and physical culture. By 1890 the Society had also estab-lished institutions for immigrants in New York, Boston and Philadelphia which assumed responsibilities for their respective neighborhoods as well as for the new arrivals.[13] Another spe-cialty was the systematic training of women, the Chicago Training School for Missions having been established in 1885 by Mrs. Lucy Rider Meyer, a physician, who had begun her career as a missionary among Negroes. Some fifteen teachers and lecturers offered Biblical, practical and medical instruc-tion. "The city," she said in 1888, "furnished an important field of usefulness for the pupils and the school in its practice becomes an efficient agency for city evangelization." The School, which by the end of the century had educated several hundred women, was in fact, though not in name, the first deaconess home in the denomination.[14]

But much of the Society's work conformed increasingly to the deaconess plan. Even before the action of the General Conference in 1888, the Society's leaders were moving in the new direction. Most influential was the highly-gifted Jane M. Bancroft, a New England minister's daughter, who typified the newly educated American woman. After teaching in Methodist schools and pursuing graduate studies in this country and abroad, she finally found a career in the deaconess movement. In Europe she followed the suggestion of the Society's secre-tary "to make a special study of the Deaconess cause, and on her return to America present the subject in its various bearings to the official Board of the Woman's Home Missionary Society, with a view of inaugurating a similar movement in the United States." [15] As chairman of the deaconess bureau, which the

[13] Gen. Conf., *Journal*, 1883, pp. 744–746; *ibid.*, 1892, pp. 758–759; *ibid.*, 1900, p. 803.   [14] *Ibid.*, 1888, pp. 744–745; Golder, *op. cit.*, pp. 345–346.
      [15] *Ibid.*, pp. 322–330, *passim*.

Society formed in 1889, Miss Bancroft in the ensuing years supervised the establishment of over thirty deaconess homes in the larger cities.

The majority of these institutions preferred a wide to a specialized social program. Thus, the Detroit Home engaged in parish work, kindergarten and manual training and nursing for the sick-poor. At its Tillman Avenue Mission, the Home overcame the opposition of Bohemians, Poles, Italians and Hungarians, and, in order to aid them further, erected a larger structure "with all modern appliances for aggressive mission work." The Baltimore Home added the Mount Tabor Industrial Institution, referred to by Miss Bancroft as "the first institutional building for deaconess work in this country and possibly in the world." But the Society stressed the training of deaconesses in a half-dozen institutions, notably in the Lucy Webb Hayes Deaconess Home and National Training School of Washington, D. C.

Besides the Woman's Home Missionary Society, other agencies, especially the church extension societies, aided the deaconess cause with gifts and personnel.[16] As for the racial and immigrant groups, the Methodist Negroes outfitted institutions in Cincinnati and elsewhere; and the German Methodists, led by Charles and Louise Golder, opened homes in various cities after 1890, including a Mother House in Cincinnati to coördinate their many activities.[17] Just as the deaconess movement enjoyed generous aid, so also it vitalized and unified Methodist philanthropy. Though the other religious workers were important, "he reads the history carelessly," said the *Christian City*, "who does not perceive the stimulating influence upon the church's thought which is created by the presence of these hundreds of consecrated women."[18] Deaconesses conducted all

---

[16] *Aggressive Methodism*, I (November 1889), 5–6; *Christian Union*, Feb. 4, 1893, p. 233; *Zion's Herald*, Nov. 24, 1897, p. 740.

[17] Golder, *op. cit.*, pp. 411–413, *passim*.

[18] *Ibid.*, XII (May 1900), 102.

but two of the twenty-six Methodist hospitals, most of which had grown up alongside deaconess homes. Deaconesses alone managed the few homes for the aged and the numerous orphanages, among them the two model ones, the St. Christopher Home at Dobbs' Ferry, New York, and the Fred Finch Home in Oakland, California. Even the elementary church schools came more and more under the direction of deaconesses. The General Conference encouraged this all-embracing tendency by empowering a Board of Bishops in 1900 to authorize "the establishment of Homes, Hospitals, Orphanages, Old People's Homes and other institutions, such as properly come under the care of deaconesses." [19]

Compared with the Methodists, the contributions of the other American denominations were insignificant. Presbyterians, for example, refused to sponsor deaconess institutions. When the Presbytery of Philadelphia in 1889 overtured the General Assembly for an order of deaconesses, a special committee, though praising the deaconess house, recommended "the immediate establishment only of the congregational deaconess (to whom alone the name appears of strict right to belong). . . ." But the Church had no real opportunity to approve or reject this conservative program, for the committee submitted two virtually contradictory amendments to be voted on separately. "It is quite obvious," the committee said, "that the vote furnishes no sufficient means of determining the mature judgment of the church," since there was presented "the anomaly of 118 Presbyteries voting to create an office which 143 Presbyteries come near saying has no scriptural warrant." [20] In view of the Church's indecision, the Assembly merely advised the various congregations to "appoint godly and competent women in full communion in the church for such ministration to bodily and spiritual needs as may properly come within their sphere." [21]

[19] Gen. Conf., *Journal*, 1900, pp. 43–44.
[20] Gen. Assembly, *Minutes*, 1890, pp. 119–121; *ibid.*, 1891, pp. 135–136.
[21] *Ibid.*, 1893, pp. 169–170.

The Assembly also authorized the Woman's Executive Committee on Home Missions to extend educational and social advantages to the "exceptional populations" of large cities.

Though Episcopalians had long favored the consecrated woman church worker, their Church had been powerless to act because of the wrangling between the deaconess institutions and the sisterhoods. But as the social crisis deepened the respective partisans concluded that women should be free to choose their own type of social service. The only canon "that can be adopted," said Henry Y. Satterlee in a carefully prepared pamphlet, "will be one that is comprehensive enough to harmonize the discordant views of all who are interested in this subject of vital importance; wide enough in its range to embrace all phases of organized woman's work in the church and catholic as the needs of human nature itself." [22] In the spirit of these convictions, the New York Diocesan Convention, in 1888, at William S. Rainsford's suggestion, drew up a Memorial to the General Convention "asking them to take steps for the revival of the primitive order of Deaconess." The request was granted the following year, Canon 10 of Title I providing for deaconesses without vows to be inducted into office by an appropriate religious service.[23] In order to provide the required training, Bishop Potter established the New York Training School for Deaconesses in October, 1890, at Grace Church. Applicants eighteen years of age followed a two years' course of study under the Reverend Randolph H. McKim and his staff of assistants. Within ten years the school had trained fifty-four women.[24]

Congregationalists thoroughly discussed the deaconess movement, and one State Association, that of Massachusetts, appointed a committee in 1892 "to report upon the expediency, and if they judge such an institution expedient to proceed to investigate and report upon the best ways and means to estab-

[22] Charles H. Brent, op. cit., p. 111.
[23] Prot. Epis. Ch., Journal, 1889, pp. 334-335.   [24] Golder, op. cit., p. 462.

lish such an institution among ourselves." The ensuing economic depression put an end to the plan.[25] But in 1901 the Illinois Association incorporated an agency, the American Congregational Deaconess Association, which opened in Chicago a training school with an able corps of instructors, as well as an orphanage and rest home in Dover, Illinois. Like the Congregationalists, the Baptists, with only two small societies in New York and Chicago, played a minor role. Although only a few denominations established deaconess institutions in large numbers, the movement was significant in the sense that it pointed the way to the fuller utilization of women in all fields of religious and social service.

The other auxiliary bodies specialized their energies: the Christian associations on the younger men and women, the brotherhoods and the sisterhoods on all men and women, and the Sunday schools and the young people's societies on youth without regard to sex. During the last two decades of the century the Christian associations greatly enlarged their programs in line with the policies formulated in the immediate post-war years. Thus the Young Men's Christian Association increased its buildings from about fifty to nearly four hundred, established schools for the training of leaders, formed associations and clubs for older boys and for college men, set up "homes away from home" for railway employees and systematized its educational work. Yet the Association was "hardly a factor" in "the industrial problem," for its excellent institutions served only clerical and skilled workers and, in effect, excluded the great class of unskilled labor. Even the Young Men's Institute of the Bowery, which intended to be a democratic social center, appealed but slightly to ordinary immigrant workingmen and the outcasts of society.[26]

But within their restricted field the Associations contributed

---

[25] Gen. Assoc. of Congreg. Churches in Mass., *Minutes*, 1892, p. 59; *ibid.*, 1893, pp. 52–53.
[26] Raymond Calkins, *Substitutes for the Saloon* (Boston, 1901), pp. 138–148; *Outlook*, Feb. 17, 1894, pp. 328–329.

more fully than most other organizations to the widening influence of social Christianity. Mainly to the Associations belonged the credit for bringing physical education within the scope of science and religion. By overstressing strength and brawn, gymnastic practice had failed to satisfy the increasing demand of urban people for rational instruction in health and hygiene. Accordingly, in 1875 the Boston Association under its new director, Robert J. Roberts, shifted the emphasis from physical prowess to "body building" — Roberts' phrase for exercise "safe, short, easy, beneficial and pleasing." For those unable or unwilling to attend the gymnasium he devised a Home Dumb-Bell Drill, which was, he said, "the Graham Bread and Butter of body-building exercises. . . . If you have time to eat you have time to exercise," he insisted.[27]

If Roberts rationalized bodily exercise, Luther H. Gulick Christianized it. As the physical director of the New York Association in the late eighties, he arrived at ideas which he presented in an address on "Our New Gymnastics" before the International Convention of 1889. More was required, he said, than attention to health and bodily symmetry. It was also necessary to educate "the physique with reference to the ultimate purpose of the whole man, body and soul." The capabilities of man, he argued, "are very much greater than simply the sum of those of the body alone, plus those of the mind alone, plus those of the soul alone." Each one "gives to the others," he concluded, "not only all that it has itself, but also enables the others to be and to do far more than they could do alone." [28] Becoming International Secretary for Promoting Physical Work and instructor in the Springfield Training School, Gulick was able to win over the Association to these views. At a meeting in 1901 in commemoration of the fiftieth anniversary of the Association, a member aptly observed that only "in the last ten years" had physical training "come to be considered simply a

---

[27] Luther Gulick, "Robert J. Roberts and His Work," in Robert J. Roberts, *Home Dumb-Bell Drill*, pp. 6–20.
[28] International Convention, *Proceedings*, 1889, pp. 98–103.

differentiated part of the great work for which the Association was founded. The historical development has been not so much in the work itself as in the idea, the conception of the place and function of physical education in the Association." [29]

The Associations for women, like those for men, improved their work, but they too passed up the golden opportunities for social service. Though reformers kept pointing to the desperate plight of the "forgotten woman," the great majority of cities lacked Young Women's Christian Associations. Thus in 1890 Fall River, Massachusetts, with fifty-eight enormous mills and "thousands of solitary young women," had "no women's Christian association, nor any boarding home under distinctly educating or uplifting auspices." [30] Where homes did exist, their rates were beyond the means of the girl earning no more than five dollars a week.[31] As if ashamed of their record, several Associations resolved to "go to the root of the worker's needs." The Baltimore Association was founded in 1883 specifically to improve the condition of working women "by providing for them a reading room, and such other departments as may be found necessary." As the outcome of an address by Grace H. Dodge in 1887 on the working girls' club movement, the Association organized two Helping Hand Societies whose work resembled that of the social settlements.[32] Some years later, the New York Association, with the aid of college women, sponsored two settlements, the Young Women's Settlement, or Christodora House, and the West Side Settlement.[33]

The Sunday school, a church adjunct of long standing, also

[29] Paul C. Phillips, "Christian Character in Athletics," *Jubilee of Work for Young Men in North America*, pp. 195–196.

[30] Clare de Graffenried, "The Needs of Self-Supporting Women," *Notes Supplementary to the Johns Hopkins Studies in History and Political Science*, VIII, Eighth Series, 1890, 9.

[31] Annie Marion MacLean, "Homes for Working Women in Large Cities," *Charities Rev.*, IX (July 1899), 219–228.

[32] Herbert Baxter Adams, *Work Among Workingmen in Baltimore. A Social Study* (Baltimore, 1889), pp. 1–9.

[33] *Commons*, II (September 1897), 13–14; *ibid.*, III (May 1898), 7; *Christian City*, XI (September 1899), 161.

shared more and more in the responsibilities of social service. "Where," asked Edward Eggleston in 1880, "has the question of the mode of decreasing pauperism through the Sunday school ever attracted any attention? What have Sunday school people done to promote the acquisition of skill in handicraft by Sunday school children?" [34] Besides having to provide satisfactory answers to these questions, the Sunday schools had to become more successful as recruiting agencies for the churches. The rapid movement of population from country to city, the increasing secularization of the public schools and the easy pitfalls of city life — all these demanded of the Sunday school greater effectiveness.[35] Yet the schools, despite a certain indigenous strength, long remained relatively inefficient. Though the number of scholars enormously increased each year, the aggregate attendance at no time exceeded forty per cent of the children of school age. Far more serious was the failure of the scholars to enter the churches. "We are confronted," said the *Christian at Work* in 1881, "with the appalling fact that in thousands of the Sunday schools of the country . . . not one scholar has been brought into the church." [36]

Most specialists attributed the comparative failure of the Sunday school to its lack of vital connection with the local congregation. Investigations undertaken by Massachusetts Congregationalists after 1881 showed that a large majority of schools received no oversight from their respective churches. "Give the Sunday school its true and dignified place as a part of the organic working body of the church," the Reverend Smith Baker implored, and then it "will be stronger and the church itself will feel a new thrill of life." [37]

[34] "Recent Phases of Sunday School Work," *Scribner's*, XIX (February 1880), 529.
[35] Nat. Council, *Minutes*, 1886, p. 152; Gen. Assoc. of Congreg. Churches in Mass., *Minutes*, 1885, pp. 58–59; *ibid.*, 1894, p. 50; Wilbur F. Crafts, "The Sabbath-School as a Factor in Public Education," *Our Day*, X (August 1892), 590.
[36] Feb. 3, 1881, p. 102; *ibid.*, Oct. 20, 1881, p. 941.
[37] Gen. Assoc. of Congreg. Churches in Mass., *Minutes*, 1886, p. 36.

Methodists had been following this prescription since 1865 when they created a department of Sunday school instruction under the leadership of Dr. J. H. Vincent. In setting up a similar organization in 1877 the Presbyterians had urged the importance of each school being under "the care and control of its own church session." [38] This timely action added so many young recruits to these denominations that most of the other ones followed their example. Thus, in the early eighties, Congregationalists, through local Conferences, State Associations and the National Council, dealt thoroughly with the situation, devoting time and effort to organizing mission Sunday schools as well as regular ones. As Sunday school secretary, the Reverend Albert E. Dunning by 1895 had founded nearly fifteen hundred out of which grew two hundred churches. By the early nineties nearly every Congregational church had an organically attached Sunday school. Financial support as well as church membership greatly increased, "all of which goes to show," as one minister said, "that the new vigor imparted to our denominational Sunday school work begins to be seen in favorable results." [39]

Besides perfecting organizations, religious forces tried in other ways to improve the Sunday schools. The many conventions and institutes evidenced the great concern about methods of teaching — an interest finding its most notable expression in the origin and growth of the Chautauqua movement. Excellent manuals were prepared for the training of teachers and schemes were devised to introduce classification and grading into the Sunday schools after the manner of the public schools. All sects widely adopted the Home Department, which the Reverend Samuel W. Dike had suggested as a means of strengthening religion in depleted areas.[40] In order to create greater interest among boys, leaders resorted to military techniques,

[38] *Ibid.*, 1883, pp. 53–54.
[39] *Ibid.*, p. 54.
[40] *Ibid.*, 1884, p. 47; *ibid.*, 1887, pp. 12–13; *ibid.*, 1889, p. 26.

organizing a United Boys' Brigade. This plan, as worked out by its founder, W. A. Smith, of the Free College Church of Glasgow, stressed compulsory attendance on classes and the weekly meetings for Bible drill. Started in 1883, the movement spread rapidly, the first American Brigade appearing in a San Francisco church in 1890. Within five years a thousand companies, with twenty-five thousand members drawn from all sections and welded in a national body, had come into existence.

In becoming more efficient agencies, many mission Sunday schools adopted philanthropic features, especially the kindergarten. The Kindergarten of the Church Association, formed in 1893 with Bishop Vincent as president, encouraged this type of instruction as an aid to the church and as a relief to congestion in the first grades of the public schools.[41] A study at the end of the century showed that the mission Sunday schools on the South Side of Chicago were busy in several other fields of social welfare also. Many of them were fully equipped, having kindergartens, sewing schools, boys and girls' clubs, relief work, fresh-air outings and educational classes. The investigator concluded that "the mission Sunday school can and does stand for a great social force in the community" and that the schools "are even now too valuable to be overlooked in the tabulating of social and ethical forces."[42] In many places the Sunday school socialized the mission chapels of wealthy congregations. Several institutional churches (though not all, as Herbert Baxter Adams rashly claimed) were also outgrowths of Sunday schools. Thus Hope Church in Springfield, Massachusetts, started in 1866 as a mission Sunday school of the South Congregational Church. Flourishing first as a chapel and then as a church, it became institutional after 1881 when David Allen Reed, a coworker of Moody, assumed its pastorate. Another

[41] W. W. Foster, "The Kindergarten of the Church," *Open Church*, I (April 1897), 84–89.

[42] H. Francis Perry, "The Mission Sunday School as a Social and Ethical Lever," *Bibliotheca Sacra*, LVI (July 1899), 481–504.

example was the Pilgrim Sunday school in Worcester, which under Charles M. Southgate's guidance developed into Pilgrim Church with a long list of social adjuncts.

Though the improved Sunday school strengthened religion at a vital point, it could not influence those in the twilight zone between youth and adult life. "Just at that age," said a Lutheran pastor, "when the exercise of the Christian life and the unfolding of the nature calls for direction, control and education, the young men and women have grown out of the position of scholars."[43] Nor could Protestants rely any longer upon the home for religious nurture. An investigation by the authorities at Harvard in 1880 showed that five-sevenths of the households sending students to the University had given up family prayer and similar practices. This discontinuance was assigned to the pressing demands of industrial life and to worldliness caused by increasing wealth and luxury.[44] Finally, the tentative plans advanced by the churches to interest young people had failed. Convinced of youth's inherent repugnance to spirituality, the churches had sugar-coated the religious pill, resorting to a myriad of literary, dramatic and musical associations which evoked no lasting response.

But, as events were to show, religion did. In the early eighties, the young Francis E. Clark, pastor of Williston Congregational Church in Portland, Maine, suggested a Society of Christian Endeavor for his juvenile converts and found to his amazement that they would gladly sign a pledge to attend the weekly prayer-meeting. Thus Clark introduced as if by accident one of the most significant religious innovations of the nineteenth century. Soon local societies were forming at the rate of five thousand a year.[45] So rapid was the growth that in 1886 a national body, the United Society of Christian Endeavor,

---

[43] C. A. Stork, "Training of the Young for the Church," *Luth. Quart. Rev.*, III (October 1873), 579–580.

[44] Pres. and Treas. of Harv. Coll., *Annual Report*, 1880–81, pp. 18–19.

[45] "Statistics of Growth," United Soc. of Christ. Endeavor, *Official Reports*, 1893, p. 81.

was formed, with Clark as president, assisted by a select board of trustees. In the autumn of 1886 the Society adopted as its official organ the Reverend W. H. H. Murray's paper, the *Golden Rule*, which after a time became the *Christian Endeavor World*. To further the movement still more, the United Society in 1889 prepared a model constitution which stressed the amenability of the various branches to the control of their respective congregations.[46]

As the movement made headway, progressive Protestants pointed to its great religious significance. It was, they urged, a reaction on the part of the young folk against worldly and aristocratic practices in church life. "It puts stress of emphasis upon the prayer-meeting," said Clark, "rather than upon a debating society; upon outward work to be done in winning others rather than upon a 'pink tea' with a piece of lemon peel in the saucer." [47] Instead of amusement the aim "is now solid Christian service," said the Reverend A. J. Gordon of Boston.[48] By means of the pledge, which was a form of outward action, the societies helped to overthrow "the doctrine of personal irresponsibility or the idleness of the conscience," so likely to ensue from the Protestant conception of freedom.[49]

These characteristics of the United Society of Christian Endeavor were present also in the various denominational young people's societies. Thus the Unitarians under the leadership of the Reverend William I. Lawrence formed societies after 1886 "to furnish both the means and the opportunity for benevolent activity, such as religious guilds provide." The "characteristic purpose" of the newer bodies, as contrasted with the earlier Lend a Hand and Unity Clubs, was, as Lawrence wrote, "something larger and more fundamental, — in attempting to arouse a wholesome interest in distinctly religious matters and to touch

---

[46] *Golden Rule*, Oct. 14, 1886, p. 8; *ibid.*, Feb. 28, 1899, p. 354.

[47] "The Christian Endeavor Movement; Its Aims and Results," *Homiletic Rev.*, XXI (June 1896), 496.

[48] "One Solution of the Amusement Question," *Golden Rule*, Oct. 4, 1888, p. 1.

[49] "The Philosophy of the Endeavor Movement," *ibid.*, May 24, 1894, p. 696.

and develop the religious life among our young people." [50] Unitarians federated their societies in 1889, and the Universalists theirs four years later — in the Universalist Young People's Union.

The many Methodist young people's societies came together in 1889 in the Epworth League, with the *Epworth Herald* as the official organ. Like the Christian Endeavor societies, the League stressed evangelism, requiring "attendance upon and support of the means of grace," and urging "the greatest activity in all lines of practical Christian work." [51] The huge membership of the Epworth League was never equalled by any other denomination, though the Baptists could point to hundreds of thousands in their Baptist Young People's Union, dating from 1891. After many societies had sprung into existence in Lutheran congregations, a Convention in Pittsburgh in 1895 arranged for a Lutheran League. The Presbyterian churches, with the Congregational and others, did not break off affiliations with the United Society of Christian Endeavor. To the demand of some presbyteries for a special society, a committee of the General Assembly replied that we "have no denominational model to which all our Sabbath schools must conform. The school is under the care of the session and may be adapted in constitution and operation to the needs of the field. So it should be with the Young People's Society." [52]

Besides Christian nurture, the young people's movement championed "practical Christianity" in all ways likely to adjust religion to the new social requirements. We "shall emphasize," said the editors of *Golden Rule*, "the idea of organization in all departments of church work; and we shall aim especially to suggest new methods of making the church what we believe it ought to be: the pioneer and exemplar in all philanthropic and benevolent enterprises." Unless the church should sound "the

<hr/>

[50] "Young People's Religious Societies," *Christian Register*, April 11, 1889, pp. 236–237. [51] Gen. Conf., *Journal*, 1892, pp. 52–53. [52] Gen. Assembly, *Minutes*, 1893, pp. 125–126.

keynote of the community in all matters of philanthropy," [53] many would conclude "that perhaps after all the essential part of religion can be practiced as well without the church as within it." [54] As another thrust at religious dualism, President Clark in 1893 advised the Christian Endeavor Societies to cultivate a larger and more intelligent spirit of patriotic citizenship. From this time on "Christian citizenship" occupied a large place in all the gatherings of the United Society. In several instances, special citizenship leagues were formed to promote a more vital sense of civic and social responsibility on the part of both young and old.[55] Though the young people's societies stressed the desirability of temperance and Sabbath observance and the electing of good men to office,[56] they did not forget the more fundamental objectives, including support for organized labor.[57]

Thus the National Christian Citizenship League, formed in 1894 by Edwin D. Wheelock, the aggressive champion of Christian citizenship in the United Society, was profoundly interested in social reconstruction. The League "does not aim," it said, "to promote surface reforms. Its object is to educate the public conscience and secure effective action on the things that are fundamental to a better state of society." [58] In its *Social Forum*, a monthly magazine, and in clubs and college classes, the League vigorously expounded the principles of Christian Socialism.[59] Some of its members established churches, the Reverend Frederick G. Strickland, for example, organizing a People's Christian Church in Chicago to agitate for the kingdom of heaven on earth. The Christian Endeavor

[53] Oct. 7, 1886, p. 8.
[54] "The Church and Philanthropy," *ibid.*, p. 9.
[55] W. H. Tolman, *Municipal Reform Movements*, 158–160; *Amer. Mag. of Civics*, VI (June 1895), 662–663; ibid., IX (January 1897), 555.
[56] *Golden Rule*, Aug. 31, 1893, p. 984; *Homiletic Rev.*, XXV (February 1893), 170–177; Gen. Assoc. of Cong. Churches in Mass., *Minutes*, 1897, pp. 110–111; *ibid.*, 1898, p. 112.
[57] *Amer. Jour. of Politics*, II (December 1894), 661; Wilbur F. Crafts, "Christian Endeavor in Reforms," *Golden Rule*, Feb. 8, 1894, p. 393.
[58] *Social Forum*, I (July 1899), 61.
[59] *Ibid.*, I (September 1899), 138.

Societies themselves did not as a rule go so far, but as a means of realizing a better social order they carried on "a vast amount of missionary and philanthropic work." [60] If the Societies in Baltimore with their social settlement were unusually progressive,[61] it was not uncommon for the Societies in most cities to engage in almost all forms of poor relief.[62] The Epworth League studied social questions in its reading course and made its Department of Mercy and Help one of the main working forces in Methodist institutional churches and social settlements.[63]

If youth received the lion's share of attention, they did not monopolize it. A brotherhood movement served men of all ages and classes. Men once had made up the majority of Protestant church attendants, but they now were turning religion over to their womenfolk. By 1880 this trend was prevalent enough to give point to the jocose remark that women gravitated toward the prayer-meeting as naturally as men toward the penitentiary. "The truth is," said the Reverend Howard A. Bridgman, "that those of them who are not in the penitentiary are at the Odd Fellows' Hall, or at the Grange, . . . interested in every conceivable kind of organization . . . , except the church of the Lord Jesus Christ." The menfolk were indifferent to the otherworldly gospel of the churches. Practical "in every other concern of life," [64] they could not appreciate religion unless it had "some relation to things seen and temporal." But men in both industry and the professions objected not so much to Christianity itself as to its counterfeits. As evidence of this, they highly approved of Henry Drummond, the Scotch professor, who lectured widely in America on "manly Christianity," defined by

[60] George W. Mead, *Modern Methods of Church Work*, p. 120.

[61] E. A. Lawrence, "An Endeavor Experiment with Social Christianity," *Congregationalist*, July 27, 1893, pp. 117–118; "The Lawrence Memorial Association," *Christian City*, X (April 1898), 429–432.

[62] *Golden Rule*, Sept. 21, 1893, p. 1044; *ibid.*, Jan. 4, 1894, p. 293.

[63] *Epworth Herald*, June 7, 1890, p. 10; *Aggressive Methodism*, V (November 1893), 7; Edwin A. Schell, "Opportunities and Perils of the Epworth League," *Meth. Rev.*, LXXVI (May 1894), 412–420.

[64] "Have We a Religion for Men?" *Andover Rev.*, XII (April 1890), 391–392.

one of his admirers as "the simple, pure practical Christianity of Jesus Christ, minus the congestive coldness and unhappy asceticism of Puritanism." [65]

In the conviction that men desired a fraternal religion, Episcopalians formed the Brotherhood of St. Andrew. A Bible class in St. James' Church of Chicago succeeded so well in its rescue work under James L. Houghteling's leadership that it organized for wider objectives in 1883. A Rule of Prayer and a Rule of Service pledged each member to pray daily for the advance of Christ's kingdom among men and to bring at least one of them each week into a religious meeting. A convention in 1886, attended by delegates from twenty societies, arranged for a national brotherhood with Charles J. Willis, a retired manufacturer and experienced missionary, as president and Houghteling as secretary.[66] Two years later Houghteling assumed the presidency, serving until succeeded in 1900 by H. D. W. English of Pittsburgh, an associate founder of the celebrated Kingsley House. Besides the annual gatherings, a magazine, *St. Andrew's Cross*, which Houghteling began in September, 1886, exerted a unifying influence. The brotherhood gained a strong foothold not only in America, but in all English-speaking countries.[67] "No other organization," said *St. Andrew's Cross*, "has ever had so wide an acceptance throughout the Anglican Communion." [68]

The Brotherhood of St. Andrew, like the young people's movement, was interested primarily in arousing a more earnest evangelism. Its constitution did not authorize a humanitarian program, and its first convention voted to refrain from parish social endeavor. But many members, favoring church work along modern lines, demanded at almost every meeting a re-

---

[65] T. G. Frost, "Professor Drummond and Athletic Christianity in Our American Colleges," *ibid.*, X (November 1888), 508.

[66] Edwin J. Gardiner, "Church Work Among Young Men," *Amer. Church Rev.*, XXXIII (May 1887), 493–494.

[67] *St. Andrew's Cross*, XV (November 1900), 34; *Churchman*, Oct. 25, 1890, pp. 523–524.   [68] *St. Andrew's Cross*, XIII (December 1898), 78.

statement of the Rules of Service. Referring to the fact it was far less comprehensive than the Rule of Prayer, Bishop Anson R. Graves declared "that this ought not to be, but that Brotherhood efforts should be pushed out in every direction, and above all to missionary work in the broad sense of the word." [69]

Though the rule was not changed, its limitations were disregarded in practice, the society participating in almost every phase of social reform. Thus, in 1889, after discussing "The Special Needs of Wage-Earners," the Reverend J. O. S. Huntington's resolution was passed: "That it is the sense of this conference that one special need of wage-earners is that they should be led to see that the cause of Jesus Christ is the cause of truth, righteousness, liberty and love in all departments of our social as well as of our individual life." [70] Speakers repeated this note in later conventions, in that of 1894, for example, when Henry Lloyd, a labor leader of Boston, stated that workingmen "were not infidels" and "would weep as often as any other class of people over the name of the Carpenter of Galilee." [71] As a blow at class distinctions, the Brotherhood insisted that "the rented pew, as in any sense proprietary, must go." [72]

The Brotherhood manifested its social faith through humanitarian endeavor. In Chicago, Philadelphia and Richmond, Brotherhood Houses, offering board and lodging at cheap rates, were established. [73] The Brotherhood also encouraged workingmen's clubs, characteristic institutions in the Protestant Episcopal Church. Thus, St. Paul's Chapter at Harvard University opened a club on Washington Street in Boston, and the St. John's Chapter in Yonkers, New York, a reading and smoking room, which expanded into Hollywood Inn, the finest of its kind

[69] "What the Brotherhood of St. Andrew Can Do for Church Extension," *ibid.*, XI (October 1900), 6.
[70] *Sectional Conference*, 1889, pp. 14, 31–32.
[71] *Churchman*, Oct. 20, 1894, pp. 493–494.   [72] *Ibid.*, Oct. 15, 1892, p. 461.
[73] *St. Andrew's Cross*, XII (October 1897), 14; *ibid.*, XI (October 1896), 6–8; *ibid.*, XV (December 1900), 70.

in America.[74] Some locals, as, for instance, Grace Church in Chicago, set up effective employment bureaus and related forms of service.[75] Mission work, particularly in hospitals, received attention.[76] Thus a St. Louis member, Charles W. Holmes, organized in 1894 a Hospital Association, which cared for patients during convalescence and secured employment for those desiring it. A Church Mission House for Convalescent Women, under the charge of Mrs. Holmes, was an outgrowth.[77]

The other Protestant churches had the Brotherhood of Andrew and Philip, founded in 1888 by the Reverend Rufus W. Miller, of Reading, Pennsylvania. His sermon, "The Ideal Church an Andrew and Philip Society," explained the work of the brotherhood in his own English-speaking Reformed (German) congregation and led to similar organizations in other parishes, particularly in the Reformed Church and the Reformed Lutheran Church. A convention in June, 1889, representing fifteen chapters with about four hundred members, formed a national body for the German and Dutch divisions of the Reformed faith. A second meeting in 1890 removed all denominational restrictions and arranged for a monthly journal, *The Brotherhood Star.*[78] The chapters, with committees on devotional, social and relief affairs, had grown to three hundred and seventy-eight with a membership of over twelve thousand by 1897. Many houses of worship, especially the Fourth Congregational of Hartford and Bethany Presbyterian of Philadelphia, found in the brotherhood a means of increasing their membership.[79]

Besides the two brotherhoods, the last decade and a half of

[74] *Ibid.*, XII (February 1898), 201; *ibid.* (October 1897), 6; *Charities Review*, VII (November 1897), 783.

[75] *Churchman*, Oct. 20, 1894, p. 467; *ibid.*, Aug. 3, 1895, pp. 119–120.

[76] *St. Andrew's Cross*, XI (November 1896), 45–46.

[77] *Ibid.*, XIV (July 1900), 241–243; *ibid.*, XI (April 1897), 203.

[78] Rufus W. Miller, "The Brotherhood of Andrew and Philip," Convention of Christian Workers, *Proceedings*, 1890, pp. 331–332.

[79] George W. Mead, "The Brotherhood of Andrew and Philip," *Open Church*, I (January 1898), 224–225.

the century witnessed the rise of hundreds of religious clubs for men. Realizing that workingmen needed Sunday morning for rest, a few congregations resorted to short gospel services, replete with lay sermons and good music, in the afternoon, after the manner of the "Pleasant Sunday Afternoon," an English practice.[80]   Far more numerous were the Sunday Evening Clubs. The Reverend Charles Murkland, later president of the New Hampshire College of Agriculture and Mechanical Arts, organized the first one in 1891 in the Franklin Street Congregational Church at Manchester. The Faville brothers, pastors of Congregational churches in La Crosse and Appleton, Wisconsin, immediately adopted the plan.[81]   Within a short time more than two hundred similar clubs were formed, many of them the direct outcome of the Reverend John Faville's address before the Evangelical Alliance Conference at Chicago in 1893.[82] What with their short sermons on practical themes, their improved music and their social and philanthropic activity, these clubs successfully appealed to formerly indifferent men and developed a "Niagara of unused power." [83]

As still another contribution to the movement, the Reverend David Allen Reed formed the Christian Industrial League in 1893 for the purpose of identifying wage-earners between the ages of sixteen and sixty with the churches and of training them for personal service among members of their class. The League provided for two groups: those desiring social privileges merely and others who wanted sickness or disability benefits in addition. The chapter at the Fourth Congregational Church in Hartford was typical, having a membership of a hundred and twenty-six, fifty-three in the first section and seventy-three in the second. The former paid an admission fee of twenty-five cents and dues of a dollar a year. The latter, for a higher fee,

[80] George W. Mead, *Modern Methods in Church Work*, pp. 111–117.
[81] John Clark Hill, *The Fishin' Jimmy Club. A Contribution to Evangelistic Liturgies* (New York, 1895), pp. 38–41.
[82] "The Sunday Evening Club," *Christianity Practically Applied*, II, 60–64.
[83] Mead, *Modern Methods in Church Work*, pp. 76–90.

received, in case of sickness, four dollars a week for thirteen weeks, two dollars a week for thirteen additional weeks and the free service of the chapter physician.[84] Taken as a whole, the various brotherhoods constituted "a movement," as the Reverend George W. Mead said, "that must stand prominent in the history of the church." Though previous to 1900 no great denominations except the Episcopal established brotherhoods, they did so early in the next century — the Methodist and Presbyterian in 1906, the Congregationalist in 1908 and others including the Baptist, the Evangelical Association and the Disciples of Christ, shortly afterwards.[85]

If women were conspicuously devout, as compared with men, class distinctions constantly challenged the hold of the churches upon them. By way of reaction, the spirit of sisterhood under a variety of forms influenced thousands of Protestants. Many congregations adopted as their own the Mary and Martha League, which the Madison Avenue Presbyterian Church of New York founded in 1894 to cultivate cordial relations between the rich and the poor.[86] In the Protestant Episcopal Church arose two hundred Girls' Friendly Societies with two boarding homes, one each in Boston and New York, and many club facilities.[87] But most effective in meeting the demands of sisterhood was the Society of King's Daughters, formed in New York in 1886 by Mrs. Frank Bottome, the wife of a Methodist minister. During a religious meeting at her home she and her nine guests hit upon the idea of an organization to exemplify the King's Daughter ideal and the Lend-a-Hand mottoes, to which they reverently added "In His Name." [88] Designed to

[84] Henry H. Kelsey, "The Christian Industrial League," *Open Church*, I (July 1897), 137–139; *Outlook*, Nov. 9, 1895, p. 761.

[85] *Laymen's Quart.*, I (June–August 1906), 14–17; *ibid.*, I (September–November 1906), 35–36; *Methodist Men*, II (June 1908), 118–119; *ibid.*, III (February 1909), 156–157; *ibid.*, III (April 1909), 213–214.

[86] Mead, *Modern Methods in Church Work*, pp. 216–222.

[87] Agnes L. Money, *History of the Girls' Friendly Society* (London, 1898), pp. 156–162, 208.

[88] *Lend a Hand*, I (April 1886), 224–225.

develop "spiritual life and to stimulate Christian activity," the Order admitted all regardless of denominational affiliations. Members were to wear as an insignia of Christian royalty a maltese silver cross tied with a purple ribbon — the symbol of a determination to break down caste or at least to emphasize mutual responsibilities. "So unsuspecting were its originators of its future success," said a contemporary, "that they dreaded any mention of it in the local press." [89] But the movement was contagious. Within two years, "circles," totalling seventy-five thousand members, existed in every section of the country, and by the time of Mrs. Bottome's death in 1906 the Society had a half-million supporters.[90]

Several influences contributed to the Order's remarkable growth. Its national organization after 1887, in which eminent men such as Jacob Riis participated, was one factor. Its yearly convention served to weld classes together on a basis of equality and fellowship. "It was new and delightful," said Ellen E. Dickinson, "to learn how the 'Daughter' living on Fifth Avenue had grasped the hand of the 'Daughter' who was a clerk in a Fifth Avenue shop, and called her 'sister,' the little silver cross being the talisman of acquaintanceship." [91] *The Silver Cross*, a monthly magazine, begun in October, 1888, with Mary Lowe Dickinson as editor, helped to extend and unify the movement. More important was the broad Christian basis of the Order. In the midst of a divided Christendom the Society was necessary, in the Reverend David H. Greer's opinion, to "show the world that there is something true and precious which we all have in common — responsibility to our Lord and Savior, Jesus Christ." [92] Finally, the social service of the Order was comprehensive, being "the broadest of all existing societies in the scope of its work." [93]

[80] Ellen E. Dickinson, *The King's Daughter* (New York, 1890), pp. 8–10.
[90] Herbert O. Crillis, "The Story of the King's Daughters," *New England Magazine*, XXV (January 1907), 553–554.
[91] *Op. cit.*, p. 11.   [92] *Silver Cross*, II (June 1890), p. 291.
[93] Mead, *Modern Methods in Church Work*, p. 210.

Within a surprisingly short time the Order established several hundred institutions to meet a wide variety of human needs. Education along university extension lines came in for much attention. By means of a Correspondence or Home Study Department, the Order aided those of defective training to pass school examinations, helped women to become bookkeepers, stenographers and school teachers, as well as gave a thorough foundation in the classics. A Library Exchange set up in 1900 furthered this aspect of the Order's program.[94] As an evidence of their vital interest in progressive church work, the Daughters opened in 1890 the Silver Cross Rescue Mission at Bayonne, New Jersey.[95] More important were the settlements. The most noted one, the King's Daughters' Settlement in New York at 48 Henry Street, began in 1890 when a Circle of Service for Tenement Work, organized by Riis and eighteen women, "agreed to coöperate with existing agencies, to visit, comfort and relieve the sick and needy of New York City, to instruct them and to better their condition physically, morally and spiritually." Supplying needs discovered by the Board of Health, the Circle was ready in 1894 to assume the full settlement status. A little later the Order founded the Harlem Settlement and the Asacog House in Brooklyn for "all sorts and conditions of girls." [96]

With a view to overcoming class distinctions among women, the sisterhood established homes for working girls in various parts of the country, the best known of which was the Gordon Rest for Working Women and Girls at Hanson, Massachusetts. The King's Sons, the auxiliary of the King's Daughters, opened gymnasiums and restaurants to attain a like objective among men. Interest in children was attested by industrial schools, boys' clubs and children's homes. In some cases, as in the Day

[94] *Silver Cross*, XIII (Jan. 20, 1900), 11.
[95] *Ibid.*, IV (December 1891), 83.
[96] *Ibid.*, II (June 1890), 267; *ibid.*, XIII (October 1900), 2; *Christian City*, XII (October 1900), 142–143.

Nursery and Children's Home at Nashua, New Hampshire, these homes operated alongside day nurseries which were favorite charities of the Order.[97] With scarcely less zeal, the Order supported the National or George Junior Republics for training youth in the principles of self-government. The Daughters also founded institutions for the diseased, as, for example, the Silver Cross Home for Epileptics at Port Deposit, Maryland, and the King's Daughters' Home for Incurables at Oakland, California. For the criminal or immoral, a Prisoners' Guild in Pennsylvania founded a Home of Industry to care for discharged convicts just as a Circle in South Carolina, in coöperation with the churches and the Woman's Christian Temperance Union, organized a Florence Crittenton Home.[98] Nor did the Order forget the charities of the older type, having to its credit by 1900 many hospitals and homes for the aged.[99]

The significance of the King's Daughters as a sisterhood of personal service is not easily exaggerated. Besides its own incredibly numerous institutions, it insisted on aiding social agencies outside its control. The Order was founded, it was recalled, "not so much to do new work as to turn new workers into fields needing helpers." [100] By forming circles for the support of this or that charity, the Daughters greatly increased their usefulness as an auxiliary form of Protestant social service.

Though less comprehensive in scope and extent, the other auxiliary forms of Protestant social service — the deaconess bodies, the Christian associations, the Sunday schools, the young people's societies and the brotherhoods — all contributed to urban welfare through philanthropies ranging from kindergartens to social settlements. Large in the aggregate, this social work filled in many gaps still open in the Protestant religio-

[97] *Silver Cross*, XII (August 1900), 11.

[98] *Ibid.*, XII (September 1900), 4; *ibid.* (October 1900), 2–3; *ibid.* (January 1901), 5.

[99] *Benevolent Institutions: 1910*, p. 184, *passim.*

[100] Clara Morehouse, "The Mission of Our Order," *Silver Cross*, XII (May 9, 1900), 10.

social system. In many instances, the local chapters of the various adjuncts were integral parts of great institutional churches. In a deeper sense, these ancillary organizations, by arousing latent spiritual energies, strengthened and reinforced the whole structure of social Christianity.

CHAPTER IX

CHANGING TRENDS IN THE SEMINARIES

INCREASINGLY the seminaries conformed their educational programs to meet urban religious needs. If earlier they had been indifferent to social Christianity, they heartily embraced it during the social crisis of the late eighties and the nineties. As training schools for the ministry, the seminaries felt the full shock of the urban impact. Many ministers and laymen, using the trial and error method, had pioneered the way to a more satisfactory religion. But mindful of the mistakes and failures growing out of their lack of formal training, they determined that the younger folk entering the field should be prepared beforehand. They looked to the theological schools to equip men and women for the task.

The movement for a socialized pastorate began under happy auspices. In the early seventies the family of Stephen Colwell endowed a Princeton professorship of Christian ethics and apologetics "to treat of the religion of Christ in its bearings upon human society and the welfare of man in general, and . . . to expound the duties which men owe to their fellow men, not only in their individual capacity, but organized and associated as churches, communities and nations." [1] Though the Reverend Charles A. Aiken resigned the Presidency of Union College to accept the chair, he construed his duties in a narrow and purely theoretical spirit. [2] As a result, really notable progress had to await a decade or more. In the meantime, Christian people kept clamoring for a more efficient ministry — for clergymen able to draw lessons from the Bible and to apply them to current religious issues. On all sides the conviction grew that, unlike the

---

[1] *Inauguration of the Rev. Charles A. Aiken* (New York, 1872), pp. 3-4.
[2] Princeton Theol. Sem., *Catalogue*, 1872, p. 15.

legal and medical professions which until recently had been deficient in theoretical training, the ministry suffered from too little practical training.[3]

A striking indication of the failure of the seminaries to satisfy new needs was the increase after the mid-eighties in the number of independent training schools for the clergy and laity. Besides the instruction which the Y.M.C.A., the Y.W.C.A., the W.C.T.U. and the Salvation Army provided, several institutional churches specialized in preparing city missionaries. For example, in 1885 the Reverend David Allen Reed, pastor of Hope Church, Springfield, Massachusetts, founded a School for Christian Workers to train Sunday-school superintendents and pastors' assistants, and a Christian Industrial and Training School for Young Men and Women to equip them for service among the wage-earning population.[4] Agencies of perhaps even broader scope included Moody's Lay Evangelistic Training School of Chicago and the School for Christian Workers at Northfield, Massachusetts, A. J. Gordon's Boston Missionary Training School and J. P. Bixby's Lay College for Christian Workers at Revere, Massachusetts. Another minister, George W. Sampson, started the Evening Theological School of New York, which in 1896 combined with Amity Baptist Church; and the Society for Education Extension of Hartford founded a School of Sociology in 1894.[5] These institutions symbolized the growing challenge to the practical usefulness of the seminaries.

Had the ministry remained a highly attractive calling, the seminaries could have met its new needs more easily. But it had sadly declined in influence and numerical strength. In the period from 1865 to 1900 a large percentage of congregations in all Protestant denominations were without pastors.[6] College

[3] George C. Shattuck, "Education of Divinity Students," Prot. Epis. Church Cong., *Essays, Debates and Discussions*, 1881, p. 250.   [4] *Report*, 1889, p. 12.
[5] *Golden Rule*, Aug. 29, 1889, p. 771; *Christian Union*, Feb. 6, 1892, pp. 271–272; *Lend a Hand*, XIII (October 1894), 303–305; *Congregationalist*, Nov. 29, 1894, p. 794; *Zion's Herald*, July 17, 1895, p. 449.
[6] Gen. Assembly of the Presby. Church, *Minutes*, 1890, p. 149.

graduates, drawn by the "mercantile spirit," passed by the ministry for "professions simply lucrative." [7] Yet financial considerations alone did not account for the ministerial famine. The methods of study in the seminaries were unsatisfactory: they sacrificed freedom of investigation to sectarian indoctrination. "Even the ignorant," said Harvard's President Eliot, "have learned to despise the process of searching for proofs of a foregone conclusion." The civilized world, thanks to "the rise and development of physical and natural science," had "set up a new standard of intellectual sincerity," he insisted, "and Protestant theologians and ministers must rise to that standard if they would continue to command the respect of mankind." [8]

The immediate remedial measures made only for futility and retrogression. In desperate need of additional clergy for the mounting population, the various denominations heavily subsidized prospective ministers in the colleges and seminaries. But, as Eliot said, indiscriminate aid of this sort appealed mainly to "young men of small mental capacity and flaccid physical or moral fibre." [9] Even the conservative Presbyterian Church, which up to 1882 had secured two-thirds of its ministry through beneficiary grants, admitted that there "is a lack of care and judgment on the part of pastors and sessions and on the part of Presbyteries and colleges in approving and continuing these men who are mentally unfit." [10] As the calibre of students declined, the seminaries diluted the content of instruction by replacing Latin, Greek and Hebrew studies with so-called "English Courses." Thus, in four Congregational seminaries, candidates of this variety rose from six and a half per cent of the total in 1885 to thirty-three and a half in 1889.[11]

---

[7] Andrew D. White, *The Message of the Nineteenth Century to the Twentieth*, p. 17, quoted in T. Edwin Brown, *Studies in Modern Socialism and Labor Problems* (New York, 1886), pp. 166–167.

[8] "On the Education of Ministers," *Princeton Rev.*, LIX (May 1883), 345–346.   [9] *Ibid.*, pp. 349–350.

[10] Gen. Assembly, *Minutes*, 1884, p. 86.

[11] *Ibid.*, 1890, p. 151; Nat. Council, *Minutes*, 1895, pp. 224–225; *ibid.*, 1898, p. 236.

Though more adaptable to average congregations than clergy of the older type, these men of mediocre intellect quailed before the tasks of the new religious leadership. When ready solutions failed to solve the problem, the seminaries analyzed their educational responsibilities from a broader viewpoint. They came to realize that, since theology had become largely a critical and historical science, it could be studied with profit only by the inductive method and in relation to the amazing advances of knowledge in other fields. Likewise, the wide variety of religious needs in the great industrial cities necessitated specialized instruction in pastoral theology.[12] For the time being, the seminaries alone must shoulder the principal burden of new curricula, for the colleges and universities more and more relegated the languages to the background and hesitated to introduce the social sciences — studies so essential to the prospective minister.

Progress along the newly projected lines was inevitably slow, although by the late seventies the Harvard Divinity School had taken steps, under Eliot's prodding, to become something more than an old-fashioned Unitarian recruiting ground. Eliot ridiculed the prevalent notion in Harvard circles that theological education should have no place in a non-sectarian university, since theology, except only Christian Dogmatics — its smallest part — was, he believed, as liberal as chemistry, philosophy or history.[13] At about the same time, the neighboring Andover Seminary fell into line with the new trends because of "the special demands for a reinvestigation of methods from our own age, evinced in the contrast it exhibits between our increased faith in a practical Christianity on the one hand, and a profounder questioning of the theology of Christianity on the other." [14]

[12] George B. Stevens, "Some Present Day Conditions Affecting Theological Education," *New World*, XVI (December 1900), 674–676.
[13] Pres. and Treas. of Harv. Coll., *Report*, 1877–78, pp. 32–37; *ibid.*, 1887–88, p. 14; *ibid.*, 1889–90, p. 123.
[14] *Catalogue*, 1879–80, p. 18.

Well before the end of the eighties, the leading seminaries were centering their scientific interests in a new subject, "Biblical Theology," which "distinctly disclaims," its defenders said, "any philosophical or speculative method." [15] Chicago Seminary introduced the new discipline as early as 1879, Andover in 1880, Bangor in 1882, Auburn in 1884 and Hartford four years later. In pressing its claims to recognition, the Reverend Charles A. Briggs of Union Seminary in New York so vehemently disparaged systematic theology that conservatives forced him and the Seminary out of the Presbyterian Church. But, as Professor George H. Gilbert said, his work "as compared with that of his accusers must be admitted to be far more scientific and scriptural." The inductive study of the Bible, apart from giving a more truthful view, "has helped," Gilbert argued, "to an appreciation of the human element in the Bible which must needs be appreciated in order to a true appreciation of the divine element." [16] Knowledge of this sort also enabled the regular ministry to direct laymen whose Biblical inductions were often as exaggerated as they were honest and sincere.

The second change in instruction resulted from an expanded and specialized curriculum. Since the traditional three-year course failed to cover the field, a fourth year, generally referred to as the Advanced Class, proved helpful. Leading seminaries — Yale in 1879, Andover in 1880, Hartford in 1882, the General Theological School in 1883 and the Divinity School of the Protestant Episcopal Church in Philadelphia somewhat later — adopted this expedient. A few seminaries, among them Andover, Hartford and Chicago, provided also for graduate study abroad. Although these modifications afforded a measure of relief, the schools gradually adopted the elective system in order the more fully to remove the "inexorable pressure of unlimited

---

[15] George B. Stevens, "What is Biblical Theology and What is its Method?" *Biblical World*, I (January 1893), 8.

[16] "Biblical Theology," *ibid.*, VI (November 1895), 360–363. Professor George B. Stevens' books, *The Pauline Theology* and *The Johannine Theology*, were the best literary expositions of the movement.

subject matter upon limited time." [17] If Harvard was the first to experiment with the new plan, Oberlin was the first to accept it wholeheartedly. In 1885, Oberlin audaciously made Hebrew and other basic subjects optional, an example soon followed, though less thoroughly, by others — Hartford in 1891, Andover in 1893 and Union in 1894.[18] But Yale did not think it wise "to abandon to any great extent the time honored course of prescribed studies." [19]

Instructors and students could not take full advantage of the elective system until a much larger number of seminarians entered upon their work after a liberal education.[20] In the hope of lifting standards in the seminaries to approximately those of the best professional schools, Harvard provided that after 1881 only students with a college education or its equivalent should be admitted to candidacy for a degree.[21] This successful experiment was widely followed, all the Congregational seminaries refusing applicants obviously lacking the necessary qualifications. The Episcopal Theological School of Cambridge required of its prospective students after 1892 a fully accredited degree, justifying its action on the ground that at least one institution in the Episcopal Communion should offer an exceptionally fine type of training.[22] Union Seminary in New York, finding in 1899 that half of those desiring entrance were unpromising, "had the conscience and courage to reject them." [23]

Improvement in the quality of ministerial students involved also the elimination of the old beneficiary system. This could

[17] E. S. Worcester, "Theological Education," *Recent Church Progress* (New York, 1909), p. 333; A. L. Gillette, "Electives in Theological Seminaries," *Hartford Sem. Rec.*, III (August 1893), 304–305.

[18] Nat. Council, *Minutes*, 1886, pp. 281–282; *ibid.*, 1892, pp. 217–218; *ibid.*, 1895, p. 223; Union Theol. Sem., *Catalogue*, 1895, p. 23.

[19] Nat. Council, *Minutes*, 1892, p. 228.

[20] John Tunis, "Social Science in the Theological Seminary," *Lend a Hand*, XVI (January 1896), 11.

[21] Pres. and Treas. of Harv. Coll., *Report*, 1881–82, p. 81.

[22] *Catalogue*, 1892–93.

[23] W. D. Hyde, "Reform in Theological Education," *Atlantic Monthly*, LXXXV (January 1900), 21.

be done by charging a regular tuition and by granting the necessary aid on a basis of merit. In this, as in so many other respects, Harvard led the way, making gradual progress after 1872 in refusing financial assistance to mediocre students.[24] But they long enjoyed privileges at Harvard. In 1890, for example, they paid only a third of the fee of the other departments. Finally in 1895 the Corporation raised it to the regular level, a step, said Eliot, which would place the school and the profession on "a footing which will commend them anew to self-respecting young men, to the parents of young men who incline to the ministry and to the Protestant community at large." [25]

At the same time the Episcopal Theological School of Cambridge imposed a small entrance charge, while others began awarding scholarships only to the deserving. The reaction against the prevalent practice gathered enough momentum to induce the Presbyterian Education Board and the Congregational Education Society to cut sharply the number of their recipients.[26] The former wrote in 1896 that, in handling "the great number of applications from every section of the country, the Board was using precaution and care." [27] The Congregational churches, with one or two exceptions, "are now endeavoring," it was said, "to administer these funds in precisely the same way in which similar funds are administered in colleges and universities." [28]

Increasingly, the seminaries seized upon city mission work by the student in his spare time as a solution to the problem of pecuniary aid. Union Seminary in New York pioneered in this sphere, developing in 1887 a plan under the Reverend A. F. Schauffler's superintendence. Only college graduates who had

---

[24] Pres. and Treas. of Harv. Coll., *Report*, 1873, pp. 15–16; *ibid.*, 1879, pp. 78–79.

[25] *Ibid.*, 1890–91, p. 19.

[26] Williston Walker, "The Churches and Their Seminaries," *Hartford Sem. Rec.*, IX (August 1899), 291–292.

[27] Gen. Assembly, *Minutes*, 1896, pp. 43, 293.

[28] George Foot Moore, "Theological Seminaries Further Defended," International Council of Congreg. Churches, *Meeting*, 1899, p. 363.

at least a seventy-five-per-cent record and maintained it in the seminary were privileged to participate. Those accepted and agreeing to teach Sunday-school classes, to visit tenements two hours each week and to help at one church service each Sunday received a hundred and fifty dollars a year.[29] Chicago Seminary adopted this plan, as did also the Divinity Department of the University of Chicago. "We expect men who receive assistance from the Education Society to do some measure of religious work," said an official of the latter institution. "Our theory is eight hours of service during the week in visitation and in holding prayer-meetings or in something of that kind and at least one service on Sunday." [30] The Episcopal Theological School of Cambridge, realizing that a high tuition was impossible, gave financial assistance on condition that candidates render its equivalent in service at the Boston City Episcopal Mission. "The school," said the dean, "does not dispense a dollar in charity." [31]

The new educational trends fared badly in isolated rural seminaries. "What medical school," asked Graham Taylor, "is thus remote from the centres of suffering men, and deprived of hospital clinics . . . How . . . can men be expected to lead whither they have never followed, or scarcely looked much less wrought?" [32] Though a few ministers feared that the city seminary might disqualify graduates for the rural parishes, the large majority agreed that the urban seminary could better prepare candidates for both fields of labor. Accordingly, some divinity schools moved to more favorable locations: the Theological Institute of Connecticut from East Windsor Hall to Hartford; Union Theological Seminary of Virginia from Hampden-Sydney to Richmond; and the Pacific Seminary from Oakland to Berkeley, California. The plans of Meadville and Andover for

[29] Francis Brown, "Field Work: Its Education Value and Relation to the Financial Aid of Students," *Christianity Practically Applied*, II, 429–430.
[30] *Christianity Practically Applied*, II, 440.
[31] *Catalogue*, 1894–1895, pp. 63–64; *ibid.*, 1898, p. 67.
[32] *Pioneering on Social Frontiers*, p. 387.

changes in sites could not be realized until the twentieth century. A few denominations consolidated their divinity schools with their universities. Thus, Methodists united Concord Biblical Institute with Boston University and made Garrett Biblical Institute the theological department of Northwestern University. Likewise, the Baptists reorganized the Baptist Union Theological Seminary as part of the new University of Chicago — an arrangement which might well have served as a model for all religious bodies. Some leaders suggested that a satisfactory solution would not be found until the numerous weak seminaries gave way to a few well-equipped ones in strategic cities.[33]

Instruction in sociology and pastoral service climaxed the movement for pedagogical reform. Three teachers, Francis G. Peabody, William J. Tucker and Graham Taylor pioneered the way at Harvard, Andover and Hartford respectively. Peabody, a professor of theology at Harvard after 1881, brought to his work, said Eliot, "an unusually prolonged training in theology and ethics, successful experience in preaching and a strong interest in teaching." [34] The traditional course in moral philosophy, with its fruitless deduction, furnished the point of departure for his fresh insights. "As a teacher of ethics," Peabody said, "I became aware of the chasm that exists between such abstract study and the practical application of moral ideals; and it seemed to me possible to approach the theory of ethics inductively, through the analysis of great moral movements, which could be easily characterized and from which principles could be deduced. I studied thus with my class the problems of charity, divorce, the Indians, the labor question, intemperance, with results of surprising interest." [35] His course, "The Ethics

[33] "The Work of the Seminary As Conditioned by Its Location," *Christianity Practically Applied*, II, 422–427.

[34] Pres. and Treas. of Harv. Coll., *Report*, 1880–81, pp. 25–26.

[35] Quoted in Frank L. Talman, "The Study of Sociology in the Educational Institutions of the United States," *Amer. Jour. of Sociology*, VII (May 1902), 823–824.

of the Social Question," which some of his colleagues thought incapable of being "seriously pursued," [36] deeply impressed the students of Harvard and finally took its true place in the University's scheme of liberal education. Besides the classroom, a Summer School of Theology, in which social Christianity had a prominent place, added to Harvard's contribution.[37]

William J. Tucker, Professor of Sacred Rhetoric in Andover from 1879 to 1893, smuggled social study into the Seminary. He took wide liberties with a Lectureship on Pastoral Theology, which at the time of his appointment was the only semblance of the Seminary's practical concern. "It seemed to me," he said, "as I looked into this lectureship that it was capable of rendering a wide and timely service. . . . It became entirely logical, under the construction put upon this lectureship, to emphasize the new and enlarged functions of the church in modern society." [38] A small number of scholarships, provided by the Winkley Fund,[39] enabled his advanced students to make investigations in various cities of subjects ranging from the Sunday school to complicated questions of labor organization. Ten additional scholarships of a hundred dollars each, with traveling expenses, permitted first-year men to participate in evangelistic and institutional church work. Many were trained at Berkeley Temple under the supervision of the Reverend Charles A. Dickinson. Others, commonly referred to as the Andover Band, labored during vacation periods in the rural districts of New England.[40] The result of classroom and extra-curricular study was the excellent course, "Social Economics," the summaries of which in the *Andover Review* greatly influenced ministers and laymen. With unusual clarity, Tucker pointed out that the church must consider (1) the relation of society to those who

---

[36] "Letter to Robert A. Woods," quoted in Woods and Kennedy, *The Settlement Horizon*, p. 40.

[37] Pres. and Treas. of Harv. Coll., *Report*, 1900–1901, p. 24.

[38] *My Generation*, p. 161.   [39] *Catalogue*, 1880–1881, p. 22.

[40] *The Theol. Sem. Bull.* (June 1888), pp. 37–38; Nat. Council, *Minutes*, 1889, pp. 182–183.

have not been fully incorporated into it, with special reference to the present aims and demands of the laboring class; (2) the relation of society to those who have forfeited their rights in it (the treatment of crime and the criminal classes); and (3) the relation of society to those who are unable, through various disabilities, to keep their place in it (the treatment of pauperism and disease).[41]

At Hartford, Graham Taylor had trained a few seminarians during the early eighties at the Fourth Church and in the Pastors' Union.[42] In 1888 the Seminary drastically reorganized its curriculum to make possible "the extended, balanced and specialized ministerial discipline which the peculiar character of our present civilization demands. . . ."[43] In his inaugural address as Samuel Hawes Professor of Practical Theology, Taylor insisted that "God's message 'to repent and believe the Gospel' cannot be fully delivered until the church is ready to offer the penitent something within her fold to turn to. . . . The adjustment of the church's thought and agencies to these social tendencies and forces is necessary both to the winning of the soul and the coming of the Kingdom." [44] In the classroom he stressed preaching, evangelistics, pastoral care, and pastoral superintendence, including church polity, fellowship, economics and Christian sociology.[45] On going to Chicago in 1892, he was succeeded by the Reverend Alexander Ross Merriam, who greatly extended the program in both its optional and prescribed features.[46] First-year men made a local study of the religious, civic and beneficent forces of Hartford by means of discussions, class visits to institutions and individual reports of assigned special investigations. "Opportunity is given in Middle and Senior years," the authorities said, "to continue the study

---

[41] W. J. Tucker, "Social Economics," *Andover Review*, XI (January 1889), 85; *ibid.*, vols. XI–XV (February 1889–June 1891).

[42] Nat. Council, *Minutes*, 1886, pp. 278–279.   [43] *Ibid.*, 1889, p. 190.

[44] *Pioneering on Social Frontiers*, pp. 387–388.

[45] *Catalogue*, 1888–89, pp. 17–18.

[46] *Ibid.*, 1892–93, pp. 22–24; *ibid.*, 1893–94, pp. 22, 24–26.

by lectures which treat some of the problems of the family, of education, of labor, of citizenship, of charity, of crime and allied themes. The scope of the lecture course," it was emphasized, "is greatly supplemented by special investigations and theses submitted by members of the class." [47]

Nearly all the leading seminaries followed in the footsteps of Harvard, Andover and Hartford. As social problems became increasingly acute, they turned to sociology for inspiration and guidance. Though an investigation in 1893 showed that in thirty-five well-known schools only five had prescribed and only nine had elective courses, not one of them "disavows responsibility for sociological teaching," and only two or three "manifest indifference toward it." If but two seminaries had complete departments in this branch, many had special or regular sociological lectureships as well as professorships in dogmatic theology which treated social themes. One professor, for example, taught "ethical and sociological theology," while another gave "large attention to the principles of ethics as developed from the moral law in the direction of social and political action." Instructors in Christian ethics, pastoral theology and homiletics were doing likewise. In some divinity schools, moreover, field work for ministerial candidates was included. Realizing, however, the need for a fuller and more systematic treatment of social science, several institutions hoped to establish chairs whose holders could devote all their time to the subject.[48]

In requesting additional equipment, the seminaries pointed to the "increasing intelligence of the communities to be served, the enlarging field of Christian effort and the broadening scope of the activity of the church and the ministry, which are characteristic of the present day." [49] Appeals like this obtained for

---

[47] *Ibid.*, 1897–98, p. 30.

[48] Graham Taylor, "Sociological Work in Theological Seminaries," *Seventh Section, International Congress of Charities, Corrections and Philanthropy, Chicago, 1893* (Baltimore, 1894), pp. 70–71.

[49] Newton Theol. Institution, *Catalogue*, 1891, pp. 26–27.

several schools, including all the Universalist ones, endowments for sociological instruction.[50] Only less indicative of the seminaries' determination to promote social Christianity was the new type of men who more and more filled the great executive positions. Thus George Hodges, who at Pittsburgh had institutionalized Calvary Church and founded the famous Kingsley House, became Dean in 1893 of the Episcopal Theological School in Cambridge. Union Seminary in New York chose as President in 1898 the Reverend Charles Cuthbert Hall, the successful pastor of the institutional First Presbyterian Church in Brooklyn. Auburn in 1899 followed Union's example, selecting the Reverend George Black Stewart, long identified with the labor movement. In his inaugural address on "The Place of the Minister in the Present Day Church," he glorified institutional churches and pledged Auburn to prepare clergy capable of managing them.[51]

Subsoiled by these trends, the field was ready for a rich sociological harvest. After Andover and Hartford, Chicago was the most important Congregational seminary, having, for example, the first department of Christian Sociology in America.[52] Aiming from the date of its opening in 1859 "to follow the practical way of training men for their work found in the legal and medical professions," the Seminary in its first years had fallen far short of its audacious plan to give as much attention to city missions as to theology.[53] But in 1891, with the creation of the Instructorship in the Use of the English Bible and Methods of Christian Work, it began realizing its early ideal. The following year this teaching expanded into a well-organized Department of Christian Sociology and the English Bible, headed by

[50] Nat. Council, *Minutes*, 1892, pp. 225–226; *Christian Leader*, March 29, 1888, p. 4.

[51] *Inauguration of the Rev. George Black Stewart as President of the Theological Seminary of Auburn and as Professor of Practical Theology* (Auburn, 1899), pp. 36–54.

[52] W. C. Gannett, "Social Economics and Ministerial Usefulness," *Lend A Hand*, XIII (October 1894), 269–270.

[53] *Year Book*, 1895, p. 47.

Taylor. Many prescribed and elective courses considered (1) Biblical Sociology, including the kingdom of God in the Old and the New Testaments and the sociological development of the Apostolic Church; (2) Sociology, dealing with the biological basis, method and terminology of social science, and with the relation of Christian facts and forces to social dynamics; and (3) Social Economics, treating of the family and its relation to the church and state, and of the function of the church in the industrial structure of modern society and its relation to the dependent, defective and delinquent classes.[54] Another strong Congregational seminary, the Divinity School at Yale, after beginning with a Lectureship on Social Ethics and the Philosophy of Religion, and with field work in the city missions, instituted in 1894 a Department of Christian Ethics and Sociology, presided over by the Reverend William F. Blackman who had won distinction as pastor of a small city institutional church in Connecticut.[55] Sociology, including economics and progressive methods of religious activity, was compulsory for Seniors, electives being available to them and to the younger men in several special studies. In addition, over ninety per cent of the candidates regularly engaged in Christian service.

In 1893 Bangor, the weakest Congregational seminary, endowed the Bond Lectureship for information on practical themes and introduced sociology as a class-room study, the teachers being John S. Sewall and Clarence A. Beckwith. The course in sociology — along with Christian Ethics, a compulsory subject — considered the various problems "that have grown to such significance in our times," such as the theories of social reconstruction, the labor question, the land question and the prevalence of crime and pauperism. Above all, the course aimed "to give the results of experience rather than the theories of the chair, and to turn upon the wants and woes of society the light of God's word." [56] In the same year Oberlin College

---

[54] *Ibid.*, 1892–93, p. 22; *ibid.*, 1893–94, pp. 15–16, 30.
[55] *Catalogue*, 1892–93, p. 172.   [56] *Catalogue*, 1894–95, pp. 22–23.

admitted theological students to its social-science studies. Two years later an alumnus, the Reverend C. H. Vincent, arranged for a series of monthly conferences upon the practical problems of the pastorate, while Z. Swift Holbrook delivered a course of lectures on Christian Sociology in which he viewed the subject "more as an art of social control than as a completed science." [57] At Pacific Seminary the Reverend Charles Kelley Jenness, one of Dr. A. G. Warner's students, gave a lecture-seminar course in 1894 on "Social Pathology and Philanthropology in Connection with the Influence of Church Charities, Medieval and Modern." Expanded and systematized, this practical, almost wholly inductive, study continued, under the Reverend Frank Hugh Foster, Jenness's successor, until the Seminary assumed quasi-official relations with the University of California.[58]

If the majority of Presbyterian seminaries were more or less indifferent to sociological study, the better ones were in the vanguard of the movement. Thus in 1894 Union Seminary in New York, through the Union Seminary Society for Christian Work, provided more fully and systematically for missionary practice, making it "a part of the regular course of training for the ministry." [59] The Union Social Settlement, established at the same time by the Alumni Club, also afforded many opportunities for student acquaintance with urban religious problems. Some years before, the Seminary had secured for its more promising men free admission to the social-science classes at Columbia and New York Universities. On adopting the elective system in 1894 the Seminary itself was ready for social studies. Professor Briggs transformed Christian Ethics into Biblical Sociology — perhaps the first formal course of this type in an American seminary — and President Hall specialized on missionary subjects, one of which was entitled, "City Evangelization and the Institutional Church." After Union, Auburn

[57] *Catalogue*, 1893, pp. 29–30; *ibid.*, 1894, p. 30.
[58] *Catalogue*, 1895, pp. 10–12; *ibid.*, 1900, p. 27.
[59] *Catalogue*, 1894–95, pp. 20–21.

Seminary was most sensitive to social currents, introducing Christian Sociology in 1891 at the hands of the Reverend Arthur S. Hoyt, an experienced pastor and teacher. The instruction included the general principles of sociology, the relation of the church to social problems and investigations in selected fields of applied Christianity. In 1896 Hoyt headed the new Department of Homiletics and Sociology.[60]

At Princeton Theological Seminary, students displayed interest in field work, and in social study through the Princeton Sociological Club. They were privileged to attend the special lectures of Graham Taylor, Wilbur F. Crafts and others, and after 1896 to follow a regular course, Biblical Sociology.[61] Financial and theological difficulties prevented Lane Seminary in Cincinnati from introducing regular study, though social problems were treated in frequent lectures and steps were taken to assure practical training. In return for service under the direction of the Cincinnati Presbytery, students were paid a maximum of a hundred dollars a year.[62] Other Presbyterian institutions such as McCormick at Chicago and Western in Allegheny, Pennsylvania, introduced similar programs.[63]

Among Baptist divinity schools, Newton Theological Institution at Newton Centre, Massachusetts, led the way. After 1883 the Reverend John M. English worked out prescribed and elective courses in the socialized pastorate.[64] George Bullen, Professor of Christian Missions during the nineties, supervised practical training, being "the personal instructor of the students in such mission work as they may, with the approval of the faculty, undertake while in the institution." [65] Hamilton Theological Seminary at Colgate University secured in 1888 a

[60] *Catalogue*, 1885, p. 12; *ibid.*, 1892, pp. 16–17; *ibid.*, 1896, p. 32.
[61] *Catalogue*, 1892–95; *ibid.*, 1896, p. 17.
[62] *Catalogue*, 1891, pp. 18–19.
[63] Gen. Assembly, *Minutes*, 1888, p. 182; *ibid.*, 1891, p. 243; McCormick Theol. Sem., *Catalogue*, 1899–1900, pp. 26, 32.
[64] *Catalogue*, 1883, p. 14; *ibid.*, 1889, p. 21; *ibid.*, 1900, p. 30.
[65] *Ibid.*, 1890, pp. 27–28; *ibid.*, 1897, p. 33.

Permanent Lectureship on Methods of Christian Work, which in 1890–1891, for example, dealt with "City Evangelization and the Evangelical Alliance." With a view to more systematic teaching, the authorities in 1890 appealed for a fund to endow a chair of Christian Sociology, pointing out that it is "now universally recognized that the minister of Christ should have a large acquaintance with social conditions, affecting the life of the individual, which he is called of God to help in Christianizing, and an intimate knowledge of the principles of Christ in their bearing on society." This desire was realized in 1892 to the extent of a lectureship.[66]

The University of Chicago Divinity School, remarkable for its advanced study in all branches of theology, devoted one of its eight undergraduate divisions to the work of missions. In the Graduate School sociology secured departmental status, under Charles Richmond Henderson, who was equally proficient in church administration and productive scholarship. By making the classes in sociology compulsory for all students, the whole Seminary stressed the practical side of the minister's vocation. Besides Henderson's courses, Shailer Mathews exegetically explored the Bible for its bearing on social theory. The material used in his courses, "Sociological Ideas of the Gospels Exegetically Investigated," and "Sociological Ideas of the Apostolic Age," he first published in the *American Journal of Sociology* and later in a book, *The Social Teachings of Jesus.*[67] Methodists showed a similar interest, especially at Boston and Vanderbilt Universities which offered electives in sociology and applied Christianity.[68]

The Episcopal seminaries made similar progress. For several years before it arranged for social study at Columbia Univer-

[66] *Catalogue*, 1888, pp. 19–20; *ibid.*, 1890, pp. 34–35, 57; *ibid.*, 1892, p. 33.

[67] *The Quarterly Calendar of the University of Chicago*, 1892–93, Divinity School Edition, No. 1, p. 20; "Introductory Statement — Department of Sociology," *Circular of Information of the University of Chicago Divinity School*, February 1895, p. 37.

[68] Boston University, *Year Book*, 1896, p. 124; *Zion's Herald*, Feb. 15, 1899, p. 198; Vanderbilt University, *Register*, 1899–1900.

sity, the General Theological Seminary had urged its professors to determine the ethical and social implications of revealed religion. In 1894, as part of a new curriculum for the advanced study of theology and its related fields, the Seminary established a Department of Moral Theology and Christian Philosophy, with the Reverend Charles Theodore Seibt in charge. Martineau's *Types of Ethical Theory*, Smyth's *Christian Ethics* and *Ely's Social Aspects of Christianity* were among the many books used as texts.[69] Three years before, the Divinity School of Philadelphia had endowed a similar chair, whose optional courses were "pursued by a considerable number of students with sustained interest." But students and faculty devoted more attention "to the practical training for the ministry," using a near-by institutional church as a clinic.[70]

At the Episcopal Theological School of Cambridge successive deans, Gray, Lawrence and Hodges, exerted their influence to favor sociological teaching. But as late as 1891 the School still believed that such instruction was "not the legitimate part of a clergyman's education." [71] Hodges's appointment in 1893, along with the adoption of the elective system two years later, resulted in sociology as an elective. A Lectureship on Sociology was the only additional provision, the appeal for a chair having failed to materialize. Practice, however, was afforded by an arrangement with the Boston City Episcopal Mission, whose head, Frederick B. Allen, was expert in social science.[72] Another Episcopal school alive to modern demands was the Seabury Divinity School at Faribault, Minnesota, one of the first five seminaries in America to prescribe sociology. Its Department of Ethics and Apologetics, headed by the Reverend J. McBride Sterrett, admirably covered the field, individual and social.[73]

[69] *Catalogue*, 1890, pp. 33–34; *ibid.*, 1896, pp. 39–40.
[70] *Catalogue*, 1892, pp. 16–18; *ibid.*, 1896, pp. 35–36.
[71] *New Nation*, Dec. 26, 1891, p. 765.
[72] *Catalogue*, 1887, pp. 59–62; *ibid.*, 1896, p. 23.
[73] Graham Taylor, "Sociological Work in Theological Seminaries," *loc. cit.*, p. 68; *Calendar*, 1887, p. 14.

In 1895 the Theological Seminary of the Diocese of Virginia was also placing emphasis "on points of theology, especially connected with the living issues of the day in Christian sociology." [74]

Lutheran seminaries mirrored the sociological trend. Thus, in 1891, the venerable W. A. Passavant organized the Chicago Lutheran Theological Seminary to train a ministry in the English language and to spread the principles of the Inner Mission of Germany. A special feature was extension study for ministers some years out of school.[75] In addition to its Christian ethics, the theological department of Wittenberg College arranged for lectures by Stuckenberg, the Lutheran sociologist.[76] In 1896 Heidelberg Seminary created a Department of Practical Theology and Christian Sociology, with John H. Bamberger and Charles F. Miller as teachers, in which, it was said, the "requirements of church, citizenship, the institutional church problem and the best methods for reaching the unchurched masses will be duly considered and emphasized." [77]

The liberal seminaries, through success in securing endowments as well as thorough interest in the question, also accomplished much. At Meadville Theological School (Unitarian), the Reverend Henry H. Barber began a survey course in 1885 in "Practical Philosophy Embracing the Relations of the Christian Church to the Pressing Questions of Political Economy, Civics and Sociology." Within five years the study, as "Christian Sociology," was minimizing theoretical issues and stressing the phases of immediate use to the minister of a modern church. In 1895 Meadville created the Caleb Brewster Hockley Professorship of Sociology and Ethics, which Nicholas Paine Gilman, the leading authority on profit-sharing, occupied for a generation. Systematic instruction in ethics came in the first year and a similar training in economics and sociology dur-

[74] *Catalogue*, 1895, p. 20.   [75] *The Record*, II (April 1897), 36, 61.
[76] *Catalogue*, 1894, p. 6.
[77] *Catalogue*, 1896, p. 16; *ibid.*, 1898, pp. 16–19.

ing the second and third years. Earlier in the decade Mrs. Abbie S. Heywood, a daughter of Adin Ballou, established the Adin Ballou Lectureship in Practical Christian Sociology to support discussions "on the social aspects of the religion of Christ, and the consequent duty and importance of applying the principles and spirit of that religion to the intercourse and conduct of man with man, in all the activities and relations of life." Gladden led off with his masterly lectures, later published under the title, *Tools and the Man,* and was followed by other speakers of equal eminence. With these facilities Meadville possessed "an unusual equipment in this important department of ministerial education." [78]

The same was true of the Universalist schools, endowed with ample funds from the Ryder estate. Ryder Divinity School in Chicago was one of the first seminaries to prescribe social study.[79] In 1891 Canton Seminary at St. Lawrence University established the Ryder Professorship of Pastoral Theology, with George Beals Fisher, an ardent Christian Socialist, as first incumbent. He immediately introduced sociology, using as texts the works of Spencer, Bascom, Ely and Gladden.[80] In the same year Tufts Divinity began a course in "Hebrew Sociology," whose first part was devoted "to tracing the origin and development of social, political and religious institutions from the rise of Judaism to its decay, and the latter part to the study of the leading Hebrew minds," with an attempt "to connect this study with practical sociological questions of the present day." As if this did not suffice, Tufts in 1893 endowed the Woodbridge Professorship of Applied Christianity.[81]

By adopting the new educational aims and methods, the seminaries had entered more fully into the intellectual and social

---

[78] *Catalogue,* 1886, p. 11; *ibid.,* 1895, pp. 14–16; Gladden, "Preface," *Tools and the Man, Property and Industry under the Christian Law.*

[79] Graham Taylor, "Sociological Study in Theological Seminaries," *loc. cit.,* p. 68.

[80] *Catalogue,* 1891, pp. 33–34.

[81] *Catalogue,* 1891, p. 87; *ibid.,* 1894, pp. 26–28.

needs of the age. The thirty or more leading schools offering subjects in sociology directly contributed to the expansion and permanence of Protestant social service. In preparing their curricula the various theological faculties had wisely avoided preconceived or dogmatic theories of social organization, stressing instead the patient study of facts with a view to tentative conclusions. So far as the seminaries were concerned, sociology was "primarily a descriptive and statistical science," the data of which were indispensable to a more intelligent application of Christianity. This attitude accounted for the city missionary practice of seminarians, the countless investigations of actual social conditions and the founding of clinics and laboratories in the form of missions, institutional churches and social settlements. Utilitarian or practical considerations explained in turn the refusal of the seminaries to teach the whole of sociology. Hartford Seminary mirrored the prevalent policy in the statement that it did not aim, "owing to the limitations of the course, at a full study of sociology as a science, but at a study of Christian principles in application to the more pressing social problems which a minister encounters." [82] Furthermore, many educators believed that, as the colleges and universities incorporated sociology into their curricula, the seminaries could limit their study to social ethics, social pathology and Christian methods of treatment.

In view of the new trends in theological training, one would expect criticism to have largely ceased by the century's turn. Yet the period closed with the seminaries under devastating attack. Thus, in 1899 at the Second International Council of Congregational Churches in Boston, President W. D. Hyde of Bowdoin College charged that the seminaries did not stress the right idea of the ministerial calling, provide proper mental drill, furnish first-hand secular knowledge or encourage the personal grasp of spiritual truth. Quite as scathingly, Presi-

[82] *Catalogue*, 1898–99, p. 30.

dent W. F. Slocum of Colorado College rebuked the seminaries for failing to insist on college-trained men, ignoring the Bible as literature, neglecting ethics and refusing to extend sociological study.[83] Leaping to the defense, Professor George Foot Moore of Andover parried these thrusts with the argument that "the change which has come over the theological curriculum in twenty years is no less great than that which has taken place in the same time in the college" and that "the theological institution has been no less prompt to respond to the demands of the new time and the new conditions." [84] Though sharing the viewpoint of Hyde and Slocum, Lyman Abbott admitted "that in all the seminaries higher standards of admission are enforced than we had supposed" and that the extensive social-study programs were above criticism.[85] In the presence of these sharply divergent attitudes, the historian may reasonably conclude that the changes in ministerial education, though rapid and radical, had only in part socialized this aspect of Protestant Christianity.

[83] *Discussions*, pp. 222–232.
[84] *Ibid.*, pp. 363–368.
[85] *Outlook*, Oct. 21, 1899, p. 438; *ibid.*, Nov. 25, 1899, p. 732.

CHAPTER X

THE BALANCE SHEET

AT THE CENTURY's close the religious scene from the social point of view was still an unfinished picture; only the broad outlines had taken on final form. In the generation then ending, the city had assumed imperial sway over the countryside, but it was destined to win additional victories in the coming years. Likewise, Protestant Christianity kept on expanding its activities, refining its procedures and clarifying its social thinking. Nevertheless, the thirty-five-year period of this study had decisively established the essential relations between the two forces. In attempting to satisfy the demands of the urban poor, Protestants had measurably Christianized their social and economic attitudes, formulated and developed a far-flung system of social service and sacrificed sectarian concerns to basic religious needs.

Though seemingly revolutionary, these changes were hardly more than the healthy response of a vital religion to a challenging environment. The urban era opened with the Protestant churches slipping into a passive alliance with the well-to-do middle classes. However advantageous the policy may have appeared at the outset, it invited disaster, for, as the cities became numerous and powerful, the churches lost the major part of their wage-earning members and failed to recoup the losses from the enlarging immigrant population. When the congregations belatedly awoke to the perilous situation, they discovered that the poor demanded social justice as well as charity, economic self-respect as well as spiritual solace. Progressive Protestants acquiesced in the working-class view, recalling that in the religion of Christ all levels of human life possessed spiritual worth. Though the dominant evolutionary philosophy of the period encouraged a humanistic religious outlook, the compelling factor in its acceptance was the labor movement. "In order to gain the laborer the church has agreed to this view," declared Anna L. Dawes, a vigorous opponent of social Christianity.[1] These years witnessed a stubborn conflict between conventional and wage-earner attitudes toward religion with the struggle terminating in a victory for labor.

Several hundred ministers and laymen influenced the course of the church's social thinking. But a few great leaders, of whom Washington Gladden, R. Heber Newton and Richard T. Ely were the most convincing, had assumed responsibility for labor's cause in the arena of religious public opinion. Aware of the Protestant tendency to ignore competitive selfishness in the industrial world, these men insisted that the individualism of the old economic science could not be reconciled with the Christian law of coöperation and self-sacrifice. As a first step toward fairness and justice, they urged the churches to recognize labor's right to organize, pointing out that when workers grew powerful enough to force employers to negotiate the ultimate result would be a joint ownership of productive property. Protestant champions of the poor also demanded state intervention. Gladden's many followers expected the state to regulate large competitive industries and to socialize the natural monopolies, while a strong minority of Christian Socialists, led by the ministers, Jesse H. Jones and W. D. P. Bliss, wished to socialize all instrumental capital.

These plans to reorganize industry in labor's interest were not viewed as substitutes for the religious life. Though progressive Protestants were fully alive to the failings of the existing capitalist system, they did not believe, whether socialist or non-socialist, that any alternative system would of itself assure the people's material welfare. Unless good personal qualities such as toil, thrift and self-reliance widely prevailed,

[1] "What Is the Purpose of the Church?" *Congregationalist*, April 19, 1894, p. 559.

even the ideally best social order could not properly function. All that was expected of coöperative forms of economic organization was better opportunities for the practice of Christian virtues and for the securing by the poor themselves of their own improvement.

These attitudes governed the continuous efforts of the church to deal adequately with the immediate aspects of urban poverty. Most Protestants realized, implicitly at least, that, first of all, the alienated poor must be brought into church relations — a program requiring modern missionary and philanthropic techniques. Although the American Christian Commission, an outgrowth of the United States Christian Commission, interpreted human brotherhood in terms of progressive church work, only a few humanitarian congregations emerged before 1880. But in the next two decades several hundred appeared in response to the accelerating urban growth, the ugly industrial conflict and the agitation of the Open or Institutional Church League. "Among the most important changes in American life within one generation," wrote Professor Peabody in 1898, "is the growth of philanthropic work in connection with churches." [2] In unanticipated measure the unit-cells of Christianity passed the test of social adaptability to cities. Thoughtful Protestants in all denominations had come to frown upon aristocratic churches as heathenish caricatures of Christianity.

Agencies ministering "to all men and to all of the man," institutional churches promoted the welfare of human beings as individuals and in their social relations. These churches thus secured for a small part of the population some of the values that the Christian labor movement hoped ultimately to make available to all persons. Like the social settlements, the institutional churches were object lessons in democracy and social justice. Increasingly, as the years passed, these churches became Christian social settlements in fact and sometimes in

[2] "Principles of Poor Relief in the United States," *Charities Rev.*, VII (January 1898), 939.

name. Of the eighty or more regularly constituted settlements in 1898, the *Churchman* showed that "a good quarter are distinctly and avowedly religious." [3]

Although the institutional church merited the attention it received, Protestants during the whole period relied upon extra-parochial organizations for the major part of their social service. Most important were the many non-sectarian missions dating from the early post-war era — a form of religious service which Jerry MacAuley, the reformed river thief, and the Convention of Christian Workers so well popularized. The denominations, notably the Protestant Episcopal Church in the fifties and sixties and the Methodists in the eighties and nineties, also consolidated their respective resources for a like purpose. In contrast to institutional churches, whose philanthropy was primarily of the preventive type, the city missionary societies specialized in remedial charity, in this respect imitating the Salvation Army whose unusual success with the submerged elements was common knowledge well before the end of the century.

Several adjuncts rendered yeoman service in mobilizing the latent social strength of Protestant Christianity. These included the mission Sunday schools, the young people's societies, the various brotherhoods and sisterhoods and, above all, the deaconess associations which gained a strong foothold in the Lutheran and Methodist Churches. By 1900 every conspicuous human need had a corresponding religious society. "The separate societies of popery have been protestantized," sneered the opponents of social Christianity.[4] But its friends defended these associations as necessary adaptations of the church to a complex urban society.

In all this conscious striving for religious success, the coöperative spirit was evident. In the social-service field, the finest

---

[3] "Notes By the Way," *Churchman*, Feb. 5, 1898, p. 191.

[4] Alexander Blackburn, "Organization for Christian Work Other than the Church," Baptist Congress, *Annual Session*, 1889, p. 22.

examples were undoubtedly the Young Men's and the Young Women's Christian Associations, mainly for middle-class youth beyond the range of the influence of the congregations. Several organizations urged united effort for social Christianity, particularly the American Congress of Churches, the Evangelical Alliance, the Convention of Christian Workers, the Brotherhood of Christian Unity and the League of Catholic Unity. These bodies presented the evangelical point of view. Through the Societies for Ethical Culture and various other organizations liberals attempted to mobilize all the forces of righteousness, Christian and non-Christian alike.

A few widely heralded associations worked zealously to acquaint the church with the social movement. Among these were the Christian Social Union, the American Institute of Christian Sociology, the Church Association for the Advancement of the Interests of Labor and the Brotherhood of the Kingdom — all aiming to elucidate the relationship of the church to sociological thinking. The various federations, on the model of the New York City Federation of Churches and Christian Workers, carried the coöperative spirit into progressive church work. After these demonstrations of unity Protestants could face the future with more serenity and confidence. Though denominational activity had vastly increased, sectarian rivalry had largely ceased. "The real interest of the sects today," said Professor Tucker, "is not in themselves but in Christianity." [5]

Likewise Protestants infused the spirit of science into their social service. When careful investigation revealed beyond doubt that most charity stemming from the Christian past was more harmful than beneficial, the churches had no choice but to incorporate modernized philanthropy into their missionary forces. The quickening of zeal in this direction, as one observer wrote in the early nineties, had "been so marked that church

[5] "The New Movement in Humanity," in his *New Reservation of Time and Other Articles* (Boston, 1916), p. 209.

leadership" in social service, "now when it is given so largely a scientific basis, is almost as pronounced as it was in the days of its strictly religious grounding." [6] Forgoing the ease and pleasure of the time-honored hand-out, Christians now helped the victims of poverty and pauperism to help themselves. They fought intemperance and prostitution in the same spirit, relying less upon preaching and repressive laws and more upon remedial and preventive charity. Protestants had readily assumed responsibility for the study and diffusion of social science in order to counteract the non-Christian philosophies often associated with it. The endeavor to make science conform to the religious outlook resulted in a Christian Sociology which found a wide audience in books, magazines and the curricula of all the leading seminaries.

By 1900 the humanitarian emphasis had in some measure restored Protestantism to its old position of influence in the nation's life. To most urban dwellers the growth of charities seemed the most important factor in social betterment. In this field the cities were best served by organized religion — Jewish, Catholic and Protestant. The churches of the latter faith also supplied most of the personnel for the associated charities and the secular social settlements. In 1905 the American Institute of Social Service found that three out of every four social workers were faithful church members. [7] Since Protestants accounted for only a fourth of the total population, their record in this respect revealed an alert social consciousness.

In a broader sense, social service mirrored the rapid progress in the mutual reconciliation of religion and labor. The two were coming to understand each other. Protestants, on their part, recognized the essential justification of the labor movement. They were now convinced, as the Reverend J. H. W. Stuckenberg discovered, "that many demands of the poorer

[6] R. Ogden, "Sociology and the Church," *Nation*, Aug. 31, 1891, pp. 114–115.
[7] W. D. P. Bliss, "The Church and Social Method," *Outlook*, Jan. 20, 1906, pp. 122–125.

classes are the demands of humanity and Christianity." [8] As for workingmen, their bitter distrust, so pronounced in the eighties and early nineties, was rapidly subsiding. One minister, C. S. Nash, could say that "the deeper socialism of England and America is looking toward, if it has not already entered, a religious phase." [9] An anonymous writer, not an apologist of Christianity, noted that church members were taking an "efficient interest in movements for social betterment and that so many in the ranks of organized labor are speaking of them as their best friends." [10] The addresses of Samuel Gompers after 1895, pointing to the fact that ministers "are becoming acquainted with us and no longer study to learn concerning us from our employers and superintendents," seemed to both sides prophetic of a new era.[11]

Thus the case for social Christianity seemed conclusive. Many had stubbornly opposed the movement on the ground either that wage-earners were without legitimate grievances or that the church's mission was only spiritual. But to most Protestants these objections were unwarranted, or of little importance as compared with the possibility of bringing immigrant labor into the churches through a social program. When this prospect failed to materialize, when experience demonstrated that the poor were more interested in the loaves and fishes than in the spiritual teachings of Christianity, a sense of futility and defeatism weighed down many minds. Though only a minority of Protestants by 1900 excluded physical welfare from the church's mission, an increasing number feared that piety was being subordinated to charity, that ideals were being lost in mechanism, that, in short, the church was being secularized.

[8] "Evolution of the Social Problem in the Churches," *Homiletic Rev.*, XXXVIII (November 1899), 464–465.

[9] Shailer Mathews, "The Significance of the Church to the Social Movement," *Amer. Jour. of Sociology*, V (January 1897), 242–243.

[10] *The Commons*, IV (July 1899), 3.

[11] Stuckenberg, "The Coöperation of the Church and Working Men," *Homiletic Rev.*, XL (December 1900), 556.

Not so much the church's social gospel as the church's social service was questioned. "It is very difficult, if not impossible, to carry on a church and a club-house under the same management," the *Churchman* pointed out. "The institutional work, being easier than the inspirational, tends to get the advantage." [12]

For these reasons a strong minority among progressive Protestants was ready to abandon social service as a general policy. At the most, the institutional church, they said, had only a temporary and special function: as a training school or clinic in social work and as a protest against any failure of the state and the voluntary societies to do their duty. When social justice was attained, the institutional church would not be needed. "The people ought to be able to provide for themselves what the churches are trying to provide for them," thought Walter Rauschenbusch. "While social conditions were simple and wholesome there were no institutional churches; . . . make social life healthy and you can simplify church work," [13] he said. The sociologists approved this attitude, Edward Allsworth Ross, for example, contending that the main purpose of the church was to socialize the human heart. The church was "not primarily an organ of philanthropy," he explained, "but preparer of the soil from which philanthropy springs." [14]

As against this extremist view, the majority of progressive Protestants asked only that the churches correlate more thoroughly the various aspects of social Christianity. Many insisted that as Christians extended the institutional church and other forms of social activity they emphasize strictly religious work. "If we want the Gospel to dominate institutions, laws, governments, industries and society," a great leader warned,

---

[12] "The Institutional Church," *Churchman*, Oct. 15, 1898, pp. 514–515.

[13] "The Stake of the Church in the Social Movement," *Amer. Jour. of Sociology*, III (July 1897), 26–27.

[14] "The Educational Function of the Church," *Outlook*, Aug. 28, 1897, pp. 1038–39.

"there must be Christian individuals to spiritualize them." First things should come first.[15]

By the same token the social service of the future should contribute more fully than formerly to the reconstruction of the social order. The institutional church, even though it had improved human life, lacked social adequacy. "It deals exclusively with individuals," concluded an experienced pastor, "and leaves untouched the conditions which make those individuals what they are." In order to realize the whole program of social Christianity, the church must continue to champion "openly and fearlessly the cause of the workingmen." [16] With this sentiment Massachusetts Congregationalists agreed, declaring in 1902 for "the entirety of Christian ethics." Besides establishing social settlements and institutional churches in every city, the church should aid workers to secure a living wage, shorter hours, the recognition of labor unions and a larger share in the heritage of culture.[17]

The misgivings with which many people viewed the future of social Christianity mirrored its uneven progress in the past. Through a social program Protestants had reproduced the compassionate life of Jesus Christ and contributed immeasurably to the growth of humanitarian democracy. In a period of transition, beset with confusion and conflict, progressive Protestants had championed orderly social reform, in this way helping the nation to surmount the perils of anarchy and despotism. Moreover, the city had entered deeply into the Protestant consciousness. What the "world" once meant to religion, said Professor Tucker, "that the city now means to Christianity, as something at once to be feared and loved, to be served and mastered." [18]

[15] Stuckenberg, "Social Study and Social Work," *Homiletic Rev.*, XXXIII (May 1897), 466.

[16] Joseph Hutcheson, "The Church's Duty in Secular Activities," Prot. Epis. Church Cong., *Papers, Debates and Discussions*, 1894, pp. 14–16.

[17] "Committee on Labor Organizations," Gen. Assoc. of Cong. Churches in Mass., *Proceedings*, 1902, pp. 47–49.

[18] "The Spiritual Life of the Modern City," *Congregationalist*, Dec. 31, 1896, p. 1038.

But Protestantism had not solved the urban religious problem. Though the missionary and social service of the churches was in the aggregate quite impressive, it affected only a relatively small portion of the immigrant working population and that in an economic and cultural more definitely than in a strictly religious manner. A more extensive social service, a keener sense of responsibility for the removal of industrial evils and, above all, a profoundly spiritual use of the agencies of social Christianity — these must be the keys to religious success in the coming century.

BIBLIOGRAPHICAL ESSAY

GENERAL STUDIES AND SOURCES

Historical Treatments. There is no definitive history of American religion since the Civil War. Several brief accounts treat the subject from all significant points of view, the most helpful being Henry F. Rowe, *The History of Religion in the United States* (New York, 1924), W. E. Garrison, *The March of Faith: The Story of Religion in America Since 1865* (New York, 1933), and Arthur Meier Schlesinger, "A Critical Period in American Religion, 1875–1900," Mass. Hist. Soc., *Proceedings*, LXIV (June 1932), 523–547. Two recent works deal exclusively with the socialization of Protestantism: James Dombrowski, *The Early Days of Christian Socialism in America* (New York, 1936), and, at greater length, Charles Howard Hopkins, *The Rise of the Social Gospel in American Protestantism, 1865–1915* (Yale Studies in Religious Education, XIV, New Haven, 1940). These are avowedly "social-gospel" histories, the former a Marxian critique and the latter a scholarly, well-arranged treatment from a broadly liberal viewpoint. Both books almost entirely ignore the influence of urban religious and social problems on the socialization of the Protestant churches, stressing evolution, liberal theology, sociology, socialism and the labor movement as the decisive factors. Of the many denominational histories, only George Willis Cooke, *Unitarianism in America* (Boston, 1902), and Allen C. Thomas, *A History of the Friends in America* (Philadelphia, 1930), are satisfactory from the social point of view.

Contemporaneous Accounts. These are indispensable for a broadly urban approach to religion. Josiah Strong, *Religious Movements for Social Betterment* (H. B. Adams, ed., Monographs on American Social Economics, XIV, New York, 1900), and Arthur T. Pierson, *Forward Movements of the Last Half Century, Being a Glance at the More Marked Philanthropic, Missionary and Spiritual Movements Characteristic of Our Time* (New York, 1900), show keen insight into the social meanings of missionary movements. The same can be said for W. H. Daniels, *The Temperance Reform and Its Great Reformers* (New York, 1878). *Stall's Lutheran Year Book and Historical Quarterly*, vols. I–IV (Lancaster, Pa., 1884–1888), edited by Sylvanus Stall, publisher and institutional-church leader, contains splendid historical sketches of Lutheran social trends. W. D. P. Bliss, ed., *Encyclopedia of Social Reform* (New York, 1897), surveys the whole reform field from the Christian social viewpoint. Daniel Dorchester, *The Problem of Religious Progress* (New York, 1881; 2d rev. ed., 1900), and H. K. Carroll, *Religious Forces in the United States,* in Philip Schaff and others, editors, American Church History Series, vol. I (New York, 1893; rev. ed., 1912), are statistical studies which only partly succeed in showing the urban impact. The Census Bureau published *Religious Bodies: 1906,* Pts. 1–2 (Washington, 1910), whose historical descriptions are useful guides to further investigation.

Personal Accounts. Most of the great figures in the movement wrote excellent autobiographies. Washington Gladden, its most influential leader, has left us his *Recollections* (Boston, 1909); William Jewett Tucker in *My Generation* (Boston, 1919) thoughtfully surveys the post-war industrial age from an urban and sanely humanistic outlook; and W. S. Rainsford in his two books, *A Preacher's Story of His Work* (New York, 1904) and *Story of a Varied Life* (Garden City, 1924), details his trying but successful efforts to rebuild St. George's Church in New York along institutional lines. Other illuminating accounts include Lyman Abbott, *Reminiscences* (Boston, 1915), Richard T. Ely, *Ground Under Our Feet* (New York, 1938), Charles M. Sheldon, *His Life Story* (New York, 1925), and Graham Taylor, *Pioneering On Social Frontiers* (Chicago, 1930).

The biographies are, as a whole, much less satisfactory. A few, however, are of exceptional merit, among them, Charles L. Slattery, *David Hummell Greer, Eighth Bishop of New York* (New York, 1921); Harriet A. Keyser, *Bishop Potter; the People's Friend* (New York, 1910); Charles H. Brent, *A Master Builder: Henry Yates Satterlee* (New York, 1916); and John O. Ovjen, *The Life of J. H. W. Stuckenberg—Theologian—Philosopher—Sociologist* (Minneapolis, 1938). *The National Cyclopedia of American Biography* (34 vols., New York, 1892–1935) is useful for contemporary estimates of religious leaders, while the *Dictionary of American Biography* (20 vols., New York, 1928–1936) is critical and scholarly.

Newspapers and Periodicals. These sources reveal the urban religious movement in all its marvelous detail and variety. Though the religious newspaper was less important than in the pre-war period, it still exerted a wide influence. *The Christian Union* (*Outlook* after 1893), founded in 1870 by Henry Ward Beecher and edited after 1880 by Lyman Abbott, held foremost place, both for intelligent reporting and for progressive views on theology and social theory. *The Independent*, though progressive-orthodox in theology, was quite conservative in social thought, failing to maintain its pre-war crusade for social justice; but many fine contributed articles make it a useful source. A few of the denominational papers yield much of interest: the *Christian Register* (Unitarian) of Boston; the *Churchman* (Episcopal) of New York; the *Congregationalist* of Boston; and *Zion's Herald* (Methodist) of Boston, a militant defender of applied Christianity. The *Watchman* (Baptist), also of Boston, just as ardently championed the "old-time religion," only towards the end of the period becoming somewhat reconciled to the new trends.

The magazines are as indispensable for the religious as for any other phase of American social history. In preparing the present study the writer scrutinized eighty-one periodicals, all of them yielding useful articles on Christian social theory and practice over the whole period or for some crucial part of it. For its many learned editorials and articles on urban topics, the *Andover Review* (Boston, 1884–1893) may be singled out, though with scarcely more justice than several others: the *Bibliotheca Sacra* (Oberlin, entire period); the *Church Review* (New York, to 1891); the *Homiletic Review* (New York, from 1876); the *Methodist Review* (New York, entire period); the *New Englander* (New Haven, to 1892); the *Princeton Review* (New York and v.p., to 1888); and the *Unitarian Review* (Boston, 1874–1891).

Among secular magazines, the *Nation* (New York, after 1865) disparaged, while the *Arena* (Boston, from 1889) rapturously approved, the increasing participation of the churches in social reform. Noteworthy articles appeared in the *Century Magazine* (New York, from 1881), the *Forum* (New York, from 1886), the *New England Magazine* (Boston, from 1884) and the *Review of Reviews* (New York, from 1890). The magazines dealing with special aspects of social Christianity are listed later at the appropriate places. Ernest Cushing Richardson, *Periodical Articles on Religion, 1890–1899* (2 vols., New York, 1907–1911), indexes by subject and author the material appearing in magazines during the last decade of the century.

URBAN RELIGIOUS PROBLEMS

Great Cities. Most of the earlier literature mirrored the difficulties and needs of the seaboard cities, especially New York. Factual information is carefully assembled in *City Evangelization* (New York, 1866), a report of the New York City Mission and Tract Society;

in the anonymous pamphlet, *Startling Facts!* . . . *The City of New York the Greatest Missionary Field on the Continent* (New York, 1864); and in Thomas Dixon, Jr., *The Failure of Protestantism in New York* (New York, 1895). *The Church's Mission to Working-men; or the Power of Christian Sympathy and Fellowship* (New York, 1863), by the Protestant Episcopal Board of Domestic Missions, is equally informative and of wider scope. The essential periodical articles include "New York City as a Field for Church Work," *Church Rev.*, XVI (July 1864), 169–193; "Church Work in Large Cities," *ibid.*, XVII (April 1865), 39–53; "Religion in New York," *Cath. World*, III (June 1866), 381–389; "The Sanitary and Moral Condition of the City of New York," *ibid.*, VII (July 1868), 553–568; Charles Wood, "The Pauperism of Our Cities; its Character, Condition, Causes and Relief," *Presby. Quart. and Princeton Rev.*, XLVI (April 1874), 217–234; and W. W. Adams, "The Spiritual Problem of the Manufacturing Town," *Andover Rev.*, V (February, April, June 1886), 117–131, 341–359, 611–631. Stephen H. Tyng, Jr., edited a magazine, *The Working Church* (New York, 1873–1874), in the interests of aggressive Christianity; W. H. H. Murray discussed religious conditions in Boston in *Sermons, Park Street Pulpit* (Series 1–2, Boston, 1870–1872), in *Music Hall Sermons* (Boston, 1870), and to a larger audience in his newspaper, the *Golden Rule* (Boston, 1875–1886).

Interpretations and Discussions. Of the many books discussing urban religious problems, Josiah Strong, *Our Country, Its Possible Future and Present Crisis* (New York, 1885), was pronounced "the most notable contribution ever yet made to home missionary literature." Samuel L. Loomis, *Modern Cities and Their Religious Problems* (New York, 1887), an even more concise and illuminating analysis, was widely read, as were also (J. B. Harrison), *Certain Dangerous Tendencies in American Life, and Other Papers* (Boston, 1880), Henry Codman Potter, *Sermons of the City* (New York, 1881), and R. H. Woods, W. T. Elsing and others, editors, *The Poor in Great Cities: Their Problems and What is Done to Solve Them* (New York, 1895).

Abel Stevens, "The Priesthood of the People," *Meth. Quart. Rev.*, LV (January 1873), 43–69, and "The Pastorate for the Times," *Princeton Review*, XL (January 1868), 83–113, broadly interpret the epoch-making American Christian Commission, whose *Reports* and *Documents* have been listed in the text. No student of social Christianity should neglect the discussions of the Evangelical Alliance

Conferences, published under the titles: *National Perils and Opportunities* (New York, 1888), *National Needs and Remedies* (New York, 1890) and *Christianity Practically Applied* (2 vols., New York, 1894). Equally important are the *Proceedings* of the Convention of Christian Workers (New Haven, from 1886); the *Papers, Addresses and Discussions* of the Protestant Episcopal Church Congress (New York, from 1874); and the *Annual Sessions* of the Baptist Congress for the Discussions of Current Questions (New York, from 1882), for which Frank Grant Lewis and Edith Maddock West prepared *An Author, Title and Subject Index . . . , 1882–1912* (Chicago, 1913). The urban impact on the denominations is further explained in the proceedings of their legislative bodies, especially in the essay-studies of the General Association of Congregational Churches in Massachusetts, *Minutes* (Boston, entire period); of the National Council of the Congregational Churches in the United States, *Minutes* (Boston, from 1871); and of the General Conference of the Unitarian and Other Christian Churches, *Proceedings* (Boston, from 1866). Important also are E. D. Morris, "Presbyterianism and the People," *Presby. Quart. and Princeton Rev.*, III n.s. (April 1874), 197–216; John Atkinson, "Methodism in the Cities of the United States," *Meth. Quart. Rev.*, LIX (July 1877), 451–505; and H. K. Carroll, "City Methodism," *ibid.*, LX (January 1878), 27–43.

LABOR'S CHALLENGE TO THE CHURCH

The growing rift between the working class and organized religion can best be studied in *John Swinton's Paper* (New York, 1882–1887); the Socialist *Workmen's Advocate* (New Haven, 1885–1890); the *American Federationist* (New York, and Indianapolis, from 1894); and John P. Coyle, "Report of the Committee on the Work of the Churches," Gen. Assoc. of the Congreg. Churches in Mass., *Minutes*, 1892, pp. 30–33. H. Francis Perry, "The Workingman's Alienation from the Church," *Amer. Jour. of Sociology*, IV (March 1899), 621–629, is a convenient summary. *Equity* (Boston, 1874–1875), "a journal of Christian labor reform," and the *Labor Balance* (North Abington, Mass., 1877–1878), "a journal devoted to the welfare of the working people," elucidate the Christian Labor Union's program, which is briefly treated in Jesse H. Jones, "The Labor Problem," *International Rev.*, IX (July 1880), 51–68.

The typical attitude of progressive Protestants appears in the writings of Washington Gladden, especially in *Working People and Their Employers* (Boston, 1876), *Applied Christianity* (Boston,

1887), *Tools and the Man* (Boston, 1893), *Christianity and Social-ism* (New York, 1905) and "The Social and Industrial Situation," *Bibliotheca Sacra*, XLIX (July 1892), 383–411; T. Edwin Brown, *Studies in Socialism and Modern Labor Problems* (New York, 1886); and R. Heber Newton, *The Present Aspect of the Labor Problem* (New York, 1886) and *Social Studies* (New York, 1887).

The Dawn, I–VIII (Boston, 1889–1896), edited by W. D. P. Bliss, is authoritative for the Christian Socialist attitude. Other attempts to reconcile Christianity with socialism appear in Philo W. Sprague, *Christian Socialism* (New York, 1893); F. M. Sprague, *Socialism from Genesis to Revelation* (Boston, 1893), the most convincing book on the subject; Philip S. Moxom, "Christian Socialism," *New England Magazine*, n.s. X (March 1894), 20–29; and Paul Monroe, "English and American Christian Socialism: An Estimate," *Amer. Jour. of Sociology*, I (July 1895), 50–68. The views of those who, while conceding the church's social mission, strongly insisted on keep-ing personal spiritual values in the foreground can be studied in A. J. F. Behrends, *Christianity and Socialism* (New York, 1886), which gives a qualified approval to the *laissez-faire* philosophy of William Graham Sumner; George Harris, *Moral Evolution* (Boston, 1896); and Francis G. Peabody's excellent *Jesus Christ and the Social Question* (Boston, 1900).

THE INSTITUTIONAL CHURCH

Progressive church work is considered analytically and factually in G. W. Shinn, *King's Handbook of Notable Episcopal Churches* (Bos-ton, 1889); Sylvanus Stall, *Methods of Church Work: Religious, Social and Financial* (New York, 1887); Washington Gladden, ed., *Parish Problems* (New York, 1887); Washington Gladden, *The Christian Minister and the Working Church* (New York, 1898); George W. Mead, *Modern Methods of Church Work: the Gospel Renaissance* (New York, 1897); and H. B. Adams, *The Church and Popular Education* (Baltimore, 1900).

Edward Everett Hale edited *Lend a Hand*, I–XVIII (Boston, 1886–1897), "a record of philanthropy and social progress," while a group of women mothered the *Altruist* (New York, from 1893), also an excellent social service journal. The *Voice* (New York, from 1883), a prohibitionist paper, and *Our Day* (Boston and Chicago, from 1888) discussed philanthropic and moral questions against the new economic and social background. For a fuller account of these ques-tions, especially in their missionary phase, the student should consult the *Reports* of the W.C.T.U. (Chicago, from 1875), of the Episcopal Church Temperance Society (New York, from 1882) and of the Presbyterian Committee on Temperance, General Assembly, *Minutes* (Philadelphia, from 1881). C. N. Crittenton in his autobiography, *The Brother of Girls* (Chicago, 1910), summarizes his efforts on behalf of the victims of prostitution, one outcome of which was the National Florence Crittenton Mission which explained its early work in *Fourteen Years' Work among Street Girls* (Washington, 1897).

The progress of the Open or Institutional Church League can be found in its *Preliminary Conference Report* (New York, 1894) and in its magazine, the *Open Church* (New York, from 1897), which contains excellent summaries of church work in typical cities. Two other magazines of great value for humanitarian churches and missions are the *Christian City* (New York, from 1889), organ of the Methodist National City Evangelization Union, and *Our Work at Home* (Albany, from 1875), in a like relation to the Albany City Mission. Excellent discussions of enlarging church work include C. S. Mills, "The Institutional Church," *Bibliotheca Sacra*, XLIX (July 1892), 453–470; G. W. Cooke, "The Institutional Church," *New England Magazine*, n.s. XIV (August 1896), 645–660; "Enlarged Church Work in Cities," Baptist Church Cong., *Annual Session*, 1890, pp. 131–167; and "The Church's Duty in Secular Activities," Prot. Epis. Church Cong., *Papers, Addresses and Discussions*, 1894, pp. 11–40. Besides many thumbnail descriptions of institutional churches, the *Christian Union* between November 21, 1891, and April 8, 1893, carried sixteen articles on "Progressive Methods of Church Work" in which qualified writers surveyed the rapidly changing scene. Similarly, the *Homiletic Review*, vols. VIII–XII (July 1884–September 1886), published eleven essays under the title, "Lay Criticism on the Ministry and the Methods of Church Work," and a "Symposium on the Institutional Church," vols. XXXII–XXXIII (December 1896–May 1897), "of permanent value, as presenting the various aspects of the subject."

Auxiliary Aids. These are briefly discussed in "Organizations for Christian Work Other than the Churches," Baptist Cong., *Annual Session*, 1889, pp. 6–47. *St. Andrew's Cross* (New York, from 1886) treats of the Episcopal Brotherhood of St. Andrew, while Ellen E. Dickinson, *The King's Daughters* (New York, 1890), and the *Silver Cross* (New York, from 1888) furnish pertinent information on the greatest of the sisterhoods. Material on the social activity of the young people's societies can be found in the *Golden Rule* (Boston, 1886–1897), "devoted to Christian nurture and practical Christianity"; its successor, the *Christian Endeavor World* (Chicago, from 1897); and W. H. Tolman, *Municipal Reform Movements* (New York, 1895). The analytical and historical study, C. Golder, *History of the Deaconess Movement in the Christian Church* (New York, 1903), is authoritative for this phase of Christian social service. *The Association Monthly*, I–IV (New York, 1870–1873), is essential for the post-war urban readjustments of the Y.M.C.A., even more so than the standard histories and the many reports of conventions and yearly activities. Elizabeth Wilson, *Fifty Years of Association Work Among Young Women, 1866–1916* (New York, 1916), and *Proceedings of* [Biennial] *Conferences* (Pittsburgh and elsewhere, from 1873) of the International Board suffice for the Y.W.C.A. The coöperative movement among the congregations for progressive church work is set out in the New York Federation of Churches and Christian Workers, *First Sociological Canvass, Fifteenth Assembly District* (New York, 1896), and its periodical, *Federation* (New York, from 1896).

Salvation Army. The indispensable sources for the Army's history in America are the *War Cry* (New York, from 1881), the *Conqueror*, I–VI (New York, 1892–1897), and *Harbor Lights* (New York, from 1897). The two books, *From Ocean to Ocean* (New York, 1891) and *Beneath Two Flags* (New York, 1891), by Ballington and Maud B. Booth respectively are highly personal defences of the Army's work. F. L. Booth-Tucker, the *Social Relief Work of the Salvation Army in the United States* (H. B. Adams, ed., Monographs in American Social Economics, vol. XX, Albany, 1900), and Edwin G. Lamb, *The Social Work of Salvation Army* (New York, 1909), are analytic summaries from the sociological point of view. The few periodical accounts are highly interpretative: "A New Advance of the Salvation Army," *Unitarian Rev.*, XXXIV (November 1890), 465–467; Gilbert Simmons, "The Salvation Army and Its Latest Project," *Catholic World*, LII (February 1891), 633–646; Charles A. Briggs, "The Salvation Army," *No. Am. Rev.*, CLIX (December 1894), 197–710; Joseph Cook, "General Booth and the Salvation Army," *Our Day*, XV (September 1895), 119–124; Maud B. Booth, "Salvation Army Work in the Slums," *Scribner's Magazine*, XVII (January 1895), 102–114; and F. L. Booth-Tucker, "The Farm Colonies of the Salvation Army," *Forum*, XXIII (August 1897), 750–760.

Christian Sociology

Sociological thinking takes on significant meaning in the luminous writings of William Jewett Tucker, notably in his "Christianity and Its Modern Competitors," *Andover Rev.*, VI–VII (December 1886–April 1887), and his Phi Beta Kappa Address at Harvard in 1892, *The New Movement in Humanity* (Boston, 1892), reprinted in his *New Reservation of Time and Other Articles* (Boston, 1916). Amory H. Bradford, *Heredity and Christian Problems* (New York, 1896), is conclusive from its special angle. Wilbur F. Crafts, *Practical Christian Sociology* (New York, 1895), is rather an urgent appeal for social reform than a reasoned defence of social Christianity. F. M. Sprague, *Laws of Social Evolution* (Boston, 1895), is a Christian Socialist's refutation of Social Darwinism. During the nineties the *Bibliotheca Sacra*, the *Homiletic Review* and the *American Journal of Sociology* (Chicago, from 1895) considered all phases of Christian sociology. The Brotherhood of the Kingdom in its *Reports* of the Annual Conference (New York, from 1894), the Christian Social Union in its *Publications* (Baltimore and Boston, from 1893) and the School of Applied Ethics, a project of the Ethical Culture Societies, in *Philanthropy and Social Progress* (New York, 1893), contributed fruitfully to the subject.

The more general attitude of the seminaries toward sociological teaching is found in John Tunis, "Social Science in the Theological Seminaries," *Lend a Hand*, XVI (January 1896), 3–15; W. D. Hyde, "Reform in Theological Education," *Atlantic Mo.*, LXXXV (January 1900), 571–578; and the *Hartford Seminary Record* (Hartford, from 1890). Graham Taylor, *Sociological Work in Theological Seminaries* (Seventh Section of International Cong. of Charities, Corrections and Philanthropy, Baltimore, 1894), is a thorough factual survey up to 1894. No true appreciation is possible without a recourse to the *Catalogues* of the leading institutions.

INDEX

INDEX

Actor's Church Alliance, 113

Adler, Felix, founds New York Society for Ethical Culture, 19

All Souls' (Chicago), institutional church, 159–160

Allen Street Memorial (New York), institutional church, 171

American Baptist Home Missionary Society, and city missions, 179, 181

American Congregational Union, and city missions, 177–178

American Congress of Churches, formation and work of, 89–90

American Congress of Liberal Religious Societies, formation and program of, 101–102

American Christian Commission, founded, 11–12; urban problems probed by, 12–14; religious adaptability to cities promoted by, 14–15, 25, 26, 27, 45, 50, 55–56

American Home Missionary Society, and city missions, 177

American Institute of Christian Sociology, formed, 110; conferences of, 110–111

Anglo-American Church Emigrants' Aid Society, 42

Asbury Methodist Church (New York), institutional, 171

Associated Churches of Cambridge (Massachusetts), purpose of, 191–192

Bailey, Joshua L., as coffee-house promoter, 50

Bamberger, John H., seminary sociology professor, 242

Bancroft, Jane M., deaconess leader, 200–201

Baptist Congress for the Discussion of Current Questions, formed, 18; industrial program of, 74–75; and city missions, 179

Baptist Young People's Union, 212

Baptists, in cities, 4; and religio-social discussion, 18, 74–75, 114–115; and institutional churches, 157–158, 180; and city missions, 179–181; and immigrants, 182–183; and deaconesses, 204; and youth, 212; and sociological instruction, 239–240

Barber, Henry H., seminary sociology professor, 242

Beacon Presbyterian (Philadelphia), institutional church, 178

Beckwith, Clarence A., seminary sociology professor, 237

Beecher, Thomas K., pioneer of enlarged church work, 28

Bellamy, Edward, on Christianity and labor, 67, 86

Bemis, Edward W., as sociological editor, 83

Berkeley Temple (Boston), institutional church, 153–154

Bethany Institute (New York), training school, 51

Bethany Presbyterian (Philadelphia), institutional church, 155–156

Blackman, William F., seminary sociology professor, 237

Bliss, W. D. P., as Christian Socialist, 75–76, 77–78, 247; as organizer for Christian Social Union, 107–108; and union of social reformers, 115, 116

Booth, Ballington, as Commander of American Salvation Army, 121–122, 128, 129; as organizer of Volunteers of America, 135–136

Booth, Maud B., and Salvation Army, 124, 126, 127, 128; and Volunteers of America, 136

Booth, William, and American Salvation Army, 118–119, 122

Booth-Tucker, F. L., as Commander

of American Salvation Army, 121, 128–129, 131–132

Bottome, Mrs. Frank, founder of King's Daughters, 219

Brent, Charles H., institutional church leader, 183

Briggs, Charles A., on Salvation Army, 123–124; as seminary professor, 228, 238

Broome Street Tabernacle (New York), institutional church, 140, 141

Brotherhood of Andrew and Philip, origin and growth of, 217

Brotherhood of Christian Unity, program of, 98–99

Brotherhood of the Kingdom, origin and program, 114–115

Brotherhood of St. Andrew, origin and growth of, 215; in social reform, 215–217

Buchanan, James R., on church and labor, 65; on union of social reformers, 116

Buffalo Plan, for church union in social service, 187–188

Byrnes, Horace W., institutional church leader, 171

Cadman, S. Parkes, institutional church leader, 159

Calvary Episcopal (New York), institutional church, 184

Calvary Methodist (New York), institutional church, 171

Central Methodist (New York), institutional church, 159

Central Union Mission (Washington, D. C.), institutional, 138–139

Chandler, Fred, institutional church leader, 175

Christian Industrial League, as part of brotherhood movement, 218–219

Christian Labor Union of Boston, formed, 21; labor unions and legislation championed by, 22–23; criticism of Protestant Church indifference to labor reform, 23–26; Christian charity deemed insufficient by, 25

Christian League of Philadelphia, formation and results of, 185–186

Christian Social Union, origin and growth of, 106–108; study program of, 108–109; in social reform, 109–110

Christian Socialism, beginnings of, 21–26; Societies of, 76–77; essentials of, 77–81

Christian Sociology, genesis of, 81–83; seminary professors of, 232–235, 237, 238, 239, 240, 241, 242, 243; bibliography of, 264

Church Association for the Advancement of the Interests of Labor (C.A.I.L.), origin and growth of, 112; industrial program of, 112–113

Church Congress of the Protestant Episcopal Church, formed, 17; Christian coöperation and social service favored by, 17–18; industrial program of, 74

Church German Society, formed, 42; and Grace Church (New York), 42–43

Church of the Holy Communion (New York), institutional, 30

Church of the Savior (Boston), institutional, 175

Cities, growth and character of, 3–4, 57; Protestant problems in, 4–11; Protestant response to, 11, 26, 27, 55–56, 81, 85–87, 88, 137, 163–165, 193, 194, 244–245, 246–255; bibliography of, 258–260

City missionaries, need for, 11, 14, 33, 50; women as, 14, 15, 51–54, 194–204; for immigrants, 181–183; training schools for, 50–52, 135, 196, 198–199, 200, 201, 203, 204, 225, 230–231. *See also* Deaconesses; Seminaries.

City missions, need for, 11–14, 15; tract societies as, 34–35, 139–142; independent, 35–37, 137–139; established by business men, 139n.; Y.M.C.A. in, 44, 204; Y.W.C.A. in, 45–46; W.C.T.U. in, 143–145, 146–147; and social purity, 145–

147; and Unitarians, 37–39, 174–175; and Episcopalians, 39–40, 183–185; and Presbyterians, 41, 178–179; and Methodists, 166–172; and Dutch Reformed, 173–174; and Congregationalists, 175–178; and Baptists, 179–181; and social reform, 25, 85–86, 145, 146, 149, 169–172, 174–175

Clark, Francis E., organizes United Society of Christian Endeavor, 210

Clark, John Bates, on ethics in industry, 68

Coe, Edward B., institutional church leader, 173–174

Cole, John H., as co-secretary of American Christian Commission, 12–14

Collens, T. Wharton, as social Catholic and a founder of Christian Labor Union, 21–22

Collins, John C., as leader in Convention of Christian Workers, 95, 97

Colwell, Stephen, economist and early champion of social Christianity, 5–6; and social ethics at Princeton, 224

Commons, John R., in Christian Social Union, 108; secretary of American Institute of Christian Sociology, 110

Congregationalists, and institutional churches, 31–34, 151–155, 164; and temperance, 47; and city missions, 175–178; and immigrants, 181–182, 183; and Sunday schools, 207, 208; and deaconesses, 203–204; and sociological instruction, 233–235, 236–238

Congress of Workingmen's Clubs and Institutes, 40

Connecticut Bible Society, and church federation, 192

Consolidation of religious forces, undenominational, 10–11, 16, 18–21, 88–106, 115–116, 185–193; denominational, 16–18, 166–185

Convention of Christian Workers, origin and discussions of, 95–96;

in city missions, 96–98, 137–139; and boys' clubs, 97

Conwell, Russell H., institutional church leader, 157; on progress of institutional church movement, 163–164.

Cook, Joseph, in Home Evangelization, 33; on Salvation Army, 124

Cornell Memorial (New York), institutional church, 171

Coyle, John P., on church and labor, 66

Crittenden, Charles Nelson, in social purity movement, 145

Deaconesses, first experiments with, 30, 52–53, 54–55; and German-American religious bodies, 195–197; and Methodists, 197–202; and Presbyterians, 202–203; and Episcopalians, 149, 203; and Congregationalists, 203–204

DeCosta, B. F., organizes Episcopal Church Temperance Society, 49; founds American White Cross Society, 146

Devins, John B., institutional church leader, 186–187

DeWitt Chapel (New York), institutional church, 174

DeWitt Memorial (New York), institutional church, 139–140, 140–141

Dickinson, Charles A., institutional church leader, 154, 161, 163

Dike, Samuel W., and Christian Sociology, 82, 83; and Sunday school extension, 208

Dodge, William E., in Y.M.C.A., 44; as president of Evangelical Alliance, 91 92; institutional church builder, 140; in Open or Institutional Church League, 161, 163

Dooly, John, city missionary, 44; institutional church leader, 140, 141

Dutch Reformed, and institutional churches, 173–174

Eggleston, Edward, and the Church of the Christian Endeavor (Brooklyn), 29

Eleventh Street Church (New York), institutional, 171

Eliot, Charles W., on education of ministers, 226, 227, 230, 232

Eliot, Christopher R., founds Unitarian Church Temperance Society, 49

Elsing, William T., institutional church leader, 140–141

Ely, Richard T., on industrial conflict, 59, 61; on workers' distrust of church, 65; promotes socialization of religion, 68–69, 99, 102, 107, 108, 110, 247

English, John M., seminary sociology professor, 239

Ensign, F. G., as co-secretary of American Christian Commission, 12–14

Episcopal Church Temperance Society, founded, 48–49; recreational centers of, 143

Episcopalians, and religio-social discussion, 17–18, 74, 106–110; and labor, 112–113; and institutional churches, 29–31, 147–151, 164; and city missions, 39–40, 183–185; and workingmen's clubs, 40, 216–217; and immigrants, 42–43; and temperance, 48–49, 142–143; and deaconesses, 30, 52, 203; and brotherhood, 215–217; and sisterhood, 219; and sociological instruction, 240–242

Epworth League. *See* Young People's Societies.

Eutaw Street Church (Baltimore), institutional, 172

Evangelical Alliance, formed, 16; religio-social program of, 90–94, 185; influence on church federation, 189, 191

Every Day Church (Boston), institutional, 160–161

Federation of East Side Workers, and social reform, 186–187

Fifth Avenue at Forty-eighth Street (New York), institutional church, 173–174

First Presbyterian (Philadelphia), institutional church, 185

Fisher, George Beals, seminary sociology professor, 243

Five Points Mission and House of Industry (New York), in social service, 36

Flower, B. O., and union for reform, 103, 104

Ford, Daniel S., institutional church promoter, 180

Foster, E. P., Christian Socialist, 76–77

Foster, Frank Hugh, seminary sociology professor, 238

Fourth Congregational Church (Hartford), institutional, 151–152

Fox, Ernest L., institutional church leader, 171

George, Henry, economico-religious theory of, 67–68; influence of, 74–75, 76, 90

Gilman, Nicholas Paine, seminary sociology professor, 242

Girls' Friendly Societies, for sisterhood, 219

Gladden, Washington, on church alienation of workingmen, 61–62, 63; on Christianity applied to industry, 70–74, 82, 111, 247; on consolidation of religious forces, 90, 99, 102, 191; as author, 70, 73, 243, 257

Godkin, E. L., on business dishonesty, 9

Gompers, Samuel, on church and labor, 63, 111, 252

Grace Baptist Church (Philadelphia), institutional, 157–158

Grace Reformed Church (New York), institutional, 174

Graham, Robert, in temperance work, 48–49

Greer, David H., institutional church leader, 150; promoter of King's Daughters, 220

Hadley, H. H., city missionary, 138

Hall, Charles Cuthbert, seminary president and teacher, 236, 238

Hegeman, J. Winthrop, church federation leader, 189
Henderson, Charles Richmond, seminary sociology professor, 240
Hepworth, George H., founder of Boston Union for Christian Work, 38
Herron, George D., champions Christian Socialism, 78–79; agitation of, 79–81, 110–111; on union of social reformers, 116
Hewitt, Abram S., on industrial problem, 74
Hodges, George, on social settlements, 85; in church federation, 191; as seminary president, 236–241
Holbrook, Z. Swift, as Christian Sociologist, 83, 111, 238
Holls, George C., as agent of American Christian Commission, 14; as administrator of Lutheran charitable institutions, 53–54
Holy Trinity Church (New York), institutional, 28–29
Home of the Evangelists, training school, 51
Home Evangelization, meaning of, 31; in Massachusetts, 32–33; applications of, 33–34
Hope Chapel (New York), institutional church, 186
Hope Congregational (Springfield, Mass.), institutional church, 209
Howard Mission (New York), social service of, 36
Hoyt, Arthur S., seminary sociology professor, 239
Hubbard, S. F., institutional church leader, 175
Huntington, J. O. S., as founder of C.A.I.L., 112; in Brotherhood of St. Andrew, 216

Immigrants, in cities, 3–4, 13, 57; and industrial conflict, 58, 59, 61; church concern for, 41–43, 141–142, 252, 255; ministry trained for, 172, 181–183.
Institutional Church Movement, beginnings of, 27–34; named, 137, 154; development of, 147–161; and Open or Institutional Church League, 161–163; influence of, 163–165; relation of city missions to, 139–141, 170–185; opposition to, 253; bibliography of, 261–262
Inter-Denominational Congress, on social Christianity, 90–91

Jackson, Alexander, on worker distrust of church, 62
Jersey City Tabernacle, institutional church, 154–155
Jesup, Morris K., institutional church builder, 139, 142
Jones, Jenkin Lloyd, as Unitarian social reformer, 101; as institutional church leader, 159–160
Jones, Jesse H., in Christian Labor Union, 22ff.; as author, 22n.
Judson, Edward, institutional church leader, 158
Judson Memorial (New York), institutional church, 158

Keyser, Harrietta A., in social reform, 112
Kindergarten of the Church Association, 209
Knox Memorial (New York), institutional church, 174

Ladies and Pastors' Christian Union, in deaconess movement, 54–55
Langdon, William Chauncey, 99
League of Catholic Unity, 99–100
Leavitt, George R., in progressive church work, 34
Lutherans, and religio-social discussion, 18; and immigrants, 41; and deaconesses, 52–53, 195–196; and charities, 53–54; and youth, 210, 212; and sociological instruction, 242

MacAuley, Jerry, in rescue mission work, 36–37, 95, 137, 249
McCulloch, Oscar Carlton, institutional church leader, 152–153
McNeill, George E., in Home Evange-

lization movement, 33; as Christian Socialist, 116

Madison Avenue Presbyterian (New York), institutional church, 156–157

Magruder, J. W., institutional church leader, 159

Mains, George P., institutional church leader, 162, 169

Mariners' Temple (New York), institutional church, 180

Mary and Martha League, for sisterhood, 219

Mathews, Shaiier, seminary sociology professor, 240

Methodists, in cities, 4, 166–167, 260; and religio-social discussion, 18, 168–170; and immigrants, 41–42, 200; and temperance, 49; and deaconesses, 54–55, 197–202; and charities, 55, 202; and institutional churches, 158–159, 170–172; and city missions, 166–170; and Sunday schools, 208; and youth, 212, 214; and sociological instruction, 240

Miller, Charles F., seminary sociology professor, 242

Miller, H. Thane, Y.W.C.A. sponsor, 45

Monroe, Paul, on Christian Socialists, 77, 78n.

Moody, Dwight L., lay evangelist, 15–16; leader in Christian Associations, 44, 45; and Christian training, 51

Morgan Chapel (Boston), institutional church, 171

Muhlenberg, William A., as "Evangelical Catholic," 10–11, 16, 42; as pioneer in Episcopal social movement, 29, 30, 40

Murphy, Francis, and gospel temperance, 47, 50

Murray, W. H. H., and social Christianity, 29

National Christian Citizenship League, and Christian Socialism, 213–214

National City Evangelization Union,

in social service, 168–170; in church federation, 192

National Federation of Churches and Christian Workers, 193

National Florence Mission Association, agent of rescue homes, 145

Nationalists, champion social Christianity, 66–67

Newton, R. Heber, and social Christianity, 48, 50, 59, 60, 70, 81, 247

New York City Mission and Tract Society, social program espoused by, 35; institutional churches of, 139–141; Women's Branch of, 142

New York Federation of Churches and Christian Workers, origin of, 189; social and religious work of, 189–191

New York Protestant Episcopal City Mission, founded, 39; agencies of, 39–40

North, Frank Mason, institutional church leader, 162, 163, 169, 170

North End Mission (Boston), institutional, 36

Noyes, Daniel P., in Home Evangelization, 32

Oberlin Institute of Christian Sociology, urges reconcilation of church and labor, 111

Ockerhausen, John H., Methodist friend of immigrants, 41

Olivet Chapel (New York), institutional church, 140, 141

Open or Institutional Church League, formation and program of, 161–163; *Open Church* of, 163; and church federation, 193

Pacific Garden Mission (Chicago), rescue and institutional, 138

Parker, Theodore, on immigrants, 4

Parkhurst, Charles H., in fight against Tammany, 81

Parmenter Street Chapel (Boston), institutional church, 175

Parton, James, on "fashionable" Christianity, 7

Passavant, William A., pioneer in

Lutheran charities, 52–53; seminary organizer, 242

Patterson Memorial (Baltimore), institutional church, 172

Peabody, Francis G., on social reform, 83; as teacher of social ethics, 232–233; on institutional church progress, 248

Pentecost, Hugh O., church rebel and socialist, 100

People's Church (St. Paul), institutional, 177

People's Temple (Philadelphia), institutional church, 171

Perin, George L., institutional church leader, 160

Philanthropy, the old, 8; the new, 84–85, 250–251

Pierson, Arthur T., institutional church leader, 155–156

Pilgrim Congregational Church (Worcester), institutional, 210

Pilgrim Congregational Church (Cambridgeport, Mass), institutional, 34

Pittsburgh Federation of Churches, work of, 191

Plymouth Church (Indianapolis), institutional, 152–153

Potter, Henry Codman, on city missions, 55, 183–184; employer-employee mediator, 113

Powderly, Terence V., approves institutional church, 155

Presbyterian Alliance of Philadelphia, in city evangelization, 41

Presbyterians, in cities, 4; and religio-social discussion, 18; and temperance, 47–48; and institutional churches, 155–157; and city missions, 178–179; and immigrants, 182, 183; and deaconesses, 202–203; and Sunday schools, 208; and sociological instruction, 238–239

Rainsford, William S., on saloons, 142; as institutional church leader, 147–150; as deaconess advocate, 203

Rauschenbusch, Walter, on social reform technique, 75; as founder of Brotherhood of the Kingdom, 114; on institutional church movement, 253

Reed, David Allen, institutional church leader, 209, 218

Reformed, and deaconesses, 196; and brotherhood, 217

Religious press, and social Christianity, 14, 18, 20, 22, 29, 44, 52, 54, 64, 76, 83, 89, 98, 100, 101, 103, 106, 108–109, 110, 120, 124, 144, 163, 170, 178, 187, 199, 211, 212, 213, 215, 217, 220; bibliography of, 257–258

Richmond, Mrs. William, as city missionary, 39–40

Riis, Jacob, as King's Son, 220, 221

Rogers, E. H., as legislator and a founder of Christian Labor Union, 21

Roman Catholics, urban strength and social program of, 7; influence on Protestants of, 11, 20, 34, 65, 137, 190, 195

Ruggles Street Baptist (Boston), institutional church, 180

Ruliffson, A. G., 51

Russell, Frank, as Field Secretary of Evangelical Alliance, 91, 93

St. Bartholomew's (New York), institutional church, 150–151

St. George's (New York), institutional church, 147–150

St. Johnland, 30

St. Mark's (Philadelphia), institutional church, 31, 40

Salvation Army, beginnings of, and opposition to, 120–121; growth of, 121–125; Auxiliary League of, 124, 127–128; Slum Brigade of, 126–128; Social Scheme of, 128–132; relief work of, 132–133; and immigrants, 133–134; and youth, 127, 128, 134–135; schism in, 120, 135; and city missions, 138, 139; bibliography of, 263

Sanford, E. B., institutional church leader, 163

Satterlee, Henry Y., institutional church leader, 184

Scudder, John L., institutional church leader, 154–155

Second Avenue and Seventh Street Church (New York), institutional, 173

Seibt, Charles Theodore, seminary sociology professor, 241

Seminaries, and decline of ministry, 224–226; improved teaching and administration in, 226–232; sociology in, 232–244; Unitarian, 227, 229, 230, 232–233, 242–243; Congregational, 226, 227, 228, 229, 230, 231, 233–235, 236–238; Presbyterian, 226, 228, 229, 230, 238–239; Episcopal, 228, 229, 230, 240–242; Baptist, 231, 232, 239–240; Methodist, 232, 240; Lutheran, 242; Universalist, 236, 243

Sewall, John S., seminary sociology professor, 237

Seward, Theodore F., 98

Sheridan, William F., institutional church leader, 172

Simpson, Matthew, on religious influence of trade unions, 10; as promoter of deaconesses among Methodists, 54

Smith, Samuel G., institutional church leader, 177

Social Christianity. See Cities.

Social Gospel, contemporary historians of, 256

Social Purity, efforts for, 13, 40, 46, 127–128, 145–147, 222, 251

Social Settlements, Christian attitudes toward, 84–85; Christian, 126, 175, 183, 187, 188n., 206, 214, 221, 238, 248–249; church members as personnel of, 251

Socialist Labor party, attitude toward social Christianity, 66

Societies for Ethical Culture, launched, 19; on theory of social reform,

19–21; in social education, 102–103

Society of King's Daughters, origin and growth of, 219–220; comprehensive social service program of, 221–222

Southgate, Charles M., institutional church leader, 210

Sterrett, J. McBride, seminary sociology professor, 241

Stewart, George Black, seminary president, 236

Stone, James S., institutional church leader, 171

Strong, Josiah, as author, 82, 90; in Evangelical Alliance, 90, 91, 93, 94; favors Salvation Army, 123; and institutional church, 161, 163

Stuckenberg, J. H. W., as leading Christian Sociologist, 82, 83, 186, 242; on progress of social Christianity, 251–252, 253–254

Sunday Evening Clubs, as part of brotherhood movement, 218

Sunday schools, need for, 206–207; better organization of, 207–209; and social work, 209; and institutional churches, 209–210

Swing, David, and progressive church work, 29

Swinton, John, on industrial conflict, 59; on attitude of workers toward church, 63, 66

Tabernacle Lay College (Brooklyn), training school, 51

Taylor, Graham, in Convention of Christian Workers, 96, 98; as institutional church leader, 151–152; as seminary professor, 234, 236–237

Temperance, revival of church interest in, 47–49; social aspects of, 49–50, 142–145

Thompson, Charles L., institutional church leader, 156, 162, 163

Tucker, William J., as champion of the new philanthropy, 82, 83, 84–85, 142; and institutional church,

137, 154; as seminary teacher of social economics, 233–234; on influence of social Christianity, 250, 254
Tunis, John, institutional church leader, 175
Tyng, Stephen H., Jr., progressive church leader, 28–29, 51

Union for Practical Progress, and social reform, 104–105; in Philadelphia and Baltimore, 105–106
Unitarian Church Temperance Society, 49
Unitarian Unions for Christian Work, as humanitarian agencies, 37–39
Unitarians, and city missions, 37–39, 174–175; and temperance, 49; and institutional churches, 159–160, 171, 175; and youth, 211–212; and sociological instruction, 232–233, 242–243
United Society of Christian Endeavor. *See* Young People's Societies.
Universalist Young People's Union, 212
Universalists, and institutional churches, 160–161; and youth, 212; and sociological instruction, 236, 243

Vincent, J. H., on institutional church, 155; in Sunday school work, 208, 209
Vrooman, Harry, 67

Wabash Avenue Church (Chicago), institutional, 172
Wage-earners, alienated from churches, 10, 61–64; social Christianity approved by, 64–65, 216, 251–252
Ward, Harry F., institutional church leader, 172

Water Street Mission (New York), founded, 35–36; work and influence of, 36–37
Weeden, William B., in social service, 38–39
Welsh, William, in early Episcopal social movement, 30–31; as founder of first workingmen's club, 40; as founder of Alonzo Potter Memorial House, 52
Wesley Chapel (Cincinnati), institutional church, 158–159
Whiton, James M., in Home Evangelization movement, 33
Willett, John, on social Christianity, 65
Wittenmeyer, Annie, journalist and deaconess promoter, 54
Woman's Christian Temperance Union, formed, 50; work of, 143–145, 146–147
Woman's Home Missionary Society of Methodist Episcopal Church, missionary and deaconess work of, 199–201

Yeatman, James E., suggests American Christian Commission, 11
Young Men's Christian Association, origin and early program of, 8–9; in New York City, 43–44, 204; for middle-class youth, 43–45; leads physical education movement, 205–206
Young People's Societies, origin and character of, 210–211; denominational, 211–212; in social reform, 212–214
Young Women's Christian Association, growth of, 45; in city mission work, 45–46; and working women, 206